Dedicated to the memory of Sir David Lean

DAVID LEAN
AND HIS FILMS

DAVID LEAN AND HIS FILMS

BY **ALAIN SILVER** AND **JAMES URSINI**

Foreword by **ROBERT WISE**

Silman-James Press
LOS ANGELES

First Silman-James Press edition 1992

Library of Congress Cataloging-in-Publication Data

Silver, Alain, 1947-
David Lean and his films/by Alain Silver and James Ursini.—
Rev. and updated ed.
p.   cm.
Includes bibliographical references and index.
Filmography: p.
1. Lean, David, 1908-1991. I. Ursini, James. II. Title.
Pn1998.3.L43A42   1991   791.43'0233'092—dc20   91-43147

ISBN: 1-879505-00-2

Cover design by Heidi Frieder

Printed and bound in the United States of America

SILMAN-JAMES PRESS
Distributed by
Samuel French Trade
7623 Sunset Blvd., Hollywood, CA 90046

CONTENTS

ACKNOWLEDGEMENTS   ix

FOREWORD   xi

INTRODUCTION   1

1   The Early Films: IN WHICH WE SERVE (1942);
     THIS HAPPY BREED (1944); BLITHE SPIRIT (1945)   11

2   BRIEF ENCOUNTER (1945)   29

3   The Dickens Adaptations: GREAT EXPECTATIONS (1946)
     and OLIVER TWIST (1948)   43

4   MADELEINE (1950)   79

5   THE SOUND BARRIER (1952)   97

6   HOBSON'S CHOICE (1954)   109

7   THE PASSIONATE FRIENDS (1949) and SUMMER
     MADNESS (1955)   121

8   THE BRIDGE ON THE RIVER KWAI (1957)   141

9   LAWRENCE OF ARABIA (1962)   153

10   DOCTOR ZHIVAGO (1965)   169

11   RYAN'S DAUGHTER (1970)   187

12   A PASSAGE TO INDIA (1984)   211

A PERSONAL AFTERWORD   229

BIOGRAPHY   231

FILMOGRAPHY   241

FOOTNOTES   267

SELECTED BIBLIOGRAPHY   275

INDEX   287

ACKNOWLEDGEMENTS

Thanks, still first of all, to David Bradley without whose kind assistance in the days before VHS (or Beta) many of the chapters could not have been written. Thanks also to Ron Garrison for aiding in the bibliographic research; Albert Hutter and members of the class of English 164 for information on Dickens and ideas about the adaptations; to Don Adams for facilitating the frame enlargements; Elaine Hofstetter and Elmer Silver for helping prepare the final manuscript; Elizabeth Ward for proofing and research on the early revisions; and Nick Peterson, Evelyn Renold, Stan Berkowitz, Howard Suber, Phil Chamberlin, and Jim Paris. Thanks as well to all our original editors, Ian Cameron then Tim Cawkwell and John Smith at November Books and Susan Tovy at Leslie Frewin. Research was done at the Margaret Herrick library of the Academy of Motion Picture Arts and Sciences, the Charles K. Feldman library of the American Film Institute, and the Theater Arts Library at the University of California, Los Angeles.

For the Second Edition,

Thanks to David Shepard, Selise Eiseman, Lamont Johnson, Andre de Toth, Guy Green, Maggie Unsworth and all the others involved in the DGA/AFI "Weekend with David Lean," in particular Ronald Neame, for clarifying questions about Cineguild.

For reviewing portions of the manuscript: Linda Brookover, Nick Redman, and again Jim Paris. For additional career information, Adrian Turner. For assisting with the stills, Bruce Kimmel; for help in the copying, Gyongyver Sovago; and for staying out of the office, Michael Rosen. Research was again done at the AMPAS and AFI libraries.

Stills courtesy of United Artists, Universal, Metro-Goldwyn-Mayer, Columbia, David Chierichetti, and Critt Davis.

FOREWORD

For most film directors, at least for those of his and surrounding generations, David Lean has increasingly been considered a "Director's Director." His determined dedication to getting his version of a film on the screen at all costs and his complete attention to every detail of the film-making process have become legend in the film industry.

Lovers of films of outstanding quality and scope are fortunate to have this thoughtful and comprehensive volume to help them more fully appreciate all the aspects of the films of this most outstanding director.

Robert Wise

INTRODUCTION

*Film is a dramatised reality and it is the
director's job to make it appear real . . .
an audience should not be conscious of
technique.*

*My distinguishing talent is the ability to put
people under the microscope, perhaps to go
one or two layers farther down than some
other directors.*

*I've just begun to dare to think I perhaps am
a bit of an artist.*[1]

Dav020id Lean directed motion pictures with an acknowledged
consciousness of his actions and a stated set of intentions and
expectations about the end product of his labor. As a worker in
an industry where that end product faces evaluation from economic criteria on the one hand and aesthetic criteria on the other,
Lean achieved a stature which few other directors could equal.

Despite this, it is no easy task to place David Lean in any
directorial hierarchy, nor is it necessarily advisable to do so. The
stories about Lean's obsessive attention to visual detail were
legion and often exaggerated. Some of Lean's colleagues may
have attributed his compulsive perfectionism to a futile hope of
avoiding that inevitable end by prolonging production. When

Claude Chabrol remarked that he and Lean were the only directors working who will wait "forever" for a perfect sunset but that he measured "forever" in terms of weeks and Lean did so in years, the observation was more than mere apocrypha. In its overstatement, it revealed the respect which Lean's peers had for his prodigious abilities. And yet when Lean spoke about himself, he was usually self-effacing. Often he would mention that fear of indecision while shooting that compelled him to take so much time and belabor such fine points in his preparations. Lean wrote about disguising technique in 1947; but it took more than fifty years of work for him to consider that he might be "a bit of an artist."

Ultimately, the aim of this book is neither to analyze Lean's prominence as a filmmaker nor the personality behind it. The focus here is David Lean's work. For those sixteen motion pictures which bear the credit "Directed by David Lean" are more than anything the definition of Lean as an artist.

In the first ten years of his directing career, from 1942 to 1952, Lean completed nine features. In the almost forty years that followed, he would make only seven more. Part of the reason for this is the change within the film industry. As budgets and shooting schedules have grown, it has become very difficult for any director to complete more than one feature per year. But even while other directors in the Forties and Fifties were making several films every twelve months, Lean never made more than one.[2] Lean's renown since 1957 has been as a maker of films on a monumental scale.

The almost all-male casts of **BRIDGE ON THE RIVER KWAI** and **LAWRENCE OF ARABIA**, the very title of the latter as well as **DOCTOR ZHIVAGO**, may also have given Lean's films the reputation of having heroes rather than heroines. In actuality, the principal characters of Lean's last two films were women; and, in all, six of his sixteen films—**BRIEF ENCOUNTER, THE PASSIONATE FRIENDS, MADELEINE, SUMMER MADNESS, RYAN'S DAUGHTER**, and **A PASSAGE TO INDIA**—had preeminent female protagonists.

Lean's thematic preoccupations or "world-view" are delineated in the chapters to come; and it will be through his characters both male and female that those preoccupations are most easily accessible. The resemblance of characters in different pictures whether separated by four or forty years is often remarkable. Even the names may be subtly similar as in Laura Jesson, Mary Justin, Jane Hudson. The themes which Lean does address repeatedly, from "ordinary" adulterous love to epic, obsessive madness, are not unique to him. Lean has said without any sense of contradiction: "I'm first and foremost interested in the story, the characters," but "I think people remember pictures not dialogue. That's why I like pictures."[3] What is unique to Lean is his visual style, one that elucidates story and characters through pictures.

In his general theory, Andre Bazin divided filmic reality into three conceivable forms: "(1) A purely logical and descriptive analysis . . . (2) A psychological analysis, from within the film, namely one that fits the point of view of one of the protagonists in a given situation . . . (3) A psychological analysis from the point of view of the spectator."[4] To simplify these types, one might call them objective, subjective, or ironic respectively. As a director Lean had to deal with all these "realities" and, as they are the only possible conventional modes, had to define his vision through them.

OLIVER TWIST (1948) is a prime illustration. In the shots of the workhouse, Lean delineates a basic "reality." His direction here is objective, although there are ironies in the very design of the set and the superimposed title, and aimed at establishing the narrative core of the film. In setting distance or angle, however, he may add to the material reality of image, something of the emotional or character reality, not "physically" present. As in the high angle medium shot of the boys drawing straws: when they leave, amidst hushed cries, Oliver is alone—his sensation is visualized by the isolation of his white-gowned figure within the gray confines of the frame and the two-dimensional reduction in height, the "flattening" imposed by placing the camera above him. Alternatively by focusing on an image within the general expository necessity of the scene, Lean may underscore its dramatic, i.e. serious or comic, quality.

The only necessary images in the sequence of Nancy's murder, for example, are those which make it clear that Sikes has killed her. Beyond that Lean may single out, still within the context of observable detail, a specific image such as the close shot of Sikes' dog scratching furiously at the door. What should be made clear here is that the fiction assumes a basic suspension of disbelief. The spectator sitting down to view the film will not be unduly surprised to discover a world of only black and white with characters dressed in and housed in early Victorian fashion, in short a world entirely incongruous with the one outside the theater. Murder and the fixtures of a room are potentially equal as observable realities, if different on a dramatic level, just as they are beyond the confines of the movie house. In the example above, the obvious point, that the episode is terrifying because the dog wants desperately to get out, is made by a selective rather than substantive manipulation within the fixed reality of the scene. In spying through a glass port on Monks and Fagin in the back of a tavern, Nancy takes in everything she can but her view of the complete "picture" is restricted. Analogously, the "objective plane" or that which provides the basic information in a film is not aligned to any predetermined standards, neither induced from the general objectivity of the whole of cinema nor reasoned out a priori, but derived from the specific "vantage" set up by the director. And the definition of that objective plane, for want of a better term, the mise-en-scene, may be taken as the first component of directional style.

That style is further refined in a substantive manner, by what Bazin calls "fit[ting on] the point of view of one of the protagonists." Instances of direct "point of view" from **OLIVER TWIST** are strikingly recorded when the camera "becomes" Oliver fleeing a crowd of pursuers: travelling forward rapidly, it slips, at his eye level, through the arms of one man then runs into the clenched fist of another, whereupon it "loses consciousness" by means of a cut to black. Later, in the courtroom, it will sway dizzily, an effect accentuated by using a wide-angle rather than a normal lens, then blur in and out of focus, and finally fall over in a faint. Here an objective view of the world is physically displaced. Going back for a moment, consider again the shot of Oliver alone after drawing the short straw. Was it truly objective, or did the staging take it beyond a simple witnessing of a narrative event?

A clearer answer may be found in the opening sequence of the film. On a country road in the midst of a sudden storm, Oliver's mother begins to give birth to him. In one travelling in, Lean simultaneously records the labor objectively—a medium shot to medium close shot, her body arched, head tilted back, grimacing—and totally externalizes not just the intangible emotion of her plight but the physical sensation, too. Knifing pain is equated with a white sheet of lightning. A contorting spasm is captured by an angular tilt from horizontal which levels off as the contraction subsides. Her complete disorientation and the distortion of her real perceptions are characterized by making her walk on a treadmill before a process screen. This device makes her move unnaturally at the edge of consciousness and introduces a secondary "reality" of reduced dimension behind the already existing one of the film itself.

Beyond this intricate subjectification, Lean may compound the frame's reality with dramatic irony. This is classically accomplished in the sequence where Nancy is followed by the Artful Dodger—the audience being privileged to observe through several shots of him lurking outside the house and trailing behind her down the rainy streets, something of vital concern of which she is unaware. Lean can also fashion a subtler ironic mode on a figurative level: as in the first conversation between Monks and Fagin in the garret. Here while Fagin's eyes stay on his body moving in and out of the shot, Monks becomes momentarily for the audience a thin, black shadow on the right side of the frame [frame 1]. This stylized rendering of Monks' form implies his malevolent character as well as the manner in which his presence looms ominously over the entire picture, a "fact" which Fagin (as the shadow is not in his line of sight) cannot know.

On a narrative level, **OLIVER TWIST** is a typical, third person film, that is the revelation of narrative "facts" is not

[frame 1]

identified with or restricted to the perceptions of a single character. Lean's subjectification of almost an entire story-line is exemplified by the even earlier **BRIEF ENCOUNTER** (1945). This is
not merely because most of the film is told in flashback, complete
with extensive voiceover narration by the female protagonist,
Laura Jesson, but because as in **OLIVER TWIST**, Lean repeatedly
uses visuals which underscore that subjectivity. Before the narration establishes the subjectivity, Lean sets it up with an exaggerated point-of-view: an extreme close shot of a woman's mouth
before Laura thinks, "I wish you'd stop talking." By having the
first thought spoken on the soundtrack be one with which the
audience is likely to empathize, the intrusiveness of the narration
is buffered and the transition smoothed. When she arrives home,
there is a more subtle effect: her husband's hat is framed in the
foreground as she climbs the stairs and he calls to her, simultaneously establishing visual and aural emblems of his presence
before he is even seen. When he is seen, various aspects of his
appearance, from his moustache to the pinstripes in his suit,
immediately contrast with the look of the man she was with in
the tea room. All these details reinforce or anticipate parts of what
Laura's flashback will reveal before it even begins.

Since most of Lean's narratives are organized in a way
which is neither "first" nor "third" person, shots or sequences like
those already cited may suddenly shift the film into either mode
without disrupting or overwhelming the basic structure. Subjec-

tivity may be accomplished in several ways. The narrative itself may be literally bracketed by being presented as a flashback from either the central character (**BRIEF ENCOUNTER, PASSIONATE FRIENDS**), a subordinate one (**DOCTOR ZHIVAGO**), or a combination (**IN WHICH WE SERVE** and, implicitly, **LAWRENCE OF ARABIA**). In any narrative context, shots may be intercut to suggest the thoughts or sensations of a character as in **OLIVER TWIST** and **BRIEF ENCOUNTER** or characters, as in the sparking streetcar terminal when Zhivago and his still-unknown, future lover, Lara, brush against each other early in that film. Shots may become literally what the character sees; or shots of the character may be manipulated to focus on an interior state. Simple instances would be the hanging in **GREAT EXPECTATIONS** or the Cossack charge in **DOCTOR ZHIVAGO**, when there is no point-of-view shot of the terrible event but merely a slow move in to reveal the horror in the actor's face. A more intricate example is found in the beginning of **BRIEF ENCOUNTER**. When Laura returns home after the final parting with her lover, she sits in the parlor and realizes that she cannot tell her husband of her affair, however platonic. A medium close shot of her slumped in the chair is cut with an over-the-shoulder view of her husband working a crossword. Lean shifts to a wide angle lens for this, suddenly extending perspective and making the man and the objects of the room in front of her seem farther away than they actually are, visually rendering her state of mind as she draws back from them into herself [**frames 2** and **3**]. Lean extends this further by bringing down the key light and dissolving back to the tea room. By using an unreal, even theatrical effect, Lean creates a hyper-real perspective, for as Laura's silhouette remains in the foreground, she "watches" Alec Harvey enter the room, the tea room and her room also, and in her imagination substitutes him for her husband whom she literally "fades out" without even leaving her chair.

All this should suggest something of the awareness of the medium which Lean brought to his material. Lean's working methods are well-documented elsewhere and seemed to vary little throughout his career. Of the script stage, one of his early

[frame 2]

[frame 3]

writing collaborators, Ronald Neame, observed: "Every line of dialogue, not just dialogue, but every line of description is studied and worked out before it's put down in that script."[5] His last collaborator was Robert Bolt: "We rewrite it about four times until we are satisfied. And, of course, it is David who must be satisfied with it."[6]

Despite the numerous awards and the frequent praise of reviewers for most of his projects, Lean has never been a critical favorite. Despite the fact that the descriptions of how Lean worked out the shooting script could easily be mistaken for remarks about the widely admired Alfred Hitchcock, this disfavor is particularly marked among *auteurists*. Andrew Sarris not only relegated him to "Less Than Meets The Eye" in the seminal

American Cinema, but concluded his assessment with a pun about "too little literary fat and too much visual lean."[7] When Ian Cameron originally contracted for this study to be written for the Movie Paperback series, he did so because "on confronting many of the film-makers I most admire, I invariably find that the film-makers *they* most admire are Messers. Lean and Fellini whose work I cannot abide."[8]

It is difficult to imagine even a superficial analysis of Lean's films that does not reveal an intensely personal filmmaker; but it was never the purpose of this study to polemicize or formulate responses to those who do not perceive this. Nor is it to make judgments of value. Rather communication, the second of I.A. Richards' "two pillars upon which a theory of criticism must rest," is the key concept.[9] The images and archetypes through which Lean's motion pictures communicate sensation or point-of-view and transfuse the narrative are the focus of the chapters which follow. It would be possible to compare Lean to other filmmakers, to weigh his early black-and-white pictorialism against that of Rex Ingram (whom he greatly admired), to contrast his "romantic" landscapes with Hitchcock[10], his construction of epics with Anthony Mann, and even his economy of expression with Renoir. All that would be an indirect approach to the subject at hand, to David Lean and his films.

1
The Early Films
IN WHICH WE SERVE (1942)
THIS HAPPY BREED (1944)
BLITHE SPIRIT (1945)

The sun was shining on the sea,
Shining with all his might:
He did his very best to make
The billows smooth and bright.

—Lewis Carroll,
"The Walrus and the Carpenter"

No coward soul is mine,
No trembler in the world's storm-
troubled sphere.

—Emily Brontë

IN WHICH WE SERVE is only one in a long list of propaganda films turned out by England and the United States during World War II. Based on the actual service record of a British destroyer recounted to Noel Coward by Lord Mountbatten, it advances the standard line of support for the war effort and follows a familiar pattern by combining the story of H.M.S. Torrin, from shipyard to the bottom of the Mediterranean Sea, with the personal lives of its captain and crew. Within this context, the film has its reputation. If it seems, at times, cloying or overeager on its way to the message of the closing title ("God bless our ships and all who sail on them."), it remains significant not just as Lean's first attempt at directing an entire feature, but as a picture singled out for admiration by its contemporaries from among scores of similar efforts.

Noel Coward hired Lean as co-director because of his reputation for the classical economy of his cutting and the dynamism of his dramatic montages but did not expect him to deal with the actors. Lean had experience shooting inserts and some second units most recently for Michael Powell on the war-themed films, **49TH PARALLEL** (1941) and **ONE OF OUR AIR-CRAFT IS MISSING** (1942). Before that Lean and stage director Harold French had worked as unofficial co-directors for Gabriel Pascal on **MAJOR BARBARA** (1941).[1] If there is any unseen hand whose stamp is clearly on this motion picture, it is playwright George Bernard Shaw's, whose hand is literally, in fact, seen signing his name to a brief, holographic prologue. If Lean did, as Rex Harrison suggests, "whisper" suggestions to Pascal[2], the result was an appropriately prosaic staging of the Shaw play consisting mostly of masters and close-ups. The film does feature travelling shots, both on stage and on location that help pace several intersequence transitions; but the emphasis is squarely on the performances, not merely on Harrison and Wendy Hiller in the title role, but on Robert Morley, Robert Newton, Emlyn Williams and a dozen others.

There is an extended montage created by Lean when the principals of the piece visit the Undershaft cannon works. Several shots, such as the panning to follow a rail of molten steel emerging from a stamper accompanied by a surging measure of William Walton's music, have isolated visual impact independent of the characterizations. One sequence does suggest the kind of subjectification that Lean would later develop. Barbara and Dolly (Hiller and Harrison) have come to the factory uncertain about their futures, alone and together. From a shot of huge tongs pulling a ten-foot ingot of metal out of a fiery furnace, there is a cut to both of them in medium close shot, with the light, ostensibly cast by the glowing metal, playing unevenly on their faces. The next shot is of a leather-aproned workman ringing a warning bell. Taken together the light and the sound of the bell are both literal events and subtle suggestions of the main characters' mixed emotions and concern.

After a few weeks of shooting **IN WHICH WE SERVE**, Coward lost interest in what he called the "fussiness" of film direction and effectively turned the reins over to Lean. Except for suggestions regarding performances, Lean was left in charge.

Lean has remarked that in "cutting a newsreel you learn

[frame 4]

[frame 5]

speed."[3] The opening sequence ("This is the story of a ship") is a
succinct montage, reminscent of that in **MAJOR BARBARA**, that
mimics the newsreel style. In the shipyard, cuts of girders dropping into place, hot rivets being passed, and sweating workmen
are juxtaposed to create a condensed but kaleidoscopic view of
the construction. As the ship is completed a series of dissolves
follows the Torrin as she slips out of dry dock for her sea-trial
accompanied by an exultant surge of music and the Union Jack is
raised on her stern. During the ship's return home, after a near-
fatal skirmish, Lean eliminates long, dull stretches of exposition
by isolating bits and pieces of the journey. This emphasis on a
visual development of the action is reminiscent of **ONE OF OUR
AIRCRAFT IS MISSING**, a picture edited by Lean a year earlier.
In the battle scenes, reaction shots intercut with antiaircraft guns
bursting, shouts mixed with shells exploding on the soundtrack,
energetically define the chaos **[frame 4]**. In the subsequent re-
flective calm as the Torrin limps back to port, static medium and
medium close shots avoid any false anticlimaxes and allow for a
dramatic detente **[frame 5]**.

Most of the film is constructed from various flashbacks as
the Torrin's sailors float in and around a tiny life-raft within sight
of the ravaged and slowly sinking ship. From this core Lean and
Coward draw the individual stories and the Torrin's history along
parallel lines. From the men's weary, oil-stained faces, the film
makers dissolve back to both domestic scenes **[frame 6]** and

[frame 6]

earlier events aboard the vessel. These interwoven flashbacks are also one of **IN WHICH WE SERVE**'s major narrative inconsistencies. Their purpose is ostensibly to allow each character to remember the events and tell his own story from his point of view. In this way a number of perspectives of the same incident may be given; but some of the flashbacks begin in the context of one person's memory yet end in the middle of another's. In some instances a character may even "remember" events with which he was never involved; for example, the three Christmas dinners are in Captain Kinross' flashback, although he was present at only one of them. As the personal stories are somewhat interrelated, occurrences leading up to climactic moments such as Blake telling Hardy of his wife's death may be divided between two flashbacks regardless of who was actually privy to them. In short, the "subjectivity" of this first film of Lean's is rather inexact.

This inexactitude carries over from the blend of memories to affect the interworking of the individual histories. The coincidence of Blake's chance meeting with Freda on the train and the fact that she is related to his petty officer by marriage is an initial storyline contrivance that seems to be exacerbated when Shorty remarks that his parents met in a similar fashion. By the time the Blakes, on their trip to Torquay after their wedding, just happen to encounter Kinross and his wife, who in their turn muse over their own honeymoon voyage taken years before to the same destination, the narrative's verisimilitude has stretched quite thin.

[frame 7]

Coward's literary irony and calculated understatement depend on this kind of plot manipulation; but Lean manages to add the same qualities on a visual level and partially to disentangle the web of plot complications. From a slow travelling in towards a newspaper announcing, "No War This Year," **[frame 7]** Lean cuts to a sea battle off Crete; and the detached, matter-of-fact flavor of the explanatory title: "Crete. May 23, 1941," reinforces the lack of emotionalism. The same "anti-momentous" impact, over space rather than time, exists in a cut from Mrs. Kinross reading her children lines from "The Walrus and the Carpenter" to a depth charge disturbing the "billows, smooth and bright." In both instances, Lean creates an ironic synthesis from the opposition of single images. On a more complex level, there is the Kinross family picnic: isolated on a rural hillside, the outing is interrupted by the appearance of several fighter planes. The scene follows one of Chief Hardy and his family viewing a newsreel of the war. The structure here is much like that of a sequence in **BRIEF ENCOUNTER**, moving from a theatre, representing artificiality, to the outdoors, naturalness. Here the natural elements of open field and sky are abruptly superseded by the inescapable, mechanistic devices of war. The personal idyll, the first of many in Lean's work, is disrupted; and the family is forced to witness a dogfight, a combat of moth-like, faceless gladiators in the no longer peaceful heavens.

IN WHICH WE SERVE also provides early evidence of Lean's awareness of camera movement and composition. When Shorty and Freda rest in a tea room, Lean distills the essence of sentimental, middle-class courtship into a single medium close two-shot, partially silhouetted against a window and anticipating similar scenes to occur in both **BRIEF ENCOUNTER** and **GREAT EXPECTATIONS**. As the crew participates in a dedication service, he uses a slowly traveling camera to scan and unite the entire company, moving across the assembly into a medium close shot of Kinross, the visual and moral center, then back again in a reflexive action. The long take as Mrs. Kinross expresses her grudging admiration for her husband's ship or the tracking into Kinross as he delivers his farewell address **[frame 8]** are equally

[frame 8]

[frame 9]

direct stagings which appropriately underscore without overemphasizing the dramatic tensions of their respective scenes.

Lean may indulge in some visual flourishes, such as the tracking shot into the tattoo ("Freda") on Shorty's forearm or the Blake wedding party posing for a photograph and reflected in the lens of the still camera **[frame 9]** but only infrequently. While these may lack a clear visual purpose, an optical device such as rippling effect superimposed over several transitions, does add figurative meaning as both a simulation of the sensation of drowning to the point of having the rippling "uncontrollably" appear and fade in the middle of flashback dialogue and a justification for the flashback itself: a man's life passing before his eyes. In contrast the most dynamic sequence in the film, the death of Mrs. Hardy and her mother and the subsequent birth of

Freda's baby, is a simple and uncluttered assemblage of shots. From the bombers flying over the Hardy house, the scene moves directly to a medium close shot of Mrs. Hardy and her mother huddled in the foreground with Freda nearby under a stairwell. Suddenly within the same shot, a bomb explodes and the building is destroyed. Only Freda is saved. Immediately after, she gives birth, an event which Lean amplifies with a panorama of the ocean and sea birds in flight. It becomes the earliest example of a birth-death cycle metaphor which Lean will use again in later pictures such as **THE SOUND BARRIER**.

With the success of **IN WHICH WE SERVE**, Cineguild, the association of Lean, cinematographer Ronald Neame, and associate producer Anthony Havelock-Allan, was on solid ground. The immediate plans for new motion pictures were not adventurous: three more to be based on Coward's material. Although Lean, Neame, and Havelock-Allan would share adaptation credit on all of them and perform the various production chores for the playwright, who was credited as producer, the marketing emphasis remained squarely on Coward. With his name coming at the end of the main titles, contrary to the traditional placing of the director's name last, and even remaining on the screen for a bit longer—on **BLITHE SPIRIT**, for instance, Lean as director and Neame as cinematographer both have their own cards which run for seven feet; Coward's follows for nine—it was clearly "Noel Coward's **BLITHE SPIRIT**" or **THIS HAPPY BREED** or **BRIEF ENCOUNTER** and never "David Lean's film of." Nor could it really have been otherwise for the fledgling members of Cineguild. The Rank Organization, despite its enlightened policy of handing money over to such satellite production units as Two Cities (Filippo Del Giudice's company, which had contracted for Coward's services) or the Archers (Michael Powell and Emeric Pressburger), would be rather more willing to continue its backing of Cineguild if it stuck to what it knew. And what it knew, for the moment at least, was Noel Coward.

The film to follow in the wake of H.M.S. Torrin was **THIS HAPPY BREED**. Begun just months after the stage production, it derives from an original that might be called a semi-sequel to

Coward's classic play *Cavalcade*. It spans the subsequent two decades from 1919 to 1939, while concentrating again on the personal history of an English family. However, the middle-class, ostensibly "democratic" cast members of *This Happy Breed* do not really follow in the bourgeois, Victorian, support-the-empire traditions of *Cavalcade*. Coward may subtly mock these "little people," caught between the upper-class and the proletariat, by

THIS HAPPY BREED: Frank Gibbons (Robert Newton) and his wife, Ethel (Celia Johnson), as they move into Clapham Common.

having a radical acquaintance accuse them of being "too busy getting all weepy over Rudolph Valentino to spare any tears for the workers of the world"; but the basic portrayal is a sympathetic one. Unlike *Cavalcade, This Happy Breed* ended on a roughly contemporary date. Because it focused on a past too immediate and too full of bitter memories of depression and Red Scare, too flavored by the hindsight ironies of appeasement, it could not give rise to a nostalgic reminiscence. The reign of Edward is easily distinguished from that of Victoria by virtue of her added half-century on a throne; but there was also the difference between tea in the dining room and chaw in the parlor, between the florid manners of Victorian gentility and the boisterousness of the working class at home.

THIS HAPPY BREED the movie does bear some resemblance to **IN WHICH WE SERVE**, specifically to the domestic scenes of the Hardys and the Blakes. The inhabitants of Number Seventeen Sycamore Road, Clapham Common are much the same people, with their irritable in-laws, their just-plain-folks camaraderie, and their unshakable belief that no matter how hard the times Mother England is forged of good stock and common sense will somehow prevail. "The people themselves, the ordinary people like you and me," Frank Gibbons tells his infant grandson, "we know what we belong to, where we come from, and where we're going. We may not know it with our brains, but we know it with our roots."

The entire play is fashioned from a simple conceit: within the context of naturalistic dialogue and decor, it proceeds to pick out the nine key scenes, the climactic or transcendent moments of a half-dozen lives over a span of twenty years. The classic problem in transposing material of this variety to the screen is how to treat the episodic structure—whether to fill it in with other scenes and transitional montages or leave it precisely as written enforcing the sensation of photographed stage play. In addition, a host of secondary considerations, such as dialogue style, had to be dealt with. For while Coward made sure that all the correct "h's" were dropped, the demands of the narrative necessitated a good many blatantly expository remarks and exchanges not made for the benefit of the character(s) to whom they were addressed but primarily designed to inform the audience of certain events. Bazin wrote in his essay on "Theater and Cinema" that "however one approaches it, a play whether classic or modern is unassailably protected by its text. There is no way of adapting the text without disposing of it and substituting something else, which may be better, but is not the play."[4] Clearly, the aim of the adaptors of both *This Happy Breed* and *Blithe Spirit* was not to supersede the text. The essential issue then becomes not how to deal with actual lines and scenes, but with basic qualities, with what the play has that the film can render better.

The results in **THIS HAPPY BREED** are not wholly satisfactory. The film itself emerges as episodic without effect, calculatedly detailed under a semblance of accidental observation, a narrative of fits and starts as characters try to become people, and people never succeed in becoming characters. The principle reason for this, aside from the aforementioned conventional problems, is the handicap of realism. What the adaptors tried to give the motion picture **THIS HAPPY BREED** and what ultimately made it imbalanced is more "credibility," more documentary reality than it could support. Under the camera eye, in Three-strip Technicolor, the Gibbons family ceases to be an assemblage of stage figures seen at a distance and becomes graphically real. Although the added expense of using this process may seem unusual, it was consistent with industry policy of generally restricting color to "theatrical" material, where studio photography would predominate and the potentially costly and uncontrollable factors involved in exterior work could be avoided. In "opening up" the play, however, Cineguild did add several exterior sequences. Inside or out, the aging that takes place between acts is a simple illusion on stage. On film, in close-up, the faces of Frank and Ethel have the authenticity of well-defined wrinkles framed by hair with subtler streaks of grey. The gradual stoop of Celia Johnson's (Ethel's) shoulders under the weight of passing years is as noticeable as the changing style of her dresses, which always retain the dowdiness befitting her station. Yet all this and a few shots of the "row" houses on Sycamore Road, giving the fictional Number 17 a physical presence it could never have on stage, still do not make those who dwell there substantively real.

Much of the problem does lie with the original, with its sterile half-truths and rigid slice-of-life posings. Many of its supporting characters are one-dimensional; and in this regard the film is an improvement, particularly in the case of Bob Mitchell, making the "chum from the war" less of a drinking partner and convenient foil and more of an individual. The film also adds some wry touches. Shifting a scene—for example, Frank's premarital lecture to Reg in the parlor now takes place in the lavatory—makes their figures seem somewhat incongruous in their formal clothes and comically underscores the pompous aspect of his advice. Inventing a new scene such as the trip to the cinema to see the incomprehensible American picture suggests the intolerant remnants of Victorian xenophobia. It can even make a small detail, such as Ethel taking down Edward's calendar after the abdication, which may have seemed too pointed a gesture on stage, a more spontaneous and artless action.

The majority of the story does continue to center on characters who do not speak words but utter lines of dialogue. Bazin's dictum holds true: the text cannot be merely appended with film effects or partially displaced by movie reality. The opening shots of the city and the travelling into the house establish one reality; then the "play" begins and asserts another. A view of the mob of people greeting Chamberlain at 10 Downing Street compounds the irony of Frank's remark, "It's exciting all right, if you like to see a lot of people yelling themselves hoarse without the faintest idea what they're yelling about," but subverts its drama. It is Queenie who says, in Noel Coward fashion but as a clear presentiment of Lean heroines yet to come, "I hate living here. I hate living in a house like a hundred other houses . . . because it's all so common." It is an empty irony, for Coward's personages are not just any inhabitants of Clapham Common, they are *the* inhabitants of Clapham Common. They are nothing more or less than lumps of observed traits, everymen and women mouthing uncertain epithets of earthly wisdom and, as such, not meant to venture out of the dramatic insulation of three walls of a parlor. They are would-be movie characters in search of a stage, like Frank Gibbons framed in medium shot between his sister and daughter rolling up yarn, trapped by a graphically mundane reality that is not inherently theirs.

BLITHE SPIRIT is, if nothing else, a radical departure from the mundane. Coward subtitled his play "An Improbable Farce in Three Acts"; but it might more accurately be termed a drawing room comedy of the supernatural, literally so in its original theatrical conception which restricts it to that one room. As a comedy, it stands almost alone in Lean's work—his only other effort in a generally comic vein being **HOBSON'S CHOICE**; but its atypical quality, the scarcity of elements that are distinctively Lean's, only begins there. **BLITHE SPIRIT** is Coward's

BLITHE SPIRIT: Charles Condomine (Rex Harrison) fends off an attack by his ghostly wife, Elvira (Kay Hammond), while his living wife, Ruth (Constance Cummings) looks on in bewilderment.

picture. His written preface, "When we are young/We read and believe/The most fantastic things./When we grow older and wiser/We learn with perhaps a little regret/That these things can never be," is qualified by Coward's own voice on the track saying, "We are quite, quite wrong." The characters who will prove this are bored ("Not by the wildest stretch of the imagination could you describe it as the first fine careless rapture,"), politely insulting ("You have a genius for understatement."), snobs ("That remark comes perilously close to impertinence."), who revel in flaunting the archetypal traits of the English petty aristocracy. Since Coward, as usual, draws his effects from wry exaggeration, it becomes essential to the comedy of the film as much as it was to that of the play that the two-time widower Charles Condomine and his wives Elvira and Ruth, dead in that order, remain faithful to his conception.

The movie Charles Condomine is still the sophisticated foil of Coward's invention, adept at the well-turned, Wildesian phrase (Charles: "It's discouraging to think how many people are shocked by honesty and how few by deceit.") and the sublimely egotistical comeback line (Ruth: "Write that down, you might forget it." Charles: "You underrate me."). When Madame Arcati, the haphazard medium, complains of a premonition that has not panned out ("I thought I was going to have a puncture so I went back to fetch my pump—and then, of course, I didn't."), Charles is ever ready with the gracious good word ("Perhaps you will on the way home."). But at heart he is true to a tradition of insensitive materialism, as evidenced by his observation, "Hmm, we must keep Edith in the house more," when he hears of a former servant girl's indiscretion or by his exploitation of Arcati to research a book. The idiosyncrasy which he shares with the likes of Frank Gibbons is the firm belief that the logical order of things is not easily subverted: "Why should having a cheese thing for lunch make me see my deceased wife after dinner?" When such a belief is finally and irrefutably contraverted, it can lead to only one conclusion: "I've gone mad—that's what it is. I've just gone raving mad."

In Coward's scheme, Charles is more prone to make the amusing "remark of a pompous ass" than an uproarious joke. Against what Elvira terms his "certain seedy grandeur" are arrayed such standard devices as the ongoing malentendu of saying unpleasant things to a ghost and having another character present think it is directed at them. Further contradiction is provided by Madame Arcati. Strengthened by her giddy naturalness and sensory awareness ("It was wonderful cycling through the woods, I was deafened by bird song."), she contrasts with Charles' mannered artificiality ("Experience has taught me to be wary of concoctions.") and attacks his triteness by a process of reversal: "Well, Madame Arcati, the time is drawing near." "Who knows? It may be receding." The cumulative result, on a narrative level, is a play that is funny without being very imaginative. Still the film version succeeds, here and there, in injecting a bit of the latter quality without compromising the former.

Bazin posits that the first thought of many directors in adapting a piece is to "conceal the theater," to "overcompensate by the 'superiority' of its [the cinema's] technique—which in turn is mistaken for aesthetic superiority," in short, to open it up. The reason for this, Bazin postulates, is that "the preconceptions of the public in these matters serve to confirm those of the filmmakers. People in general do not give much thought to the cinema. For them it means vast decor, plenty of action, and exteriors. If they are not given a minimum of what they call cinema, they feel cheated. The cinema must be more lavish than the theater." Alfred Hitchcock summarizes the formula for injecting "lavishness" in this way: "Here's the usual method: in the play a character arrives from outside and he comes by taxi; so, in the film, the adaptors show you the taxi's arrival, the characters getting out, walking up, climbing stairs, knocking at a door, and entering the room. At that point a long scene from the play begins, and if the character talks about a trip, they seize the occasion to show it to us through flashback. They forget, in this way, that the fundamental quality of the play is in its concentration."[5]

Lean does not overcompensate. There are some added bits like the comic dissolve from Arcati's "Oh, no red meat, I hope. I make it a rule never to eat red meat before I work," to a close shot of a bloody slice of roast beef being carved and passed to her or the invisible Elvira driving Charles' roadster to the bewilderment of a traffic controller or a shot of Arcati's parrot chirping, "Poltergeist, pretty Poltergeist"; but these are few and peripheral. Even the special effects are fairly restrained. The floating objects and doors opening by themselves are really nothing more than wired stagecraft. The transparent Elvira in her glowing green gown, entering suddenly via the closed French windows or having her hair disarranged as Ruth runs through her on the stairs, is a simple movie illusion.

Lean is equally restrained in his choice of angles. The sets have a theatrical depth, but the camera placement does not exploit it. Rather, the interplay between foreground and background is severely curtailed and reserved for certain useful touches: the two ghostly wives waiting impatiently on a settee while the ineffectual Arcati clambers up a ladder in the center of the room or a medium close two-shot of Ruth looking from Charles to an empty space in the background where Elvira would be if she could be seen. In the medium and long shots, characters are generally fixed in the same plane in relation to the camera; that is, in two shots the stage line is usually at ninety degrees to the camera's line of sight instead of favoring one figure over the other's shoulder. This direct and uncluttered staging flattens perspective and restricts interest to the frame's foreground. Most medium close-ups are straight on and used for reactions, the banter being delivered in medium and group shots. The cocktail sequence with the Bradmans, for example, is made up of thirteen cuts with medium and medium-long shots prevailing in eleven of them. The camera continues to function as an objective and somewhat ironic "third person," even in the most complex staging as when it tracks from a two shot of Elvira stroking Charles' head, through the hall doors, which part for it to pass, and pauses to glance in a mirror which reflects both figures in the parlor, also implying that somehow Elvira is physically present.

Throughout Lean eschews any flourishes in approaching the material. He may tamper with the time sense of the original, but only for a purpose. As Charles and Ruth argue over the "reality" of Elvira, he employs a series of dissolves over time, from morning to evening, and place, from dining room to hall to supper table to coffee on the terrace. In so doing, he infuses their purely theatrical exasperation with a growing intensity. His two inserts of a clock at 4:15 and 4:30 in the final exorcism scenes emphasize the subjectivity of the various characters' sensation of "endlessness." Most of Lean's interpretations of the text are of this sort. He underscores selected elements of genre satire, such as Arcati's mock-spectral shadow magnified on the wall in her pre-trance flitting about or the build-up of paraphernalia in the exorcism including a close shot of an urn that "smokes" moth-balls, but only lightly.

Lean's most effective "special effects" are derived from the editing. For instance, he adds visual humor in a cut from Arcati's "It upsets my vibrations" to a teakettle boiling and whistling. The tightening from medium to close two-shot and holding for ten lines as Charles quizzes Elvira on what she has done to the car is an early instance of Lean's translating dramatic apprehension into a sensible, visual correlative, narrowing the angle and withholding the cut until the emotional anxiety is dissipated with Elvira's succession of hapless exclamations. Lean makes pointed use of "technique" when Elvira demonstrates to Ruth that she is far from imaginary. The progression of details— flowers in mid-air; Elvira menacingly raising a chair over her head; curtains pulled shut; an ornament hurled from the mantel; a door thrown open—all are flawlessly timed and gradually inter- cut with close shots of the two women. The notion of confronta- tion is sharpened and concentrated, until Ruth runs out scream- ing in capitulation and a cut to long shot again coincides with a release of tension.

The question of style is never a simple one, except perhaps in its absence, if that is possible. There is something of Lean present in **THIS HAPPY BREED** and **BLITHE SPIRIT**, yet at this stage in his career, little more was required, or desired, than an application of craft to Noel Coward's art. Thematically, except for certain aspects of Madame Arcati and her breathless inquiries about "No sudden gusts of cold wind, I hope?" or Queenie in **THIS HAPPY BREED** with her "highfalutin' ideas" ("I want too much—I'm always thinking about the things I want."), there is little that foreshadows later work. The one major alteration in **BLITHE SPIRIT**, a new ending in which Charles goes to meet his wives in the "echoing vaults of eternity," seems less the personal inspiration of any of the adaptors than a matter of rounding out the retribution for questionable motives and morals for the benefit of movie censors. This does not imply that the Coward/ Cineguild collaboration lacked imagination or treated the source materials with too much respect. Certainly a good deal of **BLITHE SPIRIT**'s success was determined not just by the production unit, nor by Rex Harrison's much-praised incarnation of Charles Condomine, but also by Kay Hammond's throaty Elvira and Margaret Rutherford's dotty Arcati, both practiced performances from the stage version.

After three pictures, Lean had no particular desire to continue shining on Coward's sea, to go on doing his best to make another's billows smooth and bright. According to Neame: "David had always wanted to do something other than a stage play. We decided we had to prove ourselves apart from Coward [because] any Noel Coward film must be primarily a Noel Coward film, and we wanted to try our own wings."[2] Despite this sentiment, Cineguild had one more Coward project to film before parting company.

2
BRIEF ENCOUNTER (1945)

When I have fears that I may cease to be,
Before my pen has gleaned my teaming brain,
Before high-piléd books in charactery,
Hold like rich garners, the full-ripened grain,
When I behold, upon the night's starr'd face,
Huge cloudy symbols of a high romance,
And feel that I may never live to trace
Their shadows, with the magic hand of chance;
And when I feel, fair creature of an hour,
That I shall never look upon thee more,
Never have relish in the faery power
Of unreflecting love!—then on the shore
Of the wide world I stand alone, and think
Till Love and Fame to nothingness do sink.

—John Keats,
"When I have fears that I may cease to be"

BRIEF ENCOUNTER was Lean's first major success both in popular and critical terms. It was also the first venture into a thematic vein which Lean would mine repeatedly in future. Coward's dramatic concerns in a patriotic war film, an expansive history of a working class family, or an ironic drawing room comedy had scant fundamental appeal to Lean's sensibilities. But the story of **BRIEF ENCOUNTER**, a short-lived, quasi-adulterous romance between two ostensibly ordinary people, would reoccur in varying forms throughout Lean's work. In fact, Laura begins her flashback narration by remarking, "I'm an ordinary woman. I didn't think such violent things could happen to ordinary people," and continues with a litany of the ordinary (the day, the place, the mack Alec wears) which the station attendant closes with "ordinary cats." To escape what Lean called "ordinary dull suburban life,"[1] Alec Harvey and Laura Jesson initially do what he did: go to the movies.

The source of **BRIEF ENCOUNTER** was Coward's 1935 play *Still Life*, and the first step of the adaptors (Lean, Neame, Havelock-Allan, and Coward himself) was towards opening the play up. In keeping with Lean's considerable drive to enlarge outwardly and escape the studio (that "dark hole" as he called it), the script now spread beyond the railroad station tea room, which contained almost all the action of the original, to the train platform, the city streets, restaurants, theaters, woods, park gardens, and even drives through a picturesque countryside.

This exterior expansion lent itself to the beginning of a pantheistic imagery which Lean would from this point consistently apply to his projects. The forces of nature are meaningful participants in the lives of the characters. Both inner emotion and outward action are complemented, echoed or mirrored by natural phenomena. Wordsworth termed this effect a "sense sublime" and placed man in the continuum of Self and Nature: "To her fair works did Nature link, The human soul that through me ran." ["Lines Written in Early Spring"] In the British Romantic tradition, which Lean readily assimilates, everything is transcendentally a part of the same Spirit.

Ultimately, Alec and Laura sneak out of the movies and seek that "high romance" (of which Keats speaks) entirely outside and "in contrast to those dreary suburbs" (Lean speaking[2]) in natural surroundings. They go first to the Botanical Gardens, then to the river, and finally to a quaint bridge in the country, all to as Wordsworth might put it: "Come forth into the light of things, and let Nature be your teacher." Lean uses the particular image of the couple on the stone bridge over a stream twice, both early in the

[Frame 10]

affair and on their last day together **[frame 10]**; and it provides a striking contrast to the dark, interior overpasses and causeways of the train station. Here their love ripens in idyllic communion with their surroundings. They even rent a boat and let the flow of the river determine their course—only to be halted when a manmade barrier bars their progress. Figuratively, this obstruction represents all the repressive conventions society has arrayed against them, the artificial sense of propriety, the duty to class and family, and the resultant sexual guilt, everything that stops up the course of the river, that prevents nature from teaching them. The effect these "damming" inhibitions (Alec: "The feeling of guilt in doing wrong is too strong, isn't it? Too great a price to pay for the happiness we have together.") have on Laura is epitomized in the scene following the lovers' third meeting. On the train she squirms in her seat trying to avoid the eyes of a minister in her compartment whom she imagines is somehow aware of her "sin." She returns home to find her child hurt in an accident. In voiceover, she remembers (hovering over his bed, terrified): "I tried not to show it, but I was quite hysterical inside . . . as though the whole thing were my fault . . . a sort of punishment, an awful, sinister warning."

If there is a "sinister" as well as "dreary" element to be found in the suburbs, it must, in a pantheistic scheme, reside in the physical detail of those suburbs. The wind has frequently taken on a metaphysical implication in Romantic and Symbolist poetry. From Coleridge's "Eolian Harp" through Shelley's "Ode to the West Wind" to Yeats' "To a Child Dancing in the Wind"; and it may be viewed alternately as a source of inspiration and an omen of doom. Lean's use of it can be representative of this dual concept of a force at once beneficent and malevolent.[2] Alec and Laura's first kiss occurs in a darkly-lit alley and is played against the rush of wind generated by a passing train. If the train itself is

[Frame 11]

taken merely as an obvious sexual symbol, the wind is merely a by-product of passion [frame 11]. The train with its brute driving force is equally a symbol of the deterministic forces which throw Alec and Laura together and then pull them apart. Literally trains carry them away "in opposite directions" every Thursday, the sides of the cars physically separate them in two-shots [frame 12]

[Frame 12]

[Frame 13]

or array themselves like windowed walls through which solitary figures must pass **[frame 13]**. As it rushes by, the express first throws a cinder into Laura's eye and later almost pulls her into suicide. That express, on which they never ride alone or together, is the film's first shot; and it's absence creates the irony of the last shot. The wind, whether generated by the express when they kiss or by the later cloudburst during the lovers' emotionally stormy rendezvous at the borrowed flat, adds preternatural dimension to the scenes, as if the whole animated cosmos, even the manmade moving parts of it such as the trains participated in their affair, in their "overwhelming feeling" (Alec's words). Lean's pantheism, while not as pervasive in this film as it will be in later work, is a key concept, central to both the narrative development and selection of figurative images.

Subjectification. This technique, which was used somewhat unclearly in **IN WHICH WE SERVE**, is much more focused in **BRIEF ENCOUNTER**. The film opens objectively, as two background characters, the tea room hostess and station attendant, exchange sexual banter. As the camera noncommittally records this, a shop girl enters. The camera follows her around the bar and in the background reveals two people, sadly silent at a corner table. The girl leaves the shot, and the camera holds on the couple in medium shot but only for a moment before a cut back to the attendant and hostess at the bar. The shots are composed so that Alec and Laura take on no more importance than any other background character or object in the tea room. Of course, the viewer knows who the stars of the film and consequently who the still-unnamed central characters are. By allowing only glimpses of them, the staging externalizes their tension. The hostess' last quip to the station attendant, "Time and tide wait for no man," acts as a wry comment on the situation at that corner table, even before the details of that situation are clear.

Dolly Messiter, a matronly gossip, enters and recognizes Laura. Only then, as she accosts the couple, does the camera refocus on them. Beyond their pensiveness, the viewer still has no information about them or their relationship. Dolly proceeds to dominate the conversation with her "chattering and fussing," until it is time for Alec to catch his train. His departure is marked by no more than a light touch of the hand on Laura's shoulder. While Dolly is asking for some chocolate, Laura disappears; a train is heard rushing by and, in a moment, she is standing alone in a doorway.

This same scene is played out a second time at the end of the film but from a different perspective: Laura's. Her memory now determines the narrative direction. Lean opens immediately on the lovers in a medium close two-shot at the corner table. Everything which had dominated the earlier rendering is now unimportant. In earlier scenes in the tea room, Lean had relied on the actors' performance and the staging to add meaning. For instance, after their first day together when Laura spontaneously remarks, "You suddenly look much younger" but will not tell Alec what "makes her say that," there is no need for a voiceover explanation. Her expression fulfills the viewer's expectation and reveals that it is because she has fallen in love. Later when Alec finds her in the station long after she has fled the apartment, the entire scene plays in an unbroken two-shot. Again using viewer expectation of a cut and building tension by withholding it, the "relief" when there is a cutaway evokes part of the couple's feeling that this is the beginning of the end of their affair. Now in replaying their final scene in the tea room, the camera centers, intimately, on Laura and Alec as they speak, but their outward calm still contrasts with the words:

>ALEC
>Oh, my dear, I do love you. So very much.
>I love you with all my heart and soul.

>LAURA
>I want to die . . . if only I could die.

>ALEC
>If you died, you'd forget me. I want to be
>remembered.

>LAURA
>Yes, I know, I do too.

>ALEC
>We've still got a few minutes.

At that moment Dolly interrupts the lovers. Her disruptive appearance precipitates a cut as she literally forces her way into frame; but this time Laura's interior monologue and Rachmaninoff's music dominate the track. Her presence, her state of mind, alter the visualization of the event as well. The framing now focuses on Laura; twice the fill light goes down behind her during her

[Frame 14]

voiceovers [frame 14]. The departure bell rings, bringing her out of herself, the lights go back up. Alec stands and prepares to leave.

LAURA (voiceover)
I felt the touch of his hand on my shoulder
for a moment. And then he walked away . . .
away out of my life forever . . . Dolly still
went on talking, but I wasn't listening to her.
I was listening to the sound of his train
starting. And it did. I said to myself, "He
didn't go. At the last minute his courage
failed him; he couldn't have gone. Any
minute now he'll come back into the refreshment room pretending he's forgotten something." I prayed for him to do that . . . just so
that I could see him again, for an instant.
(pause) But the minutes went by.

"Poor, well meaning, irritating" Dolly again asks for chocolate, but this time she walks out of the shot as we stay with Laura.
The sound of an approaching train increases in volume and the
camera travels in towards her. Abruptly it tilts: suddenly as
unbalanced as her mind. As she jumps up and rushes out, the
next three shots remain severely tilted as they follow Laura out
the door. **[frame 15]** The last close shot catches her on the edge of

[Frame 15]

the platform, the wind blowing back her hair, and the light from
the passing cars pulsating across her face like waves of mental
anguish **[frame 16]**: "I meant to do it, . . . I really meant to do it. I

[Frame 16]

stood there trembling right on the edge . . . but I couldn't." The
sudden madness which began with her innocently "extravagant"
decision to purchase an expensive gift for her husband nearly
culminates in death. Then the camera moves in again, and the
frame untilts as the train finishes passing. In an extreme display of
point-of-view, Laura's emotional condition has influenced not
merely subtle elements of staging, but disrupted such standards
of naturalistic filmmaking as background fill light and a camera
plane set on horizontal. In the sequences from **OLIVER TWIST**
cited in the introduction, unnaturalistic tilted angles, process
screens, and fade outs externalized a physical sensation first and
an emotional one second. Here the externalization is primarily
emotional. While Lean reserves the most extravagant usages for
the end of the film, the start of the flashback, as described earlier,
introduced the element of hyper-reality derived from character
point-of-view. In bracketing the narrative with overt effects that
defy misreading, Lean alerts the audience and enhances its
opportunity to perceive the more subtle effects.

There are many other varied instances of intricate
subjectification. After one of their Thursday rendezvous, for
example, Laura within her own flashback imagines herself with
Alec in various exotic locations. The countryside, as seen from
her moving train, fades away and a series of fantasies are
superimposed (dancing to a waltz; at the opera in Paris; on the
Grand Canal in Venice; on a luxury liner; and beneath the palms

of a tropical island). Each expresses Laura's desire to escape her unexciting existence and live out these schoolgirl daydreams. Soon, however, these images dissolve back into the dull English countryside, just as her transient love affair will fade, and the laughter of actual schoolgirls passing the couple on the platform will become a bitter irony. The scene in the refreshment room following Laura and Alec's first kiss is another type of subjective within subjective. As she sits, half remorseful, half-glad, in the tea room and recalls within her flashback Alec's subtle invitation to go to his friend's unoccupied flat and her guarded refusal, the audience is sharing not merely Laura's memories but her memories of memories. Perhaps a more understated example is when Laura recalls the first time she conceals the truth from Fred: she sits at a dressing table with her back to him, she is seen reflected in the mirror but only the lower part of Fred's body is visible. While Laura may actually have seen his face in the mirror, the viewer never does because Laura, from her flashback vantage, cannot bear to see it as she remembers lying to him and frames the scene accordingly.

Lean structures many of his films as series of oppositions, often favoring the contrasts of reality and dreams, of the unremarkable and the exceptional. Because most of the incidents in **BRIEF ENCOUNTER**'s love affair are seen only as Laura remembers them, the viewer is necessarily subject to her interpretation of events and the most meaningful context is her personality. Seen superficially, she is a sedate, stereotyped English matron, devoted to her family, largely unemotional, and exclusively concerned with the mundane matters of daily living (witness Alec's wry observation: "What exciting lives we lead.").

This is the surface Laura Jesson; but her weekly excursions into town to shop, to go to the library, and see a movie unveil the other side of her. Watching her during these separations from her family, it is clear, even without the narration, that she is in search of something which her dull husband and monotonous home life do not offer. Until she meets Alec, it may be found in a book of poetry (Fred: "You're a poetry addict . . . "), or in a movie theater where one can, on the screen, vicariously burn with "Flames of Passion"; but it can be found. The restrictions on Laura, both real and imagined, are imposed by a world that she believes frowns on the vicarious and impractical. Like the chain that prevents the passage of a rowboat, these are artificial but strongly forged. Lean dissolves from a medium long shot of the couple outside the theater to one of them in the park, an optical device that reduces the movement and dichotomy of the entire film. In a similar vein, one might note the small credit

Dolly Messiter (Everley Gregg) offers the distracted Laura Jesson (Celia Johnson) a glass of water.

beneath the glaring main title for the fictitious FLAMES OF PASSION, "based on the novel Gentle Summer." Laura exists on the brink of life where it takes no more than a chance cinder in the eye to ignite those flames of passion, to displace her customary sublimations. As she begins to imagine, to dream, to love, and to agonize, Laura's moments with Alec are polarized between "unreflecting love" and disconsolate guilt, between elation and melancholy, a polarity made clear directly, in the dialogue, and reinforced by unconscious reactions, as in the case of the lady cellist/organist who changes from being funny to seeming sad.

All of this affects Laura's memory of the affair. Through her perceptions a dreamlike Romanticism imbues the otherwise staid events. For although Alec and Laura never become lovers in the physical sense, part of the value of their passion is in the subjective transformation of their environment, in their escape from the drab material world into sensation. Rachmaninoff's wistful "Second Piano Concerto" is played over scene as an equivalent to the lovers' emotions and as a contrast to the dismal visual reality of "ordinary" concerns. As a narrative device it is justified when Laura herself "chooses" it by switching on the radio after returning from her final parting with Alec. As Laura might well have defined her uncomplicated, middle class notion of love as "hearing beautiful music all the time," so then, within the context of her recollection, is it appropriately present on the track.

As with most dreamers, the intrusions of society and its morality ultimately prove too constricting. Laura and Alec cannot "let the great big world keep turning," as says the song which a barrel organ plays on the high street, and go about their own mad love. "Madness" itself is a word which Lean will use again and again to characterize his heroes and heroines. In **BRIEF EN-COUNTER**, madness is both the alternative and the underlying irony. For beneath the irony which Laura herself must perceive when Fred gives her the line from Keats as a crossword puzzle clue and she must fill in the word "romance" is the fact that "it goes with delirium and Baluchistan." If Laura feels enmeshed in society's orderly puzzle, if it clings vaguely to her, it also prevents her from yielding to her mad, self-destructive impulse on the platform. Although she says to Fred in interior monologue: "I couldn't. I wasn't brave enough. I should like to be able to say it was the thought of you and the children that prevented me, but it wasn't. I had no thoughts at all. Only an overwhelming desire not to feel anything ever again," it is Laura's residual sanity which holds her back.

The final sequence of the movie begins with a jump cut from Laura standing in the doorway of the tea room to the frame of the story—Laura sitting in the study with her husband. She looks disorientedly at Fred, as if the abrupt change of scene had jarred her, rudely, awake.

FRED (kneeling by her)

Laura.

LAURA

Yes, dear.

FRED

Whatever your dream was, it wasn't a very
happy one, was it?

LAURA

No.

FRED

You've been a long way away. Thank you
for coming back to me. (Laura weeps.)

Like all of Lean's most important characters, Laura is poised
between an ephemeral, self-made, or fanciful universe and the
safer, more solid, everyday world. Her brief life with Alec is
symbolized by windy excursions in a borrowed convertible and
by the trains which speed in and out of their scenes together. The
constant movement of these vehicles is representative of the
dynamic yet unstable relationship Alec and Laura have, while the
solid, wood furniture and gray fixtures of Laura's house symbol-
ize her "normal" domestic life. Even as she yearns for the magic
of the former, Laura is tied by convention, by her own insecurity,
to the latter. All this is most decisively reinforced when she flees
the apartment in the rain and goes from the high street to a small
square. A wide, high angle shot which shows her moving to a
bench also features a dark statue prominently positioned in the
left foreground. Assuming that the flashback is always fundamen-
tally from Laura's perspective, she places or imagines that black,
ominous figure in the frame like a dark god hovering over her in
disapproval. Immediately after this, a policemen, the emblem of
social order, approaches her.

Ultimately, the passion which she and Alec develop in
their wanderings, however spontaneous and natural it may be, is
not strong enough to overcome either moral or social conven-

tion. Lean has not spoken directly about Wordsworth or the British Romantic tradition, but he inserted a telling reference to them in the script of his last film, **A PASSAGE TO INDIA**, spoken by one of the minor characters: "I believe you and Ronny met in the Lake district . . . You must forgive me, but I'm an incurable Romantic." Laura is not a cliched incurable Romantic, with either a small or a capital "r." Knowing lines from Keats or visiting a nearby, if somewhat shabby, equivalent of the Lake district is one thing; having an affair is quite another. Laura's sad pronouncement, as she realizes her "dream" is almost over is "Nothing lasts really, neither happiness nor despair, not even life lasts very long." Here she verbalizes the feeling of the entire encounter: smiles, furtive glances, brief moments of happiness, longer ones of anxiety—all end. Laura "comes back" from the brink, fearful and resigned, to some obscure, predestined course of life, questioning as Wordsworth did:

> If this belief from heaven be sent,
> If such be Nature's holy plan,
> Have I not reason to lament
> What man has made of man?
> > "Lines Written in Early Spring"

3
The Dickens Adaptations:
GREAT EXPECTATIONS (1946)
OLIVER TWIST (1948)

The marshes were just a long black
horizontal line then, as I stopped
to look after him; and the river was
just another horizontal line; and the
sky was just a row of long angry red
lines and dense black lines intermixed.
>   —Charles Dickens, *Great Expectations*

Shortly after World War II ended and even before **BRIEF EN-COUNTER** was released, Lean was on location in "Dickens country," on the marshlands of East Kent along the Thames Estuary. Cineguild's new production took them, at last, into other source material than Coward's.

In choosing one of the best-known and most popular novels in the language, Lean and his associates relocated themselves not just imagistically from the conventions of a modern setting into a period atmosphere but also into a highly-charged historical context. The background of Dickens' novel is those tumultuous years of the Victorian era which witnessed the emergence of the middle-class, of monied professionals and those "in trade," and the displacement of the landed aristocracy as the governing class. Raymond Durgnat called **GREAT EXPECTA-TIONS** "accidental Marxism," and James Agee discerned traces "of Freud and perhaps to some extent of Marx."[1] Certainly if the narrative events of both the novel and the film constitute a socio-critical fiction, the person responsible is Dickens. Not only is *Great Expectations* one of Dickens' most pessimistic works on personal and character levels, but its depiction of inflexible social orders and a suffocating caste structure posits small chance for reform within the system. The myth of "upward mobility" born in the great industrial movement is a bitter irony for Dickens, who observes that whether birth or money defines the "gentleman," once made he cannot be unmade. Thus nothing could be more pathetic or unproductive than the instances of impoverished gentry. Dickens is less theoretically anti-capitalist than practically anti-industrialist, reacting against an economic revolution perfidious for both the obvious evils of sweatshops, poorhouses, and child labor and for the implicit damage done to the human spirit by its cutthroat competitiveness. Jaggers, the self-made nineteenth century man, and Wemmick, the clerk with the "post-office mouth," are serious and comic examples of the time's dehumanizing effects. Dickens' abhorrence of mechanization is a state of mind and not a statement of particulars. It is present in his prose not in passages of oratory but in patterns of images; and only in this latent form is it present in the film.

Lean and his co-screenwriters retain the character of the novel while making subtle changes in Dickens' hero, Philip Pirrip, known as "Pip." For while both may concentrate thematically on the conflicts of an individual in and at least partially against society, Dickens' established method of placing an ordinary man in unusual circumstances does not correspond with Lean's emerging one of discovering a man (or woman) with a sense of the extraordinary trapped in a commonplace situation. Lean makes Pip more dynamic but not on the scale of his later characterizations. More importantly, while he basically defines the same Pip as Dickens did, in translating the central images, Lean manages to do so on his own terms.

Pantheism. In adapting Dickens' animated universe, Lean makes more use of black-and-white exteriors than in any of his subsequent period films. The opening scene faithfully renders a contrast of dark stretches of earth and clouds against white sky; but Lean adds, silhouetted and dwarfed in extreme long shot, the figure of a boy [frame 17]. Pip is immediately caught in a tangle of

[frame 17]

pantheistic forces. He runs, and a pan follows him horizontally, as if driven by the natural lines of the landscape. Concurrently, his vertical form is in opposition to that line. Finally, the pan reveals two gibbets: the first, in the distance, seems simply to impend doom, which for Pip is the imminent manifestation of Magwitch; the second, intruding into the right foreground of the frame, is more obviously a manmade object which graphically ruptures the natural pattern. By altering Dickens so that Pip rather than Magwitch is the figure in the landscape, the background appears to propel him forward rather than trying "to get a twist upon his ankle." Lean rapidly establishes the figurative tug of natural versus artificial impulses on Pip, but he retains the graphic distinctions between the boy and the convict. After the ominous low angles of Pip against the headstones in the graveyard [frame 18] and of the wind rustling through tendrils and bare branches, Magwitch is suddenly before him as if sprung from the earth [frame 19]. His interruption of a panning shot is a geometric association which parallels Dickens' "[the other of the] black things in all the prospect that seemed to be standing upright [was]

[frame 18]

[frame 19]

a gibbet, with some chains hanging to it which had once held a pirate. The man was limping on towards this latter as if he were the pirate come to life, and come down, and going back to hook himself up again." Leaping out, posed with Pip against the hoary trees, Magwitch assumes less of a human than a preternatural dimension. The audience senses this with the character Pip at once, unlike the reader who must wait for the remarks of the narrator Pip at the end of the chapter. Coincidentally, the viewer may also recoil with a start at the unexpected appearance of the large, menacing form. For Lean, "The best thing was to frighten the audience, as the convict frightens the boy."[2]

Ultimately, the film Magwitch, delineated in a different context, cannot possess all the facets of the novel's personage. Instead of attempting to translate too much, Lean takes Dickens' "animal imagery" and makes Magwitch an integral part of the animated, somewhat hostile surroundings. He arrives for the first time as a wind sweeps the cemetery; he is devoured by the shadows rowing back to the hulks after his recapture; and he reappears at Pip's door in the midst of a storm. For the description of Magwitch which closes the first chapter, "picking his way among the nettles" like a dark, lumbering beast, Lean substitutes the dynamic image of the struggle on the mud flats, in which Magwitch sinks into the marsh and literally becomes an extension of it. In the two dimensions of the black-and-white frame Magwitch merges with the ground; in contrast, Pip and Joe, who stand watching this, are in sharp relief against the sky and distinctly detached from the natural elements within the shot.

Figurative Imagery. Many of the images in **Great Expectations** are carried over from Dickens. Pip's theft of the file and pie is a good example: His anxious voiceovers are taken from the text. "The mist was heavier yet when I got out upon the marshes, so that instead of my running at everything, everything seemed to run at me" becomes a series of travelling shots through the fog. Even the imagined cries of "Stop, thief" and "Get up, Mrs. Joe" and the grazing cattle hurling accusations ("Halloa, young thief") are adapted with the words superimposed over point-of-view medium close shots of the bull and cows. While the actual visualizations may not contain the wealth of linguistic colorations of the text, its subjective impressions are intensified—the "Stop, thief" by its very disembodied presence on the track leaves the viewer startled by it as forcefully as the boy is and uncertain for an instant whether it is conjured up by Pip or really there.

Other usages seem less arbitrary on film. The sight of Jaggers washing his hands or of Wemmick casually dusting a death mask with his coat sleeve [frames 20 and 21] are details which require individual comment for effect in novel form. In the motion picture, they become incidental bits of business which, covered by the scene's dialogue, seem more spontaneous. Since Pip is in the shot while Jaggers and Wemmick perform these actions, it is also unnecessary for him to note them in a literary aside; figurative value is added with less artifice. Similarly, the

[frame 20]

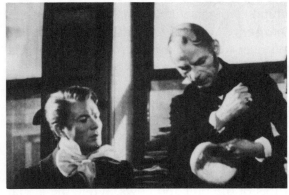

[frame 21]

impact of Pip's first sight of Miss Havisham, "the strangest lady I have ever seen," in the decaying splendor of Satis House, an event which requires several hundred words of description in the book, is instantaneous rather than cumulative. Items of decor in other scenes may also provide introductory character information: the print of a boxer on the wall of Herbert's lodgings reflecting his pugilistic aspirations; the glass-encased hangman's noose and even the severe arched doorway in Jagger's office capturing his Baroque business manner; these are unexpected, unemphatic, inserted for more the viewer's casual notice than for Pip's. The entrance into Miss Havisham's domain, however, is a climax of dramatic anticipation that is essentially Pip's. Dickens subjectifies his passage by stressing certain impressions: "white veil . . . dress . . . shoes . . . hair of white"; "Half- packed . . . not quite finished

. . . half arranged." Lean constructs the room and its inhabitants from the same passage but photographs the cobwebbed corners, the trinkets on the dressing table, all of the various contents, in point-of-view. From the beginning, with the camera peering over Pip's shoulder at eye level while the door swings open gradually to reveal the inner sanctum, Lean stages in a way that draws the viewer into Pip's childish and apprehensive frame of reference.

Lean not only adapts Dickens' literary tropes but derives and develops a variety of purely visual and/or original figurative concepts, contained within a single shot or extended over several sequences. For instance, when Jaggers enters the forge, there is a kind of synecdoche in the common film device of representing Joe and Pip by their shadows on the door [frame 22]. While this shot may not have the same implications as the like treatment of

[frame 22]

Monks in **OLIVER TWIST**, cited in the introduction, there is a suggestion of Jaggers' prejudgment of Pip and Joe as working class people being featureless, unimportant shadows. On a more elaborate level, Lean can associate a shot of arrows piercing a target back through a montage effect to Pip's fear of Estella's coldly precise behavior ("Will you always be part of Miss Havisham's plan?") or forward to the arrival of Bentley Drummle (three shots later) and, in so doing, can foreshadow both Pip's heart being pierced and his despairing conversation with Estella at the ball ("You give him looks and smiles you never give me." "Do you want me then to deceive and entrap you?"). All of this is wryly connected by the air of a stately dance on the soundtrack.

When Pip's hopes finally do expire in the conflagration at Satis House, Lean, although he adheres to the specifics of Dickens' version of the occurrence, makes two key interpolations. First, he explicitly records that Havisham's death is inadvertently caused by Pip: in slamming the door behind him, he dislodges a piece of firewood which ignites her dress. Second, in ending with a high angle long shot of Pip kneeling by her body and collapsing by the "great table," now stripped of its cloth and service and positioned on the right like a huge headstone [frame 23], Lean implicitly erects a marker over the dissolution of Havisham's

[frame 23]

perverse existence and creates a metaphor for the entombment of Pip's "great expectations" that simultaneously recalls their inception in the graveyard with Magwitch.

Lean also forges several links between Pip and the fixtures of the house. When he arrives "to play," a travelling shot back from the sunlit doorway reveals a black interior filling more and more of the frame, waiting to swallow him up like a crypt, which is exactly what its owner makes of it. Only Estella is key-lit inside; and it is she who calls him into the ominous darkness ("Don't loiter, boy"), who sets the mechanism of his fate in motion and leads him through the obscure passageways much as she will "lead" him to become a gentleman. There are also suggestions of the house as a womb—its insulated timelessness; the infantile aspects of Havisham's behavior—which Lean under-

scores when Pip leaves the house for the last time, superimpos-
ing his line, "My boyhood has ended," over an extreme long shot
of him descending the stairs with Estella. Perhaps the most
expressive sequence in the film is the escape down the river at
night: the tiny skiff is lost among the hulls of the cargo ships
(matte shots of miniatures) and on the track are the sounds of the
vessels creaking at anchor, mingling with the crewmen's songs,
and muffling the strokes of the oars. Suddenly a figurehead looms
into the foreground of a high angle shot; over a reverse someone,
unseen, cries, "Ahoy, there." The head itself looks down on them
like the face of God, as if incarnating a placid destiny that
witnesses their passage, voices a challenge, and lets them hold
their course knowing where it will lead [frame 24].

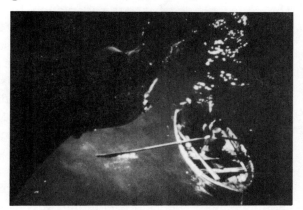

[frame 24]

Irony, Subjectivity, and Comic Relief. The ship's fig-
urehead also recalls the face of Compeyson, Magwitch's pursuer,
stitched into the visual fabric by a deterministic dissolve, as he
follows Herbert out of the shipping office [frame 25]. That incident is one of the few that Lean records in the ironic mode,
another being the start of the fire. Both incidents complement the
main thematic line. As previously noted, Havisham's death relates
the end of Pip's false hopes in her, which immediately precede
the death scene, back to the real source of his "expectations,"
which was helping Magwitch. Compeyson's face and the figurehead "hang over" the vulnerable Magwitch, but that is unknown
to Pip. The final ironic layer is that, in his ignorance, Pip causes or

[frame 25]

allows to perish, in a sense gets revenge against, both people who have fostered those deceptive and shallow expectations. This concept is peculiar to the adaptation. In the novel Pip is not responsible, except through association of his fantasy of her suicide, for Havisham's death. Nor is he so unaware of the imminence of the threat posed by Compeyson as he is in the film. By restricting the irony in this manner, Lean is more than faithful to the original's first person style; for, excepting these two brief moments and one other, equally brief, when Mrs. Joe rides up to dispatch Pip to Satis House, the film, too, is in the first person in that Pip is present in every scene.

Within that overall narrative subjectivity, Lean obtains a number of particular effects. Pip's voiceovers throughout—the sequence with the cattle, entering Miss Havisham's room as already described, the first fascinating close shot of Estella through the house gate, the low angle of the grownups at the Christmas party—are all standard devices defining a specific point-of-view. On a less obvious level, a shot may, as in **BRIEF ENCOUNTER**, catch the inner state of a protagonist. In Pip's dialogue with Estella on the stairs, for example, his own sense of inferiority is reflected in the cross-cut over-shoulder shots which angle up towards her (a step above) and down towards him [frame 26]. To approximate Pip's tension in his first adult re-encounter with Estella, Lean follows them in a long, unbroken medium two-shot as they walk through the garden. To add to his discomfort, he is forced to awkwardly sidestep hanging vines and other vegeta-

[frame 26]

tion. But the most complete externalization of sensation in **GREAT EXPECTATIONS** is contained in Pip's collapse after Magwitch's death. Lean begins with a travelling medium close shot of Pip walking unsteadily down a crowded street. Gradually the oppressive whirr inside his brain leaks onto the soundtrack; a light spins dizzily and is superimposed over his face [frame 27]. Then

[frame 27]

the camera becomes Pip, lurching forward through his front door and into his room but falling short of the bed. His loss of consciousness becomes a cut to black, an effect repeated in **OLIVER TWIST**; after a moment of silence and a dark screen, he "comes to his senses" with a slow, blurry fade-in, focusing on a close shot of the ever effusive Joe Gargery.

Between the subjective and the comedic aspects of the original, as represented principally by Joe, Lean concentrates on the former. That is not to say that the film is solemnly dramatic for

Joe, Wemmick, and Herbert Pocket—both the "young gentlemen" throwing in the sponge and Alec Guinness' interpretation of the grown Herbert—retain the innate humor Dickens gave them. The more serious caricatures, such as Francis L. Sullivan as the portly Jaggers and Martita Hunt as the grotesque Havisham, are also aptly rendered. From the standpoint of interpretation, it is John Mills' portrayal of the adult Pip which has the fewest lighter moments: posing proudly in his new, out-of-fashion suit; adding up debts with Herbert; the montage of becoming a gentleman. For the most part, the actor must fluctuate between boyish enthusiasm and forlorn brooding; and the middle third of the picture with its rapid episodes is slightly out of pace with Pip's boyhood (first third) and the events after Magwitch's return (last third).

Lean uses comedy sparingly and with greater integration as the film progresses. The cart ride with Uncle Pumblychook where the music replaces the dialogue or the dinner with Herbert where Pip receives instruction in table manners ("In London it's not the custom to put the knife in the mouth—for fear of accident") advance the plot while providing comic relief but do nothing more. Later, Joe's visit to London, which concludes with his hat floating in Pip and Herbert's teapot, occasions some serious introspection by Pip. Lean creates a visual parallel by shooting Pip reflected in a mirror and adding the figurative implication of a gilt frame around Pip in a rich dressing gown [frame 28], so that the comedy provides a lead-in for Pip to strike

[frame 28]

one of the film's most thematically serious poses. The last comic "bit" is perhaps the most telling and least amusing: Pip's meeting with the Aged Parent. By compelling Pip to nod and humor his senile father before he will pass on the information about Magwitch, Wemmick frustrates both Pip ("I am anxious to know what happened") and the viewer, who by identification and purely as one following the plot, is equally anxious to know. By altering the circumstances of his first visit to Wemmick's house at Walworth (it should be noted that an earlier scene at that location is included in the final shooting script but was cut from the picture), Lean also alters the thrust of Dickens' comedy. For the Aged Parent, in his original context, would probably seem extraneous and can only be justifiably carried over as a foil to manipulate the audience into sharing Pip's emotion and to heighten rather than relieve the dramatic suspense.

The Ending. There were two conclusions to *Great Expectations* written by Dickens: an original, pessimistic ending in which Pip and his godson speak briefly with Estella, who is widowed and remarried, that takes place in London and is, in novel time, two years later; and the revised actual ending, which was produced at the urging of Edward Bulwer-Lytton for insertion before the first serial publication in 1860. The film provides a third. Like Dickens' revised version (which, unless otherwise noted, will be the only one considered from here on), it is ostensibly a "happy ending:" the novel's final "broad expanse of

[frame 29]

GREAT EXPECTATIONS:
Pip's (John Mills) first meet-
ing with the grown Herbert
Pocket (Alec Guinness).

tranquil light [in which] I saw no shadow of another parting from her" is translated into a long shot of Pip and Estella closing the gate of Satis House behind them, locking out the past while the sentiment of the title is reaffirmed by being superimposed in large letters over the shot [frame 29]. It seems an image of abundant hope and appropriately so, fulfilling the demands of an essentially melodramatic story in a pleasing, slightly tearful, joyful, superficial, and generally satisfying manner. But, still following Dickens, it leaves several deeper implications unresolved.

    To begin with, the screenplay extensively elaborates on both the narrative and psychological lines of the novel. Dickens sets the last meeting in what has been critically dubbed a "ruined garden": " . . . no house now, no brewery, no building whatever left, but the wall of the old garden." In the film, Pip slowly walks through the still extant house up to Miss Havisham's room, recalling as he does earlier visits externalized by voiceovers from past encounters at the gate, on the stairs, and along the darkened corridors. He discovers Estella upstairs; and for the first time in the picture the dialogue and the whole thrust of the scene radically diverge from the original:

[NOVEL]

PIP
(seeing her on the garden walk)
Estella!

ESTELLA
I am greatly changed. I wonder
you know me.
[They sit on a bench]

PIP
After so many years, it is strange
that we should meet thus again,
Estella, here where our first
meeting was! Do you often come
back?

ESTELLA
I have never come here since.

PIP
Nor I.
[The moon begins to rise]

ESTELLA
(crying)
I have often hoped and intended
to come back but have been
prevented by many circum-
stances. Poor, poor old place!
Were you wondering, as you
walked along how it came to be
left in this condition?

PIP
Yes, Estella.

ESTELLA
The grounds belong to me. It is
the only possession I have not
relinquished. Everything else has
gone from me, little by little, but I
have kept this. It was the subject
of the only determined resistance
I made in all the wretched years.

[FILM]

M.S. PIP entering the room
ESTELLA'S VOICE
Pip.

M.L.S. ESTELLA (POV) by the
dressing table

M.S. PIP

PIP
Estella.

L.S. PIP over Estella's shoulder

PIP
(walking towards her)
What are you doing here? I
thought you were in Paris with
your husband.

M.C.S. ESTELLA over Pip

ESTELLA
I have no husband, Pip. Have
you not heard?

PIP
I have been ill, Estella. I have
heard nothing.

ESTELLA
When Mr. Jaggers disclosed to
Bentley Drummle my true
parentage . . . (looking down) . . .
he no longer wished to have me
for a wife.

M.C.S. PIP over Estella

ESTELLA
Well. Pip. Why don't you laugh?
You have every right.

PIP
I've no wish to laugh, Estella. I'm
truly sorry.

PIP
It is to be built on?

ESTELLA
At last it is, I come here to take leave of it before its change. And you, you live abroad still?

PIP
Still.

ESTELLA
And do well, I am sure.

PIP
I work pretty hard for a sufficient living, and therefore—Yes, I do well!

ESTELLA
I have often thought of you.

PIP
Have you?

ESTELLA
Of late very often. There was a long hard time when I kept far from me the remembrance of what I had thrown away when I was quite ignorant of its worth. But since my duty has not been incompatible with the admission of the remembrance, I have given it a place in my heart.

PIP
You have always held your place in *my* heart.

M.C.S. ESTELLA over Pip

ESTELLA
You've no need to pity me. It simplifies my life.

M.C.S. PIP over Estella

ESTELLA
There is no need to sell the house. It is mine and I shall live here.
      [She sits down. Music]

M.S. ESTELLA in Miss Havisham's chair

ESTELLA
I shall like it here, Pip. Away from the world and all its complications.

C.S. PIP looking at Estella, then to the right.

C.S. THE DRESSING TABLE (POV) a new pair of white gloves, a prayer book, and pearls which were for Estella's wedding

M.S. ESTELLA seated left and PIP standing over her on CAMERA RIGHT

PIP (gravely)
How long have you been here, Estella?

ESTELLA
I don't know.

PIP (moving closer)
Estella, you must leave this house. It's a dead house. Nothing can live here. Leave it, Estella, I beg of you.

ESTELLA
I little thought that I should take
leave of you in taking leave of
this spot. I am very glad to do so.

PIP
Glad to part again, Estella. To
me, parting is a painful thing. To
me the remembrance of our last
parting has been ever mournful
and painful.

ESTELLA
But you said to me, 'God bless
you, God forgive you!' And if you
could say that to me then, you
will not hesitate to say that to me
now—now when suffering has
been stronger than all other, and
has taught me to understand
what your heart used to be. I
have been bent and broken,
but—I hope—into a better shape.
Be as considerate and good to
me as you were, and tell me we
are friends.

PIP (standing)
We are friends.

ESTELLA
And will continue friends apart.

['I took her hand in mine, and we
went out of the ruined place; and
as the morning mists had risen
long ago when I first left the
forge, so the evening mists were

ESTELLA
What do you mean? This is the
house where I grew up. It's part
of me. It's my home.

PIP
It's Miss Havisham's home. But
she's gone, Estella. Gone from
this house, from you, from both
of us.

ESTELLA
She is not gone. She is still here
with me, in this house, in this
very room.

PIP
Then I defy her.

M.S. PIP in the middle of the
room

PIP (shouting)
I have come back, Miss
Havisham.

L.S. PIP. Estella remains in the
chair

PIP
I have come back to let in the
sunlight.

M.C.S. PIP tears down a curtain

M.S. ESTELLA suddenly backlit

L.S. PIP tearing down more
curtains

M.S. ESTELLA as light strikes her
face

L.S. ESTELLA looks up. Pip
stands behind among the
crumpled draperies

rising now, and in all the broad
expanse of tranquil light they
showed to me, I saw no shadow
of another parting from her.']

PIP
Look, Estella, look. Nothing but
dust and decay.

M.C.S. PIP walks back to Estella

PIP (bending over)
I have never ceased to love you
even when there seemed no
hope for my love. You are part of
my existence, part of myself,
Estella. Come with me. Out into
the sunlight.

[She stands. He catches her by
the shoulders]

M.S.2S. PIP and ESTELLA

PIP
Look at me.

ESTELLA (looking away)
Pip. I'm afraid.

PIP
Look at me.

[She turns slowly towards him]

PIP
We belong to each other. Let's
start again. Together.

ESTELLA (half-laughing, half-
sobbing)
Oh, Pip.

MUSIC swells.   DISSOLVE TO:

*M.L.S. CORRIDOR OF SATIS
HOUSE* as Pip and Estella run out.
They turn to look back at the
gate
GREAT
EXPECTATIONS

is superimposed over shot as
they go out into the sunlight.

GREAT EXPECTATIONS: Pip (John Mills) discovers a spellbound Estella (Valerie Hobson) sitting amid the ruins of Satis House.

Both scenes are verbally explicit, but Dickens' is more overtly directed towards character exposition and explaining what has happened emotionally in the intervening years, particularly to Estella: " . . . suffering has been stronger than all other, and has taught me to understand what your heart used to be." He ends with only a possibility of reconciliation not a fait accompli. The talk is not exactly mundane, although Pip's remarks on his career approach it, but swathed in rhetorical gentility. Pip plays an observational role noting the vegetation, the moon, the morning mists and remains conversationally passive, allowing Estella to lead him. In the film, the emphasis shifts to Pip: *he* directs the scene towards its climax. Moreover, as the dialogue is less rhetorical and the exchange more spontaneous and enlivened, a markedly less composed Estella emerges. She is still proud, much nearer arrogance than in Dickens, but, within the sequence itself, she grows more distant and distracted and finally, it becomes apparent, is on the verge of schizophrenic withdrawal. This metamorphosis into a second Miss Havisham is well outside the scope of Dickens' conception; but it does follow from the underlying notion of Estella having been bred by Havisham to "wreak revenge on the male sex." Being conditioned to patterned responses, Estella herself gives the reason for her breakdown—a deviation from the pattern: Drummle's rejection. That rejection (Dickens does not mention it or, for that matter, Drummle at all, although in the original ending he died fittingly enough "from an accident consequent on ill-treating a horse") also recreates the chief circumstances of and motivation for Miss Havisham's retreat from the exterior world.

From the opening lines Dickens actually stresses the fortuitous coincidence of the encounter, clearly establishing that both have chosen the same day to return for the first time after lengthy absences. Perhaps, speculating from the knowledge that he was in the process of an alteration and not working from the first light of inspiration, it could be argued that Dickens was anticipating and trying to undercut potential criticism of that coincidence as farfetched; and, indeed, it seems so. In any case, Lean does not have to grapple with that problem in its literary context; and he understates the chance quality of their meeting. Again he uses identification with the "first person" Pip to manipulate audience response: in Pip's preceding tour of the house, Lean restricts observable reality to what he sees and hears. When Pip enters the upstairs room, the first suggestion of Estella's presence is her over shot exclamation of his name; the first shot of her is a point-of-view. The sudden fact of her being in the room and the surprise of it shared with Pip allow the viewer no time for speculation on how she came to be there or the relative likelihood of it. Disbelief remains suspended by her very material presence and by the mutual need of Pip and the audience to make an immediate response to it.

This Estella lurking in the corners of Satis House is substantially different from Dickens'. Sitting amid the ruins, his heroine is pensive, even nostalgic, but still logical and keenly aware of her position, of not just the physical surroundings but the emotional terrain as well. Dickens gives her not only the bulk of the dialogue with four complete short speeches but also the key lines which provide most of the narrative information; Lean

defines Estella's new compulsion objectively: she arranges her
things on a dressing table and sits stiffly before them in the same
way Miss Havisham did. And the viewer shares the perception
with Pip, for he is the distinguishing factor between the two
women. As a doting lover he gave Havisham satisfaction in being
something she could not have, while reinforcing rather than
undermining Estella's aloofness; but Havisham's failure to form a
direct relationship with Pip, her emotional inability to be his or
anyone's benefactress, exacts its toll in his physical inability to
save her from the fire. Pip *can* save Estella by replacing the lost
suitor and by taking advantage of what is, for the first time, her
inferior position. Lean underscores this new position in his
staging, beginning with cross-cut medium close shots in which
Pip and Estella are "equal" then shooting from behind her, up at
Pip who stands while she sits, so that he no longer appears to be
shorter than she is. Dickens' Pip is still somewhat immature,
uncertain at best, timidly resigned at worst to waiting for direction,
a perpetual parody of the industrious Herbert Pocket's "looking
about" him. The "ruined garden" becomes an image of a new
beginning both through its archetypal associations with Eden,
and in its resemblance to the graveyard of the opening chapter.
But Lean uses each visit to Satis House as a gauge of Pip's
adulthood: his docility as a child; his hurt, adolescent anger in the
last confrontation with Havisham; and finally, in this scene, his
maturity in handling Estella.

The central metaphor in Pip's action, although it may
have been suggested by Dickens' tone or by his "tranquil light," is
also original to the film. Estella does not respond to arguments,
so Pip illuminates the situation by tearing down the curtains and
literally "let[ting] in the sunlight." In a series of three cuts [**frames
30** to **32**], Lean adds backlight and sidelight to a low-key medium
shot of Estella in Havisham's chair: her reaction is stylized—
startled, dazed, looking around in wonderment as Pip exposes
the "dust and decay." Figuratively, by allowing time, even in the
primitive movement of sun-cast shadows across the floor, to re-
enter Satis House, Miss Havisham's spell is broken. For just as
Lean can forego Dickens' verbal expressions of astonishment at

[frame 30]

[frame 31]

[frame 32]

the chance meeting in favor of equally explicit reaction shots
from his actors, he can resolve the plotted psychological conflicts
on a purely graphic level. In this, the ending is not "realistic" but

"tropistic," part of a scheme where figurative meanings become primary events. Even without the implication of reversal of Pip's earlier entry into the dark house as a child, the final image of Pip and Estella passing through the front door "out into the sunlight" still achieves its major, narrative purpose. But without the arrangement of shots to delineate the truly metaphysical effect of the light on Estella, she cannot be transformed, cannot be deterred from mental self-destruction.

In his closing chapter, Dickens sets in motion a cycle of regression on Pip's part. As if longing for the lost innocence of youth, for the period before his disillusionment, the narrator Pip so accelerates the passage of time that eleven years go by in a single sentence, and he rushes towards old age and a "second childhood." In his namesake, Joe and Biddy's son who is never conceived in the film, the young Pip of the novel's beginning reappears. Lean fashions his own link with Pip's childhood through Satis House, as previously noted, and more specifically with a single medium close shot of the grown Pip reclining on a slope and tugging at the grass in exactly the same position he assumed as a boy when Estella first caused his dissatisfaction. [frames 33 and 34] Visually Pip returns to the moment when he only dreamed of being a gentleman; now, having been made so by Magwitch, he nevertheless verbally concedes that "that poor dream has all gone by . . . all gone by." That point in the novel is, as it happens, where Dickens begins his revision. In the film, that shot in its recollection and synthesis of a past time with a stated present realization marks the instant where Lean moves beyond the book and records the completion of Pip's maturation.

That occurrence, more than anything else, also makes plausible as well as possible the "happy" ending. "Happy" with reservations, because, just as Dickens subjectively speeds up his character's regressive desires, Lean carefully outlines the frame of reference in his conclusion. The voiceovers as Pip wanders through the house are all of the young Estella and demonstrate a lingering fascination with the past. Accordingly, when the real Estella calls his name, it is initially unclear whether she is actually there or merely another imagined voice. Even the point-of-view

[frame 33]

[frame 34]

shot of her is ambiguous. One of the film's most pictorially lustrous images, it is almost a portrait, almost too stylishly lit and perfectly composed to be anything but a vision or a dream.

Obviously this line of analysis can lead, not unreasonably, to an interpretation of the ending as a complex fantasy created by Pip and culminating in the surreal, transcendent slow motion as the couple run ("float" would be more accurate) hand in hand from the house. Even as reality, there are several limitations. For example, in the last shot inside Havisham's room, the camera sees Estella in profile and Pip has a full-face view—only he is literally in a position to judge the genuineness of her expression when she says, "Oh, Pip"; and he is not above self-deception. Equally disturbing is the fact that the concluding shots build in a way that is roughly analogous, right down to the surge of exultant music, to the wait for the packet boat which ended in crushed hopes. Finally, there is the latent irony in the superimposed "Great Expectations" for the future may be only that, expectations without fulfillment, and nothing more. Many questions are never resolved. The ending achieves a certain degree of interaction with all that precedes it and certainly fulfills several functions within itself; but much as the novel's vague "shadow of another parting" does not entirely lift, traces of ambiguity linger over the film as a whole.

> *Oliver cried lustily. If he could have*
> *known that he was an orphan, left to*
> *the tender mercies of church-wardens*
> *and overseers, perhaps he would have*
> *cried the louder.*
> —Charles Dickens, *Oliver Twist*

Lean's second and last Dickens adaptation was *Oliver Twist*. This novel has the same humor and sentiment as *Great Expectations*

OLIVER TWIST: Bill Sikes (Robert Newton) threatens Oliver (John Howard Davies).

but lacks the polish and cohesion of Dickens' later work; and it tends to dwell more overtly on images of social injustice and sordid criminality: witness the early scenes in the parish workhouse. In adapting this sequence, Lean creates a series of ironic contrasts drawn directly from Dickens' detailed, atmospheric descriptions of this establishment. A lighthearted interlude between Mr. Bumble, the Beadle, and the Matron is positioned amidst the scenes of human exploitation and maltreatment. The Parish Board's pronouncement, "this workhouse has become a regular place of entertainment for the poorer classes," is met by a decisive cut to women bent over wash tubs in hard labor. A scene of house officials enjoying an opulent feast is juxtaposed with images of Oliver and the half-starved orphans, "voracious and wild with hunger" as Dickens described them. Finally, huge, sermonizing carvings proclaiming that "God is Love" loom over the heads of downtrodden scrub women [frame 35]. The film evokes the same indictment of Victorian society as its 1837 source.

OLIVER TWIST: Fagin (Alec Guinness) menaces Oliver (John Howard Davies)

[frame 35]

[frame 36]

[frame 37]

"Robert Newton's make-up and facial expressions emphasize the bestial aspect of Bill Sikes as he murders Nancy. The cutaway to the dog creates both a simile for the human terror and a metaphor for the animalistic behavior."

Oliver's final release from this "dreadful place" leads him first to the home of a mortician, where he is abused and beaten, and then to bustling, impersonal London, where he is adopted by a gang of thieves. Fagin, the leader of the young pickpockets, and his "charges" are, at first glance, rather humorous characters. They treat Oliver to a much-needed meal and entertain him; but as their situation worsens and Oliver becomes a threat to them, they are not above kidnapping him from his newly-found grandfather and imprisoning him in their hideout. The figure who most completely represents this world of criminality into which Oliver has fallen is Bill Sikes. Like Dickens, Lean never glamorizes this outlaw, his cohorts, or his society. With Sikes, in particular, there was the possibility of transforming the caricature of evil drawn by Dickens into a misunderstood, semi-tragic misfit; but the adaptors do not follow this line. Sikes remains simply a thief and murderer who commits the "unforgivable act": killing the one who loves him. His complete lack of conscience, whether in beating a child or trying to drown his own dog, lead him, by the final reel, to behave more like a wild beast than a human being [frames 36 and 37]. He ends like an animal, pursued by an angry mob, cornered and lashing out in terror. At no time during this chase nor in any other scene is the audience asked to empathize with Sikes. He is an archetypal villain whose ugly death at the end of a rope is cheered both by the mob of costumed actors on the screen and the audience in the theater.

The only person in this brood of greedy scoundrels who merits sympathy, no matter how briefly, is the pathetic Nancy. Elements such as the frail flowers on her dresser, her inexplicable love for Sikes, and her maternal affection for Oliver reveal a sensitive nature which is usually hidden beneath a cynical facade. The scene in which she first exhibits scruples comes after the recapture of Oliver. Entertaining second thoughts about exploiting the boy, she delivers a verbal attack against Fagin:

NANCY
'Civil words, civil words,' you villain. Yes,
you deserve 'em from me. I thieved for you

when I was a child not half his [Oliver's] age.
And I've thieved for you ever since, don't
you know it.

FAGIN
And if you have, it is your living.

NANCY
Aye, it is. It is my living. And the cold, wet,
dirty streets are my home. And you're the
wretch that drove me to them long ago. And
that'll keep me there . . .
(As she becomes more hysterical the
CAMERA TILTS to visualize her frenzy)
Day and night, till I die!

For all his impassioned outcries of social injustice Dickens was
too much a product of his age to act on his convictions. As with
Great Expectations, the conventions of the era demanded that he
end his tale on a sentimental if not rosy note; and he did. He even
managed to exonerate much of Victorian England very neatly in
the person of Mr. Brownlow, Oliver's grandfather. He is the
principal agent of destruction for the Fagin-Sikes-Monks ring. As
he brings the insidious Monks to justice and causes the demotion
of the workhouse tyrant, Mr. Bumble, the members of Victorian
society could identify with this avenging angel and mitigate
whatever guilt they may have felt. It would take many years and
many more novels before Dickens was to question this optimism
and find it wanting in *Great Expectations*.

Lean's task in his adaptation of novels has always been
one of condensation. In terms of not merely the practical limits of
screen time but also the very nature of the medium, transfering a
novel intact is obviously impossible. What to keep and what to
discard while maintaining the "sense" of the original should
result, according to Bazin, "in a restoration of the essence of the
letter and the spirit."[3] Lean's rendering of the dark, almost claustrophobic mood of the book is multifaceted. He uses the expressionistic and subjective style, such as the tilt during Nancy's

speech or the examples cited in the introduction. Unlike the similar treatment of Laura Jesson's emotional condition as she rushes out onto the train platform, Nancy's "imbalance" in **OLIVER TWIST**, being as much an alienation from that "ordinary" society which Laura typifies as it is her anger towards Fagin, is not a temporary state of mind.

The settings are ostensibly objective. The dreary workhouse, the morbid atmosphere of the mortician's shop, where Oliver sleeps among the coffins, as in the novel, the filth of Fagin's hideout, and the decadence of the society around the Two Boars Inn are all photographed in low-key light with attention to recreating the locales as Dickens saw them. The only exceptions to this oppressive background are, appropriately, the scenes at Mr. Brownlow's home. Oliver's light-filled bedroom

[frame 38]

[frame 39]

[frame 38] and the final shot of the film with Oliver, Brownlow and his servant, Mrs. Bedwin, framed in front of the glaring white facade of the house **[frame 39]** act as counterpoint to the general grimness of the picture's decor. This house, where Oliver has escaped the unfriendly society around him and found refuge in his grandfather's love, expressionistically reflects this aura of a sanctuary in the way it is furnished and lit. In this sense, the whiteness of the house and the contrasting darkness and decay that surround the petty tyrants and criminals in Oliver's life are not purely objective reconstructions.

The most direct visualizations of Dickens' words are in the characterizations. The author's caricatures come to life in **OLIVER TWIST** as they had in **GREAT EXPECTATIONS**. The Beadle, played by Francis L. Sullivan, who was Jaggers in **GREAT EXPECTATIONS**, is, exactly as Dickens had conjured him up, a "fat man, and a choleric." His pretensions to dignity and genteel language are as humorous on film as they were in print. Noah Claypole is a "large-headed, small-eyed youth, of lumbering make." Fagin, as interpreted by Alec Guinness, is a perfect manifestation of the greedy but comic original: "a very old shrivelled Jew, whose villainous-looking and repulsive face was obscured by a quantity of red hair. He was dressed in a greasy flannel gown, with his throat bare." Because the make-up was modeled after the traditional engravings by Cruikshank, complete with the beak nose, considerable controvery arose over the alleged anti-Semitism of this characterization. In Germany, there were riots at the film's premiere, and in the United States pressure from various organizations caused the code office of the MPAA repeatedly to deny its certificate of approval. After cuts were made, primarily involving comic scenes with Fagin, **OLIVER TWIST** was released in the United States nearly three years after its British run.

Various visual elements create a continuity in rearranging the novel's jumbled plot. As in **GREAT EXPECTATIONS**, the adaptors had a surfeit of narrative elements from which to select. Consequently the complex meanderings of the original became, in the film, a few, simple plot twists. The Monks character, a

OLIVER TWIST: The Beadle (Francis L. Sullivan) leads Oliver (John Howard Davies) out of the dining hall after his incontinent request for more.

rather involved and melodramatic figure in Dickens' original who continually popped up like a clichéd bad penny, appears in very few of the movie's scenes and only as a narrative-furthering *deus ex machina* or a symbol of evil. The benevolent Rose and Harry, who like Monks were related in some obscure way to Oliver, were dropped entirely, as the adaptors combined all the "do-gooders" into one person, Mr. Brownlow. In addition, the eloquent diction of the child Oliver is replaced by a speech more natural to someone his age.

Lean exploits the inherent condensing quality of the image with which he can in a few seconds with a minimum of shots "describe" what may have taken even as visually-oriented a novelist as Dickens several pages. The workhouse sequence is again illustrative: while Dickens devotes four chapters to Oliver's abuse and misery in this place, Lean uses a montage of short scenes to convey all the drudgery, starvation, and regimentation. With the facility of an experienced editor, Lean creates mood and atmosphere through montages like this one. In fact, as Lean

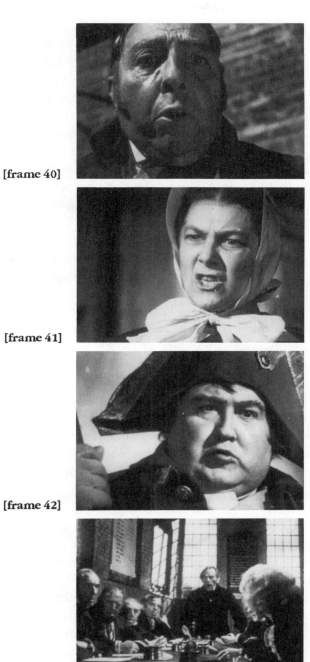

[frame 40]

[frame 41]

[frame 42]

[frame 43]

developed his personal style in both Dickens adaptations, some of the most striking instances are in the editing. Besides its economy, there is its precision in sequences such as the final chase, in which a constantly enlarging crowd follows Sikes' dog to the murderer's hideout and which is framed and cut to match their growing frenzy. As the dog and the mass of people rush, diagonally and dynamically, across the frame and through the London streets, the audience is caught up with them in the race to find Sikes. Lean's cutting can also be ironic, almost dialectical. as in the juxtaposition of animals being herded through the London streets mixed with shots of stifling crowds milling by. Equally ironic is the cut from Fagin assuring the Dodger that the spying will be "a pleasant piece of work" to the miserable boy standing outside in a rainstorm. There is at least one instance where Lean is directly inspired by Dickens for his cutting. The author, within approximately fifteen sentences in the novel, describes the responses to Oliver's request for "more food." The writing leaps across space and time to accommodate rapid and humorous glimpses of the elders' reactions. Lean translates this into four cuts from the overseer, to the Beadle, to the Matron, and finally to the assembled Parish Board [frames 40 to 43]. Dickens often seemed to anticipate the motion picture in his writings, in minor instances such as these or in a major plot device such as the suspenseful cross-cutting across wide expanses of space in *A Tale of Two Cities*, where Eisenstein claimed to have discovered a "dissolve" in the second paragraph of the final chapter.[4]

Like the book, the movie is not strictly a first person narrative; but this does not prevent the adaptors from straying from the observational mode Dickens has established. Several prominent examples have already been mentioned; and whether it is the subjective camera in the courtroom or Sikes' hallucinations after Nancy's murder, all subjective treatments forcefully add another, more personal level to the film. Although Dickens' original is almost completely confined to urban scenes, Lean adds a number of nature images. The opening storm is not found in the book but forms an original prologue to the workhouse. The combination of pantheistic and subjective elements, thunder and

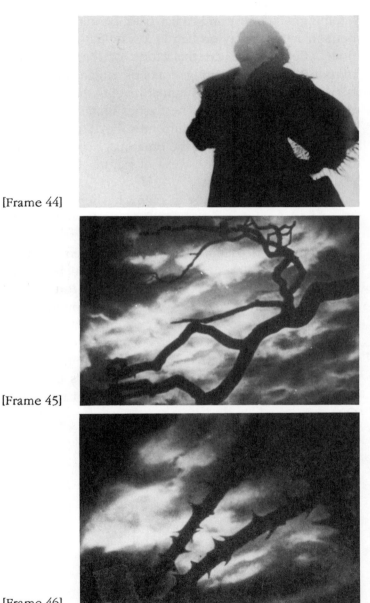

[Frame 44]

[Frame 45]

[Frame 46]

"Visualizing the sensation of labor: a figure on a treadmill outlined by lightning on a process screen; jagged branches and twisted briars outlined against a stormy sky suggest the shooting and gnawing pain of childbirth."

lightning which respond to her pain, bending briars symbolizing her sorrow, interplay on film in a way that is not possible in the novel. Beyond the externalization of feeling analyzed in the introduction, the opening contains suggestions of interaction between the cosmos and human events in the mother's ordeal that are typical of Lean. The flashes illuminate the sign on the workhouse gate; but concurrently the ditches in the grounds cause her to stumble and the ominous, howling winds hold her back. In Lean's dualistic view of nature, both beneficent and maleficent forces coexist.

At some point in Lean's films his heroes or heroines must assert or defend their freedom of action. Oliver's moment comes when Noah defiles the memory of his dead mother. He leaps at and pommels the defamer, only to be beaten in turn by Noah's reinforcements. In a series of shots, which are echoed in **LAWRENCE OF ARABIA** during Lawrence's torture by the Turks, Oliver is spread-eagled and whipped. Though the beating is severe, he refuses to wince or cry out, much to the consternation of Noah. For as Mrs. Sowerberry remarked earlier, "He must be mad." If Oliver is mad indeed, it is with the exhilaration of independence. It is a step further in Lean's developing world view towards the madness of Nicholson, Lawrence, or Adela Quested.

4
MADELEINE (1950)

*I know from experience that the world is not
lenient in its observations. But I don't care
for the world's remarks so long as my own
heart tells me I am doing nothing wrong.*
                    —Letter from Madeleine Smith
                    to Pierre Emile L'Angelier, 1855

*Certainly these letters show as extra-
ordinary a frame of mind and as unhallowed
a passion as perhaps ever appeared in a Court
of Justice.*
                    —John Hope, Lord Justice Clerk
                    at the trial of Madeleine Smith, 1857

MADELEINE is Lean's most serious examination of Nineteenth Century Great Britain, deadly serious in both its subject
matter and tone. Almost devoid of comic relief, it deals with
murder—not with the compulsive, agonized killings of a misfit
such as Bill Sikes—but murder of convenience, murder of a
discarded lover planned and executed by a woman of twenty-
one years fresh from a London finishing school. The film makes
use not only of trial records but of Madeleine Smith's letters and
Emile L'Angelier's memorandum book (not admitted as evidence)
to follow the course of actual occurrences. There are several

books on the case, most recently two editions of the *Notable British Trials* series, edited by A. Duncan Smith (1907) and F. Tennyson Jesse (1927) and *The Madeleine Smith Affair* by Peter Hunt (1950) which derived partly from research material assembled by the filmmakers. The case was also the subject of two novels, the first published in 1864, and a tragicomedy in two acts in 1928. In short, it typifies those Victorian murders which George Orwell remarked "have given the greatest amount of [reading] pleasure to the British public, the murders whose story is known in its general outline to almost everyone and which have been rehashed over and over again."[1]

In this day and age the case of Madeleine Hamilton Smith may seem if not innocuous certainly far from extraordinary in its characters and events. Yet the kind of contemporary notoriety it received and the solemn social judgments it engendered are typical of the formal hypocrisy that has come to be associated with mid-Victorianism, with the unconscious tug-of-war that pitted outward insistence on "proper behavior" against the inward fascination of passion. If that passion was, in the public eye, "criminal" and if those who corresponded with it fallen men and women, it is clear in light of such studies as Steven Marcus' *Other Victorians*, if not in the socio-economic history of the time, that sexual transgression was not all that uncommon. It is equally clear these "immoral" acts were either kept secret or politely overlooked by a strange code of conduct that objected less to any given "illicit" acts than to being compelled to the distasteful extreme of having to speak openly about them.

Lean and his screenwriters were not out to judge Madeleine Smith, that had been accomplished a hundred years before, but rather to interpret her "exceptional" story from this mid-Twentieth Century perspective, to explain what the prologue calls "an interest [in her] which time can never change." Accordingly, **MADELEINE** begins in a quasi-documentary style: a view of modern Glasgow, factory chimneys and white smoke, the low relief of two and three-story grey brick houses, and "in this great city of Glasgow there is a square . . . Blytheswood Square . . . there's nothing very remarkable about its appearance . . ." As simply and unobtrusively as that, the picture's underlying tension is introduced. For just as her city and her house are genuinely commonplace (then and, the images suggest, now), Madeleine Smith will prove an outwardly conventional, somewhat undistinguished young woman. The real question, the one that makes the whole drama possible, is why she should so startle the good citizens of Glasgow, should so arouse their prurient interest or incite their moral indignation. Why should the name of the well-bred, slightly spoiled, second daughter of a prosperous member of the Scottish gentry, a girl who quite possibly poisoned her lowborn suitor with arsenic in 1857, still be known? For if Madeleine Smith was singled out by society, her character and her story in its peculiar "exceptionalness" reflect more on the prejudices and driving mores of the unrecorded faces that watched her during her trial than on herself.

The past slips in so gradually: the long shot of Glasgow at the film's beginning is not that conspicuously modern. The blare of auto horns over the shot only vaguely suggests anything beyond 1910. The footsteps on the soundtrack might just as well be those of Emile L'Angelier. All these elements confuse past and present and anticipate the ambiguity of the ending. For like the variant conclusions of *Great Expectations*, the issue of Madeleine's culpability is genuinely uncertain. Moreover, it can remain central only as long as it is unresolved. **MADELEINE** is neither fact nor fable. The film refuses to do more than speculate on what really happened not because of historical accuracy in which the trial jury recorded a noncommittal verdict of "Not proven," but because it is appropriate to the historical ambivalence that confronted the real Madeleine Smith. A large part of this personal history's impact derives from changing values, from the reasons why Madeleine's letters now seem so full of girlish frivolity and cloying gentility in their ardor. How else can one explain the lingering chastity of the affair and the hundreds of guilty words exchanged trying to justify the "sin" that finally overcame it; "Am I not your wife? Yes I am. And you may rest assured that after what has passed I cannot be the wife of any other but dear Emile [though] we should, I suppose, have waited till we were married."

[May 6, 1856] Letters such as these were labeled scandalous, torrid, and "frightful," the term used by John Inglis, Madeleine's defense attorney, at the time. In the end the only answer one could honorably make to the accusing finger of Victorian society, the one Madeleine tries unsuccessfully to make to its most prominent representative, her father, was no answer at all.

Despite all the words written about the case, **MADELEINE** is essentially original material, not based on a Coward play or Dickens novel. It is the character and "her strange Romantic story" which fall, with a minimum of manipulation, into line with Lean's thematic proclivities. As has been noted, beginning with **BRIEF ENCOUNTER** and culminating in **A PASSAGE TO INDIA**, Lean has constructed several of his films around a heroine. Like Laura Jesson and Mary Justin in **PASSIONATE FRIENDS** before her, Madeleine is caught in a stifling trap of social conventions, but that trap was much more rigidly constructed in 1857 and could more easily bring its victims to destruction. In this instance, the character of Madeleine is, as the title suggests, more than Laura or Mary, more than Jane Hudson in **SUMMER MADNESS** or Rosy Ryan, the entire film. It is not from as subjective a viewpoint as Pip's or Laura Jesson's, although several images emerge directly from her imagination. Since the indeterminate quality of her motives, her "secret," is the focal point of her trial, it would not be appropriate to reveal the "truth" by externalizing her emotions. Whatever the real Madeleine Smith felt, whatever her actions, however sordid or everyday, whatever the authentic Emile, or William Minnoch, or Glasgow of 1857 were, Lean displaces them all to concentrate on a somewhat Romantic portrait of an enigmatic young girl. As the film develops that girl becomes a woman who may be the unhappiest of his heroines.

Madeleine's personal fantasies are caught in a deterministic undercurrent first established in the quasi-objectivity of the prologue with its dry, narrative voiceover. From the modern street a period figure emerges and casts her compelling shadow over a "for sale" sign; Madeleine (Ann Todd) appears from somewhere, from anywhere, and smiles vaguely. "Madeleine . . . come, my dear, we're going in," her mother calls; inside the house the camera and the Smith family glide fatefully towards each other. Mr. Smith, the architect, the cold pragmatist, is impressed ("It has solidity"); Madeleine is fascinated. A panning shot strays with her as she drifts to the stairwell and descends to the basement rooms—there she fixes on a barred window and a tracking shot follows her over. As light from it strikes the wall behind her, a shadow falls across her face and is greeted by another smile. Quickly the muted symbols of the room are suggested: the predestined pull of the travelling and panning; the window which draws Madeleine forward like an unseen hand; the images of the bars and her shadow which prefigure the prison and Emile's appearance, both in the way he is first seen and in the figurative sense of a "shadow over her existence"; the furtiveness of a "lower" room, the sexuality of its womb-like security and the narrow opening which Emile will violate with his cane. The meaning of Madeleine's look, transfigured as violins swell over shot, a lyrical solo followed by anticipatory tremolos, is purposely not specified. How well she knows Emile, whether she knows him at all at this point, is never specified either, although her mother's remark later, "Madeleine, I've never heard you sing in French before," intimates that her acquaintance with him is not too long standing. Uncertainty is a factor from the beginning. L'Angelier arrives as if created to fit the opportunity, as if conceived and conjured up by Madeleine as she enters that dark chamber. With that darkness clinging to him, a dream-lover or a demon-lover or both, he is sprung from the depths of her house and her soul to fulfill her Romantic yearnings.

That aspect, at least, is clear from the start. Madeleine's romantic fancies are reflected in her ending to Janet's bedtime story ("You haven't finished telling me what happened to the Prince?" "He went far away across the sea . . . and never came back again.") with even a presentiment of tragedy. Immediately after, while she sings a French ballad in the parlor, her "foreign prince" arrives outside. At first, he is only a long, black shadow across the pavement, then a pair of glistening boots as a medium close shot slowly moves up the length of his body. The real Pierre Emile L'Angelier was the son of an immigrant French nurseryman;

he worked as an unimportant clerk in a warehouse. The film
L'Angelier also holds this position. He too takes drugs (laudanum)
for energy, lives in a modest flat in Franklin Place, and even
seems a trifle pathetic in his struggle against his own foppish
outlays for financial security. But when he stands outside
Madeleine's basement window at night, he bears only a superficial resemblance to either of those L'Angeliers. His eyes are
inflamed in a dusky face, and a pleased, almost smug smile
disturbs the line of his pencil moustache. **[frame 47]** Swathed in a

[frame 47]

velvet cape and twirling a silver-topped cane, he looms up
suddenly, brooding and awesome in stature, a consummate
Byronic figure in full regalia. Madeleine is trapped inside for a
moment, confined in a long medium shot as the family and her
formal suitor, William Minnoch, make their ritual good nights.
Then, like a good stage director, she brings down the lights. A cut
to high angle causes her figure to be distorted by the lamp glass
in the foreground as she moves about the room foreshadowing a
latter distortion by an apothecary jar at the druggist's; a rapturous
waltz surges on the soundtrack; a low angle medium close shot
catches the edge of her dress swirling excitedly past. Four cane
taps, a key is passed, Emile is waiting in the alley. They stand
together silhouetted against the street light **[frame 48]**; their faces
intercut in deeply backlit close-ups, obscure, barely discernible
features with highlights on the eyes and lips, a stylized vision.
They kiss and ignite a real storm, a torrent of passion that

[frame 48]

threatens to drench them as thoroughly as any physical love would.

Much of the magnetism of L'Angelier's character is rendered figuratively or in archetype. Superficially he is something of a poseur; metaphysically, storms seem to accompany his passage. In the first actual lovemaking, Madeleine meets him on the grounds of the country house at Rowaleyn. There on an idyllic, sheltered hilltop, overlooking the moonlit sea, they listen to the raucous strains of a distant dance. Impulsively, she invites Emile to join her in a highland reel: "Dance with me. We are quite alone." "I do not know how." "Danse avec moi." At first, he will do no more than prance satyr-like and tap his palm with his cane; she weaves slowly around him. Lean cuts to the dancers in the village then back as an impatient Madeleine snatches away his symbolic stick ("It should go faster . . . You can't dance with that in your hand."). Another cut: a travelling shot with those below as they pick up speed. In the woods, Madeleine falls. In close shot Emile's self-assured smile reasserts itself, and he bends towards her. The sequence ends on the other dancers, in various cuts, spinning, gyrating, shouting, until one feverish couple can dance no more, turns, and runs out.

This event is nearer the end than the beginning of the affair. The fact that her attitude is changing is apparent when she visits L'Angelier's shabby room:

> MADELEINE
>
> Emile, I wonder if you know what you have
> done to me. I . . . I thought we loved each
> other. I wanted to leave my family and go
> away with you. But, until now, I have never
> really known you.
>
> EMILE
> Nothing has changed.
>
> MADELEINE
> It has, Emile.

Why it has changed is clarified only in the shifting imagery that characterizes L'Angelier's scenes, in his diminishing stature in Madeleine's eyes. Madeleine's real disillusionment comes later. Throughout the initial two thirds of the picture, the events before the trial, Lean uses certain motifs and interior moods to expand the implications of these scenes. As Madeleine's disenchantment grows, L'Angelier degenerates from Byronic hero to an affected, intemperate dandy. Part of his appeal had always been simply his foreignness and his good looks, and the very forbidden aspect of the affair. That was evident from the first scene in the parlor: "Dis moi tu m'aime," Madeleine sang, obviously enjoying the thrill of addressing her lover in the very midst of her unknowing family; and at the same time vaguely aware of the immaturity of her conduct: "I was clumsy; I sang many wrong notes." Her breathless observation to Emile that "we are like children hiding" and her later invitation to dance were simply exhortations to him to play the "illicit" game with her. Nor is L'Angelier completely immune: his neighbor, Thuau, calls Madeleine an "enchantress" and quotes Emile's remark, "It is a perfect fascination I have for that girl," at the trial. Yet he clings to the notion of marrying only into Madeleine's life and caste of society; and his smug remark about his new necktie, "I chose it with care," might easily apply to Madeleine herself. Much of this is fraught with irony. "There is such a thing as keeping up appearances," he tells Thuau, defending the purchase of an expensive suit. "There is such a thing as paying the rent, too," his friend replies, not comprehending that for L'Angelier the one depends on the other. To "protect his investment" and maintain his hold on Madeleine, L'Angelier must, literally and figuratively, make his presence felt, a necessity which Lean underscores visually. When, for example, Madeleine accepts Minnoch at the ball, he opens his mouth to answer her, but a wail of bagpipes drowns him out. Shortly thereafter, a cut to a high angle view of the ballroom discloses L'Angelier's figure on a balcony in the foreground of the shot [frame 49]. A reverse shot

[frame 49]

frames him, sullen and almost satanic, closely and at a low angle. The music is associated with the tryst at Rowaleyn, and the manner of its inclusion here, while L'Angelier lurks ubiquitously and seems from his position to hold sway over the entire room and its occupants, suggests that Minnoch is "drowned out." He might still be easily displaced by the former lover, will be displaced but more by the effects of Emile's ceasing to be present than anything else.

L'Angelier's threat to blackmail Madeleine into wedlock ("You made yourself my wife.") may be understandable to the audience, which is aware of his all-too-human failings. For the acutely disappointed Madeleine it is her Don Juan cast into a dismal flat and exuding vulgar insecurity. The rendering of the sequence in which L'Angelier forces his way into the house is pointedly melodramatic: her childish amusement in gazing at her new hat in the mirror yielding to a tracking shot which is suddenly interrupted; the ominous rasp of the cane behind the closed curtain; the equally ominous geometry of an abrupt tilt from the taut door chain to a face wedged in the narrow vertical opening by the jamb; low light moving hesitantly with Madeleine down the corridor; the panning medium close shot across her prostrate, sobbing form. All this fittingly marks the end of a "Romance," of which Madeleine is author as much as participant, the brutish transformation of Lochinvar into Caliban.

The grimmest irony is that more than anything vanity works against L'Angelier, perhaps doubly so. First, there is the vanity of his own posturing. Second, if Madeleine does give him arsenic, there is the cosmetic purpose for which she originally purchased the poison. In this vein, Lean adds numerous sardonic touches to the scene with the cocoa. Some are obvious, such as the sound montage of the doorbell rung by L'Angelier over an extra close shot of the bottle of poison. The constant favoring of the fateful cup in the framing is so marked that it is the subject of a follow focus shot; but it has a tensely ambiguous effect later, in a high angle medium close shot of her, when it hovers hazily at the bottom of the frame [frame 50]. Some are fairly subtle: Emile's casual "I fear that . . ." interrupted by the maid's entry with the tray of chocolate and the empty cups. Others are complex visual

[frame 50]

and aural metaphors, as when Madeleine pours some of the arsenic into a wash basin while Janet bathes in the background and sings, "Who killed Cock Robin." The inference is not just of murder in general. By this point it is clear that it refers more specifically to L'Angelier, the cockerel with fancy tie displayed like a coxcomb. Moments later Emile enters with exaggerated sound effects: the clack of his walking stick into the stand, the thump of his gloves into his hand, as he struts through the parlor, preening in front of the mirror, condescendingly appreciating the furnishings and boasting just a little: "I have inherited the feelings and delicacies of a person well bred . . ." But, as he leans against the mantelpiece, his real stature and his imminent demise are reflected behind him in the form of a small statuette: a brass rooster [frame 51]. The metamorphosis is complete. The symbolic

[frame 51]

reduction of Emile from an almost preternatural level to an animal one defines the change in him which Madeleine had sensed only inexactly before.

There are two principal consequences. The first, Emile's death, occurs within the context of Lean's pantheistic forces. A brief shot catches the wind sweeping a cobbled street. Again L'Angelier's shadow stretches over it; but this time he wears a light colored coat, as if the loss of aura forbade anything as dark as in his first appearance. Again it starts to rain. The next sequence begins with an establishing shot of a clock face reading

11:25. Lean condenses the passage of ninety-five minutes into a half dozen deterministic cuts: L'Angelier outside pondering the unlit windows of the house; Madeleine and Janet asleep within. Then, as if the course of things were truly beyond human intervention, come four shots that are purely "objective": a corridor filled with creaking noises; the front door straining against the gusts; the lock, its bolt rattling; and finally a street clock. In a distant tower one a.m. sounds like a knell; it sets in motion a precipitous tilt down which reveals L'Angelier's figure: a walking stick detaches itself and falls to the wet pavement, the form sags.

The second consequence is on a subjective level. For just as L'Angelier's death will be carried, literally, in the wind, Madeleine unconsciously discerns the need to shelter herself from the storms that attend his passing and buffet the house in the night, the need for a safe harbor. That this is her view of Minnoch is clearly established in one of their exchanges:

> MINNOCH
> Madeleine, will you wear this ring . . . till we
> choose you one.
> (He shows it to her)
> It will be clumsy on your hand, but I should
> like to think of it there.
>
> MADELEINE
> I will wear it. I like it. 'Tis solid. Is it your crest?
>
> MINNOCH (nodding)
> A crossbow.
>
> MADELEINE
> Ah. I thought it was an anchor.

Like his ring Minnoch is solid; like Fred Jesson, or Howard Justin pulling his wife back from the subway tracks, he is the anchor that will keep Madeleine from emotional shipwreck on the shoals of passion. Caught as she is in the opposing currents of social convention and adventurous infatuation, threatened leewardly and windwardly by their respective incarnations in her father and L'Angelier, Minnoch offers the refuge of a relationship free of anxiety. And if he lacks fire, Lean compensates partially by setting his proposals to Madeleine against backgrounds that are "acceptably" Romantic: riding by the sea and at the ball.

Like her antecedents in Lean's work, Madeleine is poised between domestic security and the frightening abyss of independence. What makes Madeleine unique, if not her willingness, at one point at least, to abandon all and leave with her lover, is the bifocal quality of her character, partly deriving from the ill-defined nature of the actual Madeleine Smith and partly a synthesis of fictional personalities as diverse as Laura Jesson and Estella. The likeness with the former, between Madeleine's idealization of Emile and Laura's fantasy visions of Romantic love through the train window, is clear enough. The links with Estella, the beginnings of an aloof demeanor, are not forged until the last third of the picture. As surely as Emile ceases being analogous to the noble Alec Harvey of **BRIEF ENCOUNTER** and changes into the arrogant Bentley Drummle of **GREAT EXPECTATIONS**, as Minnoch becomes less a weak Fred Jesson and acquires some of Pip's final resolution, Madeleine, to save herself, must become as intangible, mysterious, and coldly inaccessible as Estella. For when the real and imagined L'Angelier both perish, it is no longer possible to hide from the fury of righteous winds.

Until that point Madeleine had used her father's ignorance of her lover to heighten her own sense of security, to rise above his unfeeling reserve, while psychologically compensating for his lack of affectionate display towards her, and to insulate herself from his gruff authoritarianism. Even in the scene where she knelt at his feet, helping with his boots and listening to his chastisement ("There seems to be something about your character that prevents you from acting naturally"), she remained mentally above him. This position was reinforced by the sea of crinoline dress spread about her which materially simulates the expansiveness of her inner sensation and allows her to dominate the frame. By means of the two-dimensional area which the dress as an extension of self occupies and in the whiteness of it against her father's black

[frame 52]

and grey in the dimly lit room, she is made, despite being at his feet, the visual center [frame 52].

Immediately after L'Angelier's death, a medium shot catches Madeleine in white again wearing her wedding dress, again unconcernedly trying something on before a mirror but this time made ominously double-headed by the framing. When she confronts Thuau, who has come to expose her, with Mr. Smith in the study, the last two shots disclose a subtle shift of psychological balance [frames 53 and 54]. Smith stands in the foreground. The camera adjusts to a slightly higher angle, looking down as she comes up behind him. His line, "We are naked," applies chiefly to Madeleine, stripped of her secrecy. The decor underlines her assailability, a pale figure all in white surrounded by Smith and Thuau's dark suits and the dark wood paneling and leather chairs. Again she goes down on her knees before her father, but this time she falls clutching his legs for support. The medium close shot of her as Smith frees himself and leaves the room is in marked contrast with the earlier scene. The angle and framing now accentuate the physical vulnerability. With everything out in the open, she can no longer control the situation.

As her superior position deteriorates, Madeleine's ability to resist the encroachments of the real world into her personal universe diminishes. At the railway station, her physical escape from Glasgow is rendered unfeasible by Minnoch. She returns his ring ("It may get lost.") with all its implications. She drifts away

[frame 53]

[frame 54]

from him, out of safe harbor, and loses herself in the crowd, in
her own thoughts.

Various images reappear decisively in the trial, a sequence
which occupies the final third of the film. With only her interior
resolve and a black veil to shield her, Madeleine enters the
courtroom from the cellar prison; and a low angle pan upwards
stresses the steepness of the ascent, as if she were being drawn
out of her own room in the basement of Blytheswood Square.
The sound of the trap door dropping shut startles her and
suggests her disorientation at being pulled up forcibly out of her
own world. The previous exterior shot of the courthouse itself
revealed it against the sky, cut off from the grey solidity of the
city. Her loss of privacy in the thronging court is emphasized by

an insert of faces peering through oval-shaped ports in the doors of the room and a shot of an artist sketching her in stern profile. The clerk reading the indictment, the judge squinting over his spectacles, the murmurs of the officials—all are contiguous to her anxious emergence. As Madeleine has mentally withdrawn into unperturbable silence, as casually it seems as she lowered her black veil over her face, Lean divides the trial episode clearly between subjective and objective.

Among the sights and sounds of the proceedings, Madeleine fixes on the ringing of the court bell; the table with her possessions on exhibit; and, as Minnoch is being cross- examined, the black boots of the prosecutor moving across the floor. The details Madeleine picks out—or those Lean selects for her—build a psychological rather than physical reality. Her disinterest in Minnoch on the stand, for example, stems from her realization that she can no longer anchor herself for safety to anyone. Beyond that, Lean is stacking the case in Madeleine's favor. The trial is intricately but precisely arranged. The prosecution has but four witnesses on screen: the defense has nine. Moreover the Lord Advocate is "forced" to present his case in capsule chronology; Inglis develops his out of the framework of his impassioned closing remarks with witnesses recalled in flashback close ups at the appropriate moments. By the time he finally concludes, striding dramatically into a tight close shot, Lean has edited the prosecution out of any chance of victory.

While this scheme merely affirms the course of the genuine trial, it is also the climax to a consistent pattern through which, by using actual events but altering them slightly, Lean manages simultaneously to reconstruct and to circumvent historical reality. Lean subliminally prepares the viewer for the trial in the composition of shots, like the empty medicine glass in the foreground with Madeleine's picture, visually anticipating Inglis' suggestions of possible suicide; in simple narrative selection, as when the movie Madeleine is seen using the arsenic on her skin, something the real Madeleine Smith claimed but could never prove; and in the direction of action, such as Ann Todd's expression of faint but apparently genuine surprise on hearing that Emile is dead. These touches more than the lengthy speeches delivered by prosecution and defense directly to the camera, which equate the jury and the audience, forecast the final verdict.

By the second time the trap door falls, destiny has already ruled in Madeleine's favor. Lean cuts to a long shot: the courtroom is less crowded, not as constricting, the tension dissipated. At the verdict, a tracking shot towards Madeleine in the dock dissolves to a view of her on the steps of the courthouse, parasol in hand, again a portrait of aloof beauty and gentility. Unlike most of Lean's dreamers and visionaries, who are either destroyed by their dream or compelled to abandon it, Madeleine has retained her integrity and isolation. Her remark to Minnoch—"I do not regret things"—is prophetic and at the same time characteristic. As the calm face and Gioconda smile appear in final medium close shot, **[frame 55]** the narrator asks, "Madeleine

[frame 55]

Smith, Ye have heard the indictment. Were ye guilty or not guilty?" She moves her head slightly from side to side, but her eyes remain fixed on the camera as it travels in slowly towards her. There is no answer.

Nor should there be one. Objective recreation has never been the real aim of Lean's pictures. Just as the artist who sat sketching Madeleine was not rendering a likeness of Ann Todd, of the reality before him, but of what he imagined a murderess should resemble, Lean "interprets" history. In fact, the artist's sketch is an authentic one, taken from a contemporary newspaper drawing. Since no photographs of Madeleine Smith are extant, questioning the reliability of the artist's graphics is a way of suggesting that the legends of her beauty might be true after all. This in turn "justifies" her being portrayed by Ann Todd rather than a character actress who "looked" the part. The real sketch also reveals that the black veil is a concept original to the film. These manipulations or even more fleeting ones, such as the equation of the two Madeleines' handwriting in a brief insert close shot of a letter addressed to L'Angelier, are obviously not revealed to the general audience. Unlike the sketch artist, Lean does not phenomenologically fit people to real occurrences, but conversely molds events to his characters. If this film is to remain textured by dreams or as Coleridge suggests "to venture into twilight realms . . . and feel deep interest in modes of inmost being," those modes cannot be restricted. The vague smile and barely perceptible travelling in of the opening scene return and fade again; the enigma is all that remains.

5
THE SOUND BARRIER (1952)

Thou art a symbol and a sign
To Mortals of their fate and force;
Like thee, Man is in part divine,
A troubled stream from a pure source;
And Man in portions can foresee
His own funereal destiny,
His wretchedness, and his resistance,
And his sad unallied existence;
To which his Spirit may oppose
Itself—and equal to all woes,
And a firm will, and a deep sense,
Which even in torture can descry
Its own concenter'd recompense,
Triumphant where it dares defy,
And making death a Victory.
　　—George Gordon, Lord Byron, "Prometheus"

It would be possible to characterize **THE SOUND BARRIER** as
a semi-documentary about the men who challenged the speed of
sound, and, for Lean, as a turn back up the "documentarian" road
in the direction of **IN WHICH WE SERVE**. It would also be inac-
curate. In Lean's films, the definition of milieu, whether the brick
and cobblestone of Victorian London or the tinted glass and

Sir John Ridgefield (Ralph Richardson) uncrates and examines the model of his experimental jet aircraft.

concrete of supersonic aviation, is a means not an end. "Appearance" is only one facet of a more complex reality; it is not surprising that contemporary critical assessments of **THE SOUND BARRIER** often overlooked what Lean was actually detailing.

Man in flight is the central narrative concern of the script, which Terence Rattigan fashioned from Lean's concept, and of the motion picture. Initially, all the conventions of documentary which characterize the detached, understated tradition of the GPO shorts and the faithful recreations of Humphrey Jennings seem present. The scientific or technical details of the actual endeavor, from Ridgefield's explanation of the "sound barrier" or his demonstration of jet propulsion in the factory and the many faithfully recreated test flights, are included; but the elevation of events over the characters, the definition of the objective at the expense of the personal are only inherent tendencies in the form. Their application in **THE SOUND BARRIER** is restricted and never becomes part of a true, documentary exposition.

The scene of Ridgefield's explanation of the barrier, for example, is only superficially technical. In the middle of an informal supper with his daughter, Sue, and son-in-law, Tony, he uses a ruler as a prop and delivers an impromptu lecture, trying to outline the intangible in simple terms for the uncomprehending Sue. As he does, her expression reveals a lingering uncertainty, not just over the "how's" of the operation but over the "why's" as well. She verbalizes her qualms later that evening:

> SUE
> Father, answer me a question, will you?
>
> RIDGEFIELD
> Yes.
>
> SUE
> Is the ability to travel at two thousand miles an hour going to be a blessing to the human race?
>
> RIDGEFIELD
> Well, I'd say that's up to the human race.
>
> SUE
> As a member of it I can't say that I'm duly optimistic. In fact, if that's all that lies beyond this barrier, what purpose is there in risking lives to crash it?
>
> RIDGEFIELD
> Well, I could talk about the national security . . . beating the potential enemy bomber . . . flying to New York in two hours. But that's not the real point. The real point is it's just got to be done. What purpose did Scott have in going to the South Pole?
>
> SUE
> I wish I knew. I really wish I knew.

This dialogue describes the basis of the most important

personal conflict in the film—the visionary versus the pragmatist. Ridgefield is alone in medium close shot when he speaks, figuratively and literally separated from his daughter. He is too caught up, too fascinated by the concept he "holds in his hand" to take note of his alienation from her and, by extension, from the world in general.

The scene in the test bed, where Ridgefield gives another demonstration, this time of his new jet engine, functions similarly. Again Ridgefield, with Tony, is separated from Sue: in the first scene by their shared knowledge of the sound barrier, in the second by a safety screen of wire and glass. Although Tony is clearly not driven by any abstract ideals or sense of "mission," his feelings are a reflection of admiration for those qualities embodied in Ridgefield. His scatterbrained inanities, such as singing "I'd rather have a bow-wow-wow-wow-wow" or irritating his wife with trite phrases like "piece of cake," mask him as a boorish but likeable fellow. His drive and intensity places him side-by-side with Ridgefield in that chamber and on the brink of the equally perilous realms of the unexplored. During Sue's first jet flight she continually stares down at the earth (the Alps, the Greek ruins) below her, until a newly-inspired Tony tells her, echoing Ridgefield's own words, "Why do you want to look at the poor old earth? Look up there. There's our future: Space. You can't make that insignificant." Tony, Will Sparks, the engineer, Philip Peel, and the other test pilots are instruments of the "old man's" vision but not unconscious ones. Like Icarus in legend, these men revel in the exhilaration of flight. By means of the unnatural wind from the jet's engines which disturbs the stalks at the edge of the airfield, they have the power to affect nature, even if only temporarily. The curving white jet trail is their mark emblazoned over the sky; and, as that shot dissolves to one of the Andromeda Galaxy, that mark extends over the entire universe. In this context, the test flights assume mythic proportions. The impassioned voices of the aviators with the sun glinting off their dusky face masks as they buffet towards the unknown connote costumed ritual or religious litany, when they shout the mach numbers, as much as scientific experiment. In these vehicles, veering towards

the sun, there is a chance for apotheosis. They may disappear
into the void but not before a personal, almost existential,
assertion of identity. "And man in portions can foresee/His own
funereal destiny . . . To which his spirit may oppose." It is
Ridgefield, watching the flights from the ground, who has the
acute awareness of "destiny," who fulfills the archetypal imagery:

> TONY
> Oh, by the way, Will wants a name for her [the
> new jet]. Got any ideas, Dad?

> RIDGEFIELD
> Yes. "Prometheus."

> TONY
> Prometheus? Who was he?

> SUE
> He was a Greek god.

> RIDGEFIELD
> He stole fire from heaven.

> TONY
> Oh, yes, I remember. He came to a sticky end,
> didn't he?

> RIDGEFIELD
> He did. But the world got fire.

Ridgefield is the "modern Prometheus." Instead of stealing fire,
his fate is to break through the gods' mysterious wall of sound. As
a pilot, he had once experienced the elation of flight with metal
wings. Now, in his later years, he has taken to the world of
"imagination" in the sense Coleridge described "as a repetition in
the finite mind of the eternal act of creation in the infinite I AM."
He designs the kind of vehicles which will someday trace a
course to the very stars he studies so fervently in his observatory.
He has, in fact, withdrawn so far into his own world that he
seems void of human emotions. His "way of feeling grief" after
his son's fiery death is to examine a model of his new jet and,

after Tony's annihilation, to listen to the tapes of the crash. His vision is his one, insular passion. As Will Sparks remarks to him, "I don't know what devil it is that's eating you up, but it can't make life any too happy for you." As a character, Ridgefield anticipates Nicholson in **KWAI** and T.E. Lawrence. It was Lawrence who observed that "the dreamers of the day are dangerous men," and Ridgefield, so easily lost in thought or distracted, is such a "daydreamer." Like Lawrence, he consciously denies the human side of his character and purposely separates himself from normal society. Alone in his observatory he can watch "the process of continuous creation" without danger; outside of it, the threat of extinction is needed to sustain and compel his actions. The crisis in Ridgefield's life, like that in Lawrence's, comes when his humanity reasserts itself.

> SUE
> You want me to think of you as a man with
> a vision. Well, that vision has killed both my
> husband and my brother. And while I'm
> alive it's not going to kill my son, too. There
> are evil visions as well as good ones, you
> know, father . . . [Ridgefield answers while
> waiting fearfully for Philip Peel's attempt to
> break through the barrier.]

> RIDGEFIELD (shaken)
> Can a vision be evil, Sue? Can it, can it? It's a
> terrible thing to make a man doubt everything
> he's ever lived for . . . as if I've killed them
> both for nothing. But it can't be true. Can it?
> Can it?

As Peel's plane dives, the camera is in close on the terrified Ridgefield and tilts as it did for Laura Jesson, to subjectify a moment of emotional instability. This time the test succeeds; the barrier is broken. In the final scene, Ridgefield has again withdrawn into his observatory, his doubts buried. He survives the psychological buffeting of uncertainty because his visionary shield, his mental conditioning is strong enough.

So central is that vision, good or evil, to **THE SOUND BARRIER** that all the secondary characters are defined in terms of their relationship to it. Of those who perish, Chris, Ridgefield's only son, on whom he initially builds his hopes by forcing him to become a flier, functions primarily as a symbol of Ridgefield's inability to regenerate his vision, to pass on its adventurous spirit. Chris' fear of flight, which his many lessons cannot dispel, and his cowering before his tyrannical father—the force of whose presence is captured even before he appears by the imposing portrait in his study—evidence that he has inherited the very character weaknesses which Ridgefield has suppressed in himself. In that sense, Ridgefield's mute acceptance of Chris' crash during his first solo becomes another tacit assertion of his own unique vision. Tony replaces Chris as Ridgefield's protegé and student. Immediately after the funeral, Ridgefield uses the glistening model to draw Tony away from Sue, to enmesh him. Framed with Ridgefield in two shot by the window or leaving his wife's bed to gaze out from the terrace into the black abyss, accompanied by strains of atonal music which often suggest, in Lean's films, fear and wonder, Tony is the Icarus who flies too near the sun and is thrown back to earth. His ship, upon impact, is buried in the ground.

The visual imagery which Lean associates with this destruction can also suggest regeneration. Beginning with the unnatural whine of the engine which intrudes on the shot of the falling hawk before Tony's last test flight, Lean again uses the contrast of science and nature to color narrative events. Just before the crash, the sound drops out entirely and the camera is on Ridgefield in the tower surrounded by windows. In the silence, the power of the natural which lurks in the landscape just outside is at once calm and menacing. From Ridgefield, there is a cut to a farmer as he runs up to a smouldering fragments of the plane. Then a pan reveals the crash site and a craning movement looks down into the black smouldering crater from a high angle. As it would with the disposal of the constable's body in **RYAN'S DAUGHTER**, Lean's treatment transforms that hole in the earth

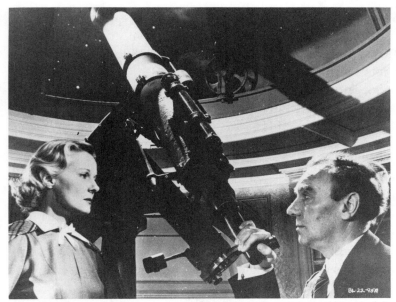

Ridgefield (Ralph Richardson) and his daughter, Susan (Ann Todd), come to an understanding in his observatory at the end of the film.

Susan surprises her father as he listens to a recording of her husband's final radio transmission.

into nature's spiritual womb. After Sue has learned of Tony's death, Lean uses camera movement and optical transitions from a close shot of her through three windows to the starry sky dissolving to the pit at sunrise and then to Sue and Tony's newborn child to create a pantheistic metaphor of rebirth.

Of those who survive, Philip Peel, the war pilot who tries to quit flying, is probably the most balanced character. His return to aviation is partially in response to an addictive impulse: as he watches Tony and Sue leave Egypt in a jet transport, the music soars and the camera moves into his eager, anticipatory expression; it is not treated as a regression. It is rather a step forward, out of the Egyptian kind of antiquity which Tony had rejected earlier. Mentally, Peel is keener than Tony. He respects Ridgefield's vision and, unlike Tony who is hard put to explain his father-in-law, can detachedly express his admiration, as he says to Sue: "You know I don't think that sort of understanding comes from up here [pointing to his head] . . . only from here [pointing to his heart]." But Peel has not subdued his common human feelings. He remains devoted to his family and provides a refuge for Sue after her husband's death. His admirable ability to balance between the two worlds is best exemplified in the scene following his "historic" flight. He returns to his locker room and tries to tell his wife what he has just accomplished:

JESS (entering)
Oh, good. I found you.

PHILIP
Hello, darling . . . I . . . I

JESS
Hello, darling . . . I want to see you today . . .
[their dialogue overlaps]
They won't take it back until closing time tonight.
[showing him some material]
So we've got to make up our minds now.
Do you think the color's too much?

[Philip is unable to get a word in]
Because they've got one, sort of a daisy color
with stripes going down here . . . I . . . well,
it seemed a bit dull to me, but if you . . . Look,
darling, pay attention. This is very important.
Is it all right?

PHILIP
Yes, I'm sorry, darling. Yes, it's fine. Come
and see the . . .

JESS (cutting him off)
Good, that's lovely . . . If I can only get back
in time. Well, 'bye. 'Bye, all. See you at
home. [She leaves. Philip begins to laugh,
then breaks down completely]

Although he has tasted briefly of the "part divine," Peel must now
readjust to the ordinary. Alone among the protagonists, he
possesses the equanimity both to crash through the barrier and to

Ridgefield (Ralph Richardson) and Tony (Nigel Patrick).

confront the mundane aspects of life with a similar if unequal enthusiasm.

Sue, finally, is the vision's antagonist. She neither understands nor meekly condones the venture. Because her life is built upon home and a family, because her worries are those of "everyday" life, the sound barrier has no meaning in her scheme of things. To her it is only a "great wall in the sky strong enough to smash an airplane to pieces . . . beyond it nothing, nothing at all." Because her father seems so cruel and unfeeling, it is only after witnessing the human and comprehensible fear of failure in him during Peel's test run can she even consider a reconciliation. She brings her son with her to Ridgefield's home and sets the child christened John after his grandfather on a map of the moon

Ridgefield (Ralph Richardson) anxiously scans the skies from his office window after losing radio contact with the experimental aircraft.

presaging, possibly, his astronautical future. The final image of Ridgefield's telescope and a model aircraft nosed towards the distant stars recapitulates within a single frame the central thrust of the film: Ridgefield, the Promethean man, and his legacy of questing for the infinite.

6
HOBSONS'S CHOICE (1954)

*The brain may devise laws for the blood,
but a hot temper leaps o'er
a cold decree . . . this reasoning
is not in the fashion to choose me a
husband.*

—William Shakespeare,
The Merchant of Venice

HOBSON'S CHOICE is Lean's last film in black-and-white and last portrayal of period England, the concluding installment in an informal series begun with **GREAT EXPECTATIONS**. The opening is closer to the startling, expressionistic prologue of **OLIVER TWIST** than the documentary-like introduction of **MADELEINE**. The wind sweeps loudly down a wet, cobbled street at night. A black boot hangs forebodingly at the top of the frame, as the camera travels back past a trade sign swaying noisily on its rusty hinges to the flickering lamp of Henry Hobson's shoe store. A cut inside permits the travelling to continue down a display of Hobson's wares before panning abruptly to a branch tapping against a skylight in the rear. As the camera turns back towards the center of the room, the door suddenly bursts open. A shadow looms across the floor, and in the doorway a dark figure lurches like a drunken ghost, until a loud belch on the soundtrack reveals that it is just a plain drunk. Only then does it become apparent that **HOBSON'S CHOICE** is a comedy.

Lean's use of the fixtures of a period for dramatic effect culminated in **MADELEINE**. In **HOBSON'S CHOICE**, the comic anagram of this becomes a parody of genre style, in particular his own. The atmosphere of the opening is built on ominously exaggerated details: the streets must be wet, the wind must be blowing, a branch must be striking the skylight with its twisted silhouette. This staging precipitates an even greater comic deflation when a character staggers in and turns out to have been neither shot nor stabbed nor plagued by any demon other than rum.

A similar reversal is applied in the scenes of courtship between Maggie Hobson and Will Mossop. Their Sunday meeting starts out as vaguely reminiscent of Alec and Laura's boating excursion in **BRIEF ENCOUNTER**. An extra long shot of them strolling through the green parkways laid out in a complex geometrical pattern dissolves to a medium shot by a river bank. But the river Irwell is nothing like the pleasant stream in the earlier film. An almost-capsized, iron fence fronts a single, paint-flecked bench by a stunted flower bed. The clouds in the background are of smoke sent up by the factory chimneys of Salford. In this less than idyllic spot the couple sit and talk; but Lean photographs them in a long take from behind, at a slight high angle, so that the river remains prominently visible for a considerable time. Near them bits of debris drift through its oily surface; beyond a frothy layer of detergent residue floats, almost motionless except for the occasional clusters of bubbles that detach themselves and arise, with perverse romanticism, skyward. Lean is not above satirizing his own images of love and nature (and in this scene, at least, has even anticipated an ecological relevance). Not even the first kiss is sacred. Alec and Laura's took place spontaneously in a dark passageway amid the noise of rushing engines. Maggie must command hers ("Right here in the street?" "Come on, lad, get it over."), retreating into a dingy causeway where the only sound on the track is the shallow gurgling of a small sewer that divides the alley behind the couple.

Rather than Rachmaninoff, who might in this instance be, as Madame Arcati suggests, "too florid," **HOBSON'S CHOICE** is reinforced with a subtly humorous score by Malcolm Arnold. It

makes its presence felt in the initial tracking shots over the rows
of pumps and clogs. Calliope-like notes sound a restrained,
waltzing air over the ladies' high-top shoes, a more boisterous
clip-clopping for the riding boots, and a music box chiming when
the children's footwear appears. A few moments later, as Hobson
"falls" upstairs, a precipitous drum roll accompanies the action.
Much of the music and effects—from the comic clarinet when he
gets up the next morning to a squeaking medicine cabinet near
the end echoing the trombone's lament of the main theme—is
geared to Hobson, most effectively perhaps in the strange,
vibrato orchestration when he chases the moon in a puddle.

Since **HOBSON'S CHOICE** is a character comedy, the title
role, as portrayed by Charles Laughton, is appropriately in the
Dickens tradition. The red-nosed tradesman spending too much
time at the local tavern is a familiar type. With his round, slightly
besotted face and a double chin under a flat-topped hat, his large
belly protruding behind an extremely wide belt with a huge,
glistening buckle, and his thumbs cocked confidently behind the
armholes of his waistcoat, Hobson is mostly bluster. He rants
against lawyers ("It's a lawyer's job to squeeze a man and
squeeze him where his squirming's seen most."); women ("Female
perversity comes from leading an indoor life. Women think
they're important because they're washing kitchens."); and tee-
totaling ("Life's got to be worth living before I'll live it.") with
equal vigor. Yet his shouts of "I'm master here!" in his own
household are easily circumvented, as in this exchange:

MAGGIE
Dinner's at one o'clock, remember.

HOBSON
Now, look here, Maggie, I set the hours in
this house. It's at one o'clock because I say
it is, not because you do.

MAGGIE (wearily)
Yes, father.

HOBSON
So long as that's clear, I'll go. [He exits.]

MAGGIE
Dinner's at half past. That'll give him half
an hour.

It is quickly established that Hobson's eldest daughter, Maggie, runs both house and shop behind her father's back. She is the primmest and most efficient, the best at avoiding "muddles" and least likely to incur Hobson's disapproval by affecting a "waggin' hump" (a bustle). She is also the cause of much of his exasperation by being "uppish" and by refusing to give any approbation to his drinking. Maggie describes herself as "strong and proud" and her lack of servility is in marked contrast to the sight of her father on his knees before Mrs. Hepworth, a wealthy patron, who is prompted to remark, "Get up, Hobson, you look ridiculous." "Courting's like that, my lass," Maggie tells her sister while tapping a sequined shoe, "all glitter and no use to anybody"; yet for all her cold pragmatism, she harbors certain Romantic urges, which, like the rose from her bridal bouquet that she saves from the trash to press in her Bible, are quietly concealed.

Maggie is the least sentimental, most aggressive of Lean's heroines; so aggressive, in fact, that she could probably never exist in his work except in a comedy. Like that of the married Laura Jesson or the spinsterish Jane Hudson, her lot seems somehow preordained, as when Hobson announces his intentions for his younger offspring:

MAGGIE
If you're dealing husbands round, don't I
get one?

HOBSON (surprised)
You, with a husband? (laughing uncontrollably)
Aye, that's a good one.

MAGGIE (coldly)
Why not?

HOBSON
Why not? (pacing about) Now, Maggie, I
thought you'd sense enough to know. Well,
if you want brutal truth, you're past marrying age.

MAGGIE
I'm thirty.

HOBSON
Aye. Thirty and shelved. Well, all the
women can't have husbands, Maggie.

Within Maggie's utilitarian principles resides the firm belief that a
husband would serve. Accordingly, while another Lean heroine
might do no more than wait restlessly for something to happen,
Maggie attacks the question frontally ("It's a poor sort of woman
that will stay lazy when she sees her best chance slipping from
her."). She announces her own intention to an awed Will Mossop,
dismisses his former fiancée ("You're treading on my foot."),
picks up a ring (Alice: "A brass ring? Out of stock?" Maggie: "Why
not? It's always from someone's stock."), and summons a wedding
party to the church. While it may not occur quite as rapidly as all
that, it does come about by a willful design, a design which
simultaneously affirms and contradicts her father's sarcastic observation: "It's a great relief to know your mind's taken up with
ideas; I thought for a moment it was taken up with a real man."

In one sense, Maggie's mind is only taken up with an
idea. When she says, "Will Mossop, you're my man," it may have
less to do with Will himself than with the abstract notion of using
him to find her own independence. She, unlike the less fortunate
Madeleine, realizes it must be sought in a way the established
social order approves of, or rather, as her society did not approve
of independent women at all, in a way that was not overtly anti-
establishmentarian. In this instance it is through marriage. Will's
confusion reflects the contradictions in Maggie's action, for she
must break several minor traditions (waiting for some man to
propose; marrying within her class) in order to fulfill this more

basic one (getting a "man") which, in turn, is only a means towards the end of personal enfranchisement. Maggie views Will as an implement for fashioning her own destiny. As she tells him, "You're a business idea in the shape of a man. My brains and your hands'll make a working partnership." The speech she makes to Mrs. Hepworth to secure a loan reveals that she does see Will as something more than a tool. Maggie has a basic sympathy, if not respect for Will. This is evident from Will's first appearance, when he pops up through the cellar trap and squints at the world like a myopic mole **[frame 56]**. Maggie makes an excuse for his inability to read a calling card ("It's the italics.") while

[frame 56]

the editing establishes that she is the only one who can see that he is holding it upside down. Her consideration here and the relationship she subsequently finds with Will involve more than her protecting him or teaching him how to write with the aid of inspirational maxims ("Great things grow from small," "There is always room at the top."). By a kind of transference, she projects her own drives (those socially unacceptable in a female) onto him and succeeds in altering both his outward appearance and his personality. He becomes genuinely "her man" not just in terms of possession but because she, quite literally, "makes him."

In the early stages, Lean clarifies Will's pliability through a variety of comic scenes. The outing in the park is followed by a trip to Will's lodgings. There while Maggie disentangles him from his fiancée and her mother (his landlady), a temperance parade passes advising him to "Beware the Wrath to Come." But he is already too caught up in the various possibilities which Maggie has opened up and loses himself in reverie until a blow from his would-be mother-in-law jars him awake. It is too late for him to be wary—Maggie has intoxicated him with dreams of advancement. Gradually, as Will—much like Madeleine was—is figuratively pulled up from the security of his cellar, changes take place. Hobson's attempted intimidation with his black belt ("You've got an ailment and I've got the cure. We'll beat the love from your body.") only succeeds in dispelling his remaining hesitancy. He even puns in reply: "You'll not beat loving me." From a shot of Will fidgeting and embarrassed as he watches Maggie test the springs of a double bed, Lean dissolves to him self-assuredly examining sheets of leather. His physical aspect is transformed; the dark circles disappear from under his eyes, the eyebrows become less bushy, his bowl haircut fills out below the ears, and his suits begin to fit. Even his voice mellows and no longer cracks when threatened, as it did when Hobson summoned him up for chastisement. There are implications of maturity in his dialogue with Maggie:

> WILL
> I'm going to give you a shock.

> MAGGIE
> I doubt it.

> WILL
> I've just paid out 120 pounds.

> MAGGIE (shocked)
> What?

> WILL
> To Mrs. Hepworth. That's her capital plus
> twenty percent. We can do without her now.

> MAGGIE
> It looks as though you can do without me, too.

WILL
Maggie! I thought to please you.

MAGGIE
You do. You do. Only I like to have a finger
in the pie.

WILL
God knows, Maggie, you made the whole pie.

As Will's awareness expands, he moves from his earlier ecstatic
visions ("It's like a happy dream.") to a calmer, more stable
confidence in the situation. His ultimate realizations are confided
to Maggie after he confronts Hobson on equal terms ("You told me
to be strong and use the power that's come to me through you.
Words came to me mouth that made me jump at me own boldness
. . . I said such things . . . to him, while he's the old master." Maggie:
"And you're the new."), but the joy of them, like his persistent "By
gum's" remains his own. The dreams return, this time in concrete
and attainable form, because, as Maggie observes (in vicarious
triumph), "You're the man I made you. And I'm proud."

Throughout **HOBSON'S CHOICE** the framing serves to
underscore the relationships. From the direct and economic
establishment of the setting and period with travelling shots
down Chappell Street, Lean elects to insert an over-the-shoulder
of Beenstock Senior peering down sternly at the pub and Hobson
("There's a small spark of decency in that man that's telling him,
at this very moment, that my eye is on him."). Inside Moonrakers,
an insouciant Hobson is framed tightly by his staunch drinking
cronies; but during a later visit when Maggie's conduct makes
him the object of some ridicule he will be isolated in medium
close shots. In both instances, the framing reflects the attitude of
those around Hobson.

On a more complex level, Hobson's own domineering
attitude is marked in a scene where Vicky helps him with his boots.
As in Madeleine, the staging (she is at his feet), angle (over
shoulder: up towards him and down at her), and costuming (she
is in black; he is white-shirted) favor the dominant character (but

this time without the daughter-over-father, against-appearances thrust of the similar sequence in the earlier picture). In many ways, Maggie's defiance is bolder than Madeleine's; and her father's failure to bring her into line is visualized in a four-shot of the family at supper that evening. While he tyrannizes his younger daughters, Hobson stations himself in the foreground taking up a large portion of the frame with his head and shoulders. They stand meekly beyond him to the right; then Maggie enters. As she comes forward unhesitatingly, the visual focus realigns itself on her form moving through the shot [frame 57]. When she announces, "I'm going to marry Will, Father," she literally turns Hobson's head around,

[frame 57]

forcibly breaking his overbearing gaze by brushing past him. After the others have been sent out so that they may talk, Lean uses a slight low angle, he sits and she stands determinedly over him ("I've to settle my life's course . . . I'll tell you my terms.").

The dynamic shift away from Hobson, initiated here, culminates in the final confrontation between the three principals. Lean begins by intercutting a slight high angle medium shot of Hobson and all three daughters with a slight low angle of Will in medium close. All are arrayed against his lone figure—his tactic is to imitate Hobson's own swaggering manner. With a haughty tone and his thumbs wedged under his vest, he copies the old master's habitual poses. Hobson, perhaps sensing his ploy, waits until only Will and Maggie remain in the room with him before offering her husband a seat. Then he stands hovering over his daughter and son-in-law, tucks in his thumbs, and tries to gesticulate his way back into control of the scene while making his "generous proposal." But Will rises, backs him down into a chair with a few hard, economic facts ("And all you think you can offer me is me old job at eighteen shillings a week, me, the owner of a business that's starving yours to death."), and wins the game of dominance and submission handily. When the question of a name for the shop is settled, a panning medium close shot carries Maggie, gazing admiringly, from the loser's (Hobson's) side to Will's. The presence of three main characters, all significantly interacting, necessarily prevents Lean from subjectifying much of the material by restricting it to any one viewpoint.

Nevertheless, there are several instances where a first person attitude is momentarily adopted, generally for comic effect. Will's reverie outside his old lodgings, for example, is subjectively intensified by a travelling in to close shot and a crescendo on the track. The jolt of being brought out of it is approximated for the audience by cutting back with the sound of the landlady's blow and abruptly replacing the music with street sounds and raucous shouts. A smaller, similar touch is added when Will leaves the new shop for the first time. As he stops to inspect the sign with his name on it, a key light comes up on the letters and sets them glowing like the pride inside him. Much of the subjective sensation in an instance like this depends less on a formal manipulation than on a sustained identification with the character. Although Will's painful self-consciousness is heightened by such things as the "fweeping" sound of the bedroom door, the wedding night is basically a silent exposition of his emotion rather than an externalization of it. It is easy to feel embarrassment with him, as he arranges his starched collar front and cuffs on the mantelpiece or fumbles awkwardly out of his pants.

The most overtly manipulated stagings are keyed to Hobson's drunk scenes. His falling movement upstairs at the film's start is a good illustration: the camera hurtles back from him in high angle medium shot as he trips rapidly up each step. At Moonrakers, after Maggie's departure, wide angle medium close shots accentuate Hobson's tipsy swaying; then the camera itself staggers to and fro with him as he gropes his way out. An occurrence of *delirium tremens* features a number of fantasy point-of-view shots. A swarm of imaginary locusts descending onto the bed **[frame 58]** and a man-sized grey mouse grinning over the footboard are intercut with reaction shots of Laughton squirming

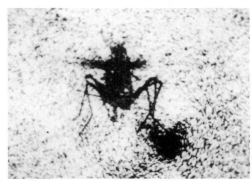

[frame 58]

[frame 59]

in his long johns **[frame 59]**. The sight of one of his drinking companions sticking out his tongue in the mirror instead of Hobson's own reflection is composed over-shoulder, reinforcing the reality of it for the hallucination's victim and helping build to his climactic yell as he drops a pitcher of wash water.

For all the accuracy of its dialect and period characterizations, for all its slapstick moments, **HOBSON'S CHOICE** is not a standard, middle-country farce centered on the title's dilemma of having to take what's offered or nothing. This is partly because of its exploration of themes of social relationships and personal maturation. It is also because of Lean's additions and extrapolations. A scene like Hobson's alcohol-addled pursuit of the moon's reflection is a tour-de-force of comic surrealism. Lean develops it precisely: from the first quizzical glances of Laughton, while he leans against a traditional lamppost, at the rippling likeness in the water [frame 60]; as he pulls up his trouser legs and hops after it from puddle to puddle like an oversized frog; to his antics below Beenstock and Son's window, unwarily circling the open trap to the grain cellar. With the tremulous chords of Arnold's "moon theme" on the track, Lean moves from the humorously absurd image of Laughton on his back with his feet caught on the guard chains and floundering like an overturned tortoise, to the chillingly eerie tumble down the grain shaft: a matte of Hobson, mouth gaping and eyes widened in surprise, over a forced perspective of bricks—the moon still looming unnaturally overhead after the body has dropped from sight, its theme sounding a note of final victory over his crash landing [frame 61].

[frame 60]

[frame 61]

7
THE PASSIONATE FRIENDS (1949) SUMMER MADNESS (1955)

*There come and go and come again in
the sky the threatening clouds, the
ethereal cirrus, the red dawns and
glowing afternoons of that passion
of love which is the source and
renewal of being.*
—H.G. Wells, *Passionate Friends*

PASSIONATE FRIENDS is a transitional work for Lean on
several levels. Made immediately after **OLIVER TWIST**, the last
picture with second wife Kay Walsh, **PASSIONATE FRIENDS** is
the first picture with third wife Ann Todd. It is also Lean's first
taste of foreign locations, the Swiss Alps in which a portion of the
film is set. Finally, it is a return to a contemporary setting,
although the Wells novel is set before World War I.

The modernization of Wells' novel is, in itself, curious and
somewhat revealing. **PASSIONATE FRIENDS** falls most conspicuously between **BRIEF ENCOUNTER** (four years earlier) and
SUMMER MADNESS (six years later), with Mary Justin forging a

clear link between Laura Jesson and Jane Hudson. All three characters have a love affair which becomes the focal point and is concluded concurrently with each film; but while Laura remains faithful out of continuing love for her husband, Mary Justin's marriage is one of convenience, and Jane is a spinster. **PASSIONATE FRIENDS** also anticipates **MADELEINE**, on a direct (it was made immediately prior to it; both pictures star Ann Todd) and thematic level. Wells' original story was a combination epistle and first person history written by its protagonist, Steven Stratton, for his son, tracing events before the turn of the century to 1911. It explored, much as Lean would in **MADELEINE**, rigid social conventions; and these are the real antagonists to the human figures in both novel and film. The movie's Mary Justin becomes, along with Madeleine Smith, the most unstable of Lean's heroines. Vacillating, as Madeleine would, between passion and a union for purely material satisfaction, Mary Justin in the novel is also driven to murder—in this instance, her own. Laura's flirtation with suicide is a momentary impulse; but while Mary is dissuaded from the attempt at the end of the screen version, much of the compulsive, increasingly schizophrenic behavior that drove her to suicide in Well's conception remains.

In this first picture with Ann Todd, Lean emphasized the qualities which caused her to be dubbed "the English Garbo," the cool, distended expressions and whispery voice that he would deliberately play against in **MADELEINE**. For part of the underlying normality of the other heroines, even at the height of their fantasies, is in their physical aspect. The wide-eyed, tweedy Laura Jesson and the energetic, accident-prone Jane Hudson with her constant "Oh golly's" and "Wow's" contrast markedly with the expensive wardrobe and aristocratic manner of Mary Justin. Even in everyday surroundings, Lean catches her wistfully contemplating in the moody sidelight of a bed lamp or airily resplendent in evening gown and veil and makes her the most pictorially attractive of his women.

As a consequence, there is a dichotomy in **PASSIONATE FRIENDS**. At times, it recaptures the glistening black-and-white compositions of the period films. The action, which derives from

THE PASSIONATE FRIENDS: Mary Justin (Ann Todd) and Steven Stratton (Trevor Howard).

an intricate flashback plot development, and characterizations become melodramatically stylized. At other moments, though, particularly in the scenes with Steven Stratton—who, as played by Trevor Howard, is a literal reincarnation of Alec Harvey—Lean may verge back past the realistic, middle-class romance of **BRIEF ENCOUNTER**. In the flashbacks of Mary before her marriage, girlishly holding hands in her ruffled print dress and lying next to Steven in the grass, Lean recalls the juvenile love of Shorty and Freda in **IN WHICH WE SERVE**. This bifocal style is appropriate to Mary's own indecisiveness. As did Emile L'Angelier and William Minnoch, Stratton and Justin appeal to divergent aspects of the heroine's personality; but, more in the manner of Alec Harvey and Fred Jesson, the associations are less absolute, less polarized between rapturous abandon and dull security.

There are, however, aspects of Mary's character which are never resolved. By evading the possibility of Mary's death, which the preceding narrative has at least suggested if not firmly established, the conclusion compromises her. Vindicated neither by her innocence nor by overwhelming strength of passion, she returns to her husband to face his unfounded accusations. For whatever reason Wells' ending was abandoned; but there are other, more fundamental divergences from the novel. As the entire focus of the story shifts from Stratton to Mary and as the events are recounted in the context of her life rather than his, the film neither follows through on Laura's rush to the edge of the tracks in **BRIEF ENCOUNTER** nor fully anticipates the ordeal of **MADELEINE**.

The imagery of Mary and Steven's last idyll in the mountains clearly reflects back to the excursions into the countryside in **BRIEF ENCOUNTER**. The sequence in which they go boating on an Alpine lake might almost be match cut with a similar outing in **SUMMER MADNESS**. But the strongest resemblance is one of basic attitudes on a character level. Mary Justin's remark, "I want to belong to myself," gives voice to an aspiration held in common with Madeleine Smith and perhaps Lean's last heroine Adela Quested, but not as clearly by Laura Jesson, Jane Hudson, or even Maggie Hobson. Maggie's forceful pragmatism and Jane's career-woman status (which she is not above deprecating: "Oh, [I'm just] a fancy secretary, really.") are only partially the result of a search for personal liberation. More importantly, they are actively (Maggie) and passively (Jane) aimed at fulfilling or facilitating the realization of essentially romantic notions. The self-assessments of Mary ("I'm a hard woman") and Madeleine ("I do not regret things") reflect an awareness of individual identity which will hold up under stress. The failure of their respective relationships arises from a struggle to maintain that awareness within a repressive social order, an order which throws their desires for love and independence into conflict. In this regard, despite its contemporary setting, **PASSIONATE FRIENDS** seems closer to **MADELEINE** or **A PASSAGE TO INDIA**.

Lean has frequently employed a narrative framework which, if not an actual series of flashbacks, as from the raft in **IN WHICH WE SERVE**, is triggered by a movement backwards in time, as from "T.E. Shaw's" funeral in **LAWRENCE OF ARABIA**.

Often he has exploited the technique for novel or revealing effects: Yevgraf's third-person voiceovers during scenes from his memory in **DOCTOR ZHIVAGO** or the subjective "replay" of the parting in **BRIEF ENCOUNTER**; but nowhere is it more compounded—perhaps, confounded—than in **PASSIONATE FRIENDS**. The meetings of Steven and Mary, separated by several years, could almost be viewed as an elaboration on a conversation in **BRIEF ENCOUNTER** (Laura: "You think we shall ever see each other again?" Alec: "I don't know. Not for years anyway."). The scenes of their affair before her marriage, which Mary recalls after their first re-encounter, becomes a flurry of brief events, a montage reminiscent of Laura Jesson's romantic musings while gazing out the window of her train compartment and part of an abbreviated process of selective, almost fanciful remembering by Mary. The overall structure, with overlapping flashbacks forming a narrative that is episodic yet static in terms of change, seems more analogous to Wells' "threatening clouds [that] come and go and come again." Most of the film drifts aimlessly, the past strung out like a bridge of hazy clouds interlaced with a present that may threaten but never bursts into dramatic intensity.

The climactic and central sequences in the Alps are part of the film's most consistent imagery. The lovers' last day together in the mountains completes the cycle which began in the natural settings of rural England. In the novel, a supporting character, representing societal judgment of the illicit affair, advises Stratton to stop being "romantic and uncivilized." The same values, the same antipathy between civilized behavior and unbridled ardor holds true in the movie. The final progression from Mary on a snow-capped peak with Steven to the white-tiled subway with Justin represents a movement away from the natural into the artificial, away from precarious independence towards conformity, back into what Henry James called "a full-fed material insular world, a world of hideous florid plate and ponderous order and thin conversation." It is equally a regression from a natural height of passion—an image transposed from Wells—to an artificial subterranean depth of repression—a striking extension of the original's direction. Again the film backs away from intensity. Relieved of the burden of Mary's suicide, the ending is, in various ways, Lean's most ambiguous, in terms of what will happen "after," and most realistic in the sacrifice of sensation for security. Where Laura and Rosy Ryan return to husbands whom they loved, Mary returns to a marriage of convenience. In this final sense, she may be the most frustrated of Lean's heroines, cut off from Romantic fulfillment as firmly as Adela Quested, but without even her solitude to console her.

SUMMER MADNESS (1955) occupies a clear middle position in Lean's career. Between the black-and-white period pictures and the color/widescreen productions of later years, it is his last contemporary film. While not his initial effort in color, it is the first photographed entirely on location, particular values which Lean refused to abandon in the films that followed. For the first time also, both his principal actors (Katharine Hepburn and Rossano Brazzi) and the source material (Arthur Laurents' play) were non-English. It was, in short, Lean's first step away from being a British director of British pictures aimed at a predominantly home audience towards becoming an international filmmaker working with "foreign" producers and stars in a world market.

Thematically, though, **SUMMER MADNESS** has much in common with its antecedents in Lean's work. Again, the imaginings of Laura Jesson aboard the train are an obvious referent. The very locale of **SUMMER MADNESS** is anticipated by Laura's dream image of riding with Alec Harvey in a gondola on the Grand Canal. The city of Venice is cast in a major role in **SUMMER MADNESS**. The film begins with Jane's arrival and ends with her departure. The opening scene on the train:

ENGLISH PASSENGER
Is this your first visit to Venice?

JANE
Yes. Is it yours?

PASSENGER
No, I've been here several times.

JANE (mildly astonished)
Several times! You have!

PASSENGER
Yes. I hope you're going to like it.

JANE
Like it? I've got to. I've come such a long
way. I've saved up such a long time for this
trip. Do you think I, maybe, won't like it?

PASSENGER (reassuring)
I'm sure you will. Not everybody likes it the
same way . . . but the majority find it very
beautiful.

JANE (still a bit apprehensive)
Yeah. Well, I guess I'll settle with the majority.

reveals something about Venice, something about Jane, and
something about the invisible "majority" which will, as in the
stories of Laura Jesson, Mary Justin, and Madeleine Smith, play its
own part. The obvious analogies between Jane Hudson and these
others have already been drawn. Yet in her particular way, Jane is
a more *re*fined and less *de*fined characterization closer in shared
traits, if not in time, to Rosy Ryan. The admixture of opposing
qualities makes her outgoing yet repressed, eager but anxious,
brash yet self-conscious, graceful but a bit clumsy: she is sharply
delineated and outwardly a most realistic figure. Few of the
events of her past and little of her present occupation, almost
nothing of her personal history is specified; and inwardly she is
as much if not more prone to fantasy as any Lean heroine.

Jane is not "put into context." Her encounter with Venice
is a dual synthesis of the everyday with the extraordinary, not just
of the Romantic city and the plain American tourist but also of the
commonplace streets and shops with the unusually romantic girl.
"In America every female under fifty calls herself a 'girl'." For all its
directness of plot—there are no flashbacks in **SUMMER MAD-
NESS**; it is restricted in terms of place and Jane's week-long stay—

the film's action seems suspended in time while that synthesis takes place. It is, as the title suggests, a slightly delirious idyll momentarily detached from any simple progression of days on a calendar while Jane searches for "what she's been missing all her life."

That synthesis also involves coming to distinguish surface values from genuine ones, material experience from emotional. For instance, she pauses to take in a gondola drifting on a glistening canal to the strains of a distant serenade, only to have her view temporarily obstructed by garbage being thrown into the water. Just as Jane's notion of postcard Venice is gradually undermined, so are her personal illusions about herself and others. Both the Jaegers and the McIlhennys aid in this process. The younger, ostensibly happy Eddie and Phyl Jaeger are not really the ideal couple which Jane imagines. This realization distresses her most because it upsets her scheme of things. On a more figurative level, Jaeger is a painter. Phyl has an art book under her arm, as she tries to understand his work. Even the methodical Lloyd McIlhenny, despite his timetables ("Independent activity—we're allowed two hours of it every day") and crass remarks ("To me it's just Luna Park on water") is impressed by the museum ("That place certainly sold me Art. That you gotta see, Miss Hudson"). All are caught up in a superficial, two-dimensional world with no more substance than a landscape. Jane herself looks at the city through the viewfinder of her camera. The compulsion she has with it is introduced in the first scene: "Oh, boy, gotta get a shot of this [the lagoon]. Oh, golly! Fifth one of these I've used already. Haven't even got there yet." On film, she reduces the world to two dimensions, until it becomes, as in McIlhenny's comment on the art museum: "hundreds of pictures, all done by hand," not only something she can possess, can take home and see again, but also a reality which she can selectively manipulate by screening out the discordant sights or bracketing it with her own title, as when she has the English passenger on the train hold a travel brochure for "Venice—City of Romance" while she photographs it. The camera is a tool for creating that "romance" and a habitual sublimation, the value of which Jane must reassess during the course of the film.

Materially, the red goblet and the white gardenia are

more important, more varied symbols than the camera. Like her home movies they are souvenirs; but they are also tangible, three-dimensional objects, and they are central to Jane's understanding of her situation. For whether the goblet she buys from Renato is truly an Eighteenth Century antique or one like the half dozen others purchased by the McIlhennys at the glass works is another superficial consideration. The valuation of people is not. The gardenia is a remnant of schoolgirl dreams:

> RENATO
> Why did you choose that flower?

> JANE
> I once went to a ball. Not just an ordinary
> dance, but a real ball. It was the first one I'd
> ever been to. Somehow I'd got it into my
> mind that I had to wear a gardenia. I don't
> know why. I guess I'd read about gardenias
> in a book or something. I must have—I
> didn't even know what they were.

> RENATO
> And did you wear one?

> JANE
> Gardenias turned out to cost two dollars a
> piece; and the boy I was going with was still
> in college. But it was a nice dream.

> RENATO
> Well, now you have your gardenia.

> JANE
> Yes.

> RENATO
> Everything happens sooner or later.

> JANE
> Yeah, that's what they say. Everything
> happens to him who waits . . .

Like the film itself, the elements in this scene alternate between those dreams and actuality. The dialogue lingers over the illogical, youthful wish and the rich associations of "not just ordinary" ballrooms, while violins in the background play "Summertime in Venice," a song linked with the couple throughout the picture— almost an archetypal underscoring as was the Rachmaninoff concerto in **BRIEF ENCOUNTER**. But pragmatic necessities dispel her dream. And as the physically present Renato supersedes the memory of the "boy," Jane becomes anxious, falls back into conversational generalities and subtly dodges any kind of involvement—as with the use of an impersonal "him" rather than a more affirmative "her" in the last line.

Both the goblet and the flower bring up the question of Jane's willingness to trust others, to risk becoming involved. For that question and the answers found in the affair with Renato are the film's major concern. There is an initial explicitness which can leave little doubt about what Jane wants; but her guardedness, her way of talking to Signora Fiorina about "a girl on the boat coming over" rather than herself:

> JANE (by the balcony of her room)
> Way back, way back in the back of her mind
> was something she was looking for.
>
> SIGNORA FIORINA
> What?
>
> JANE (spreading her arms out over the city)
> A wonderful, magical, mystical miracle!
>
> FIORINA
> No? To do what?
>
> JANE (after a moment's hesitation)
> Beats me.

and her cynical remark at the end, all suggest that the greatest hindrance to finding her miracle, what really "beats her," is her own insecurity. Unlike Mary Justin or Maggie Hobson, heroines inclined to take a more active part in the resolution of their desires, Jane just spreads her arms out over the city and waits.

The subjectification in **SUMMER MADNESS** is certainly not as pervasive as in **BRIEF ENCOUNTER**; nor, operating from a different plot referent, should it be. Lean does employ the technique to expose Jane's sensations at the *pensione*. Contrasting with the exultant stance on the balcony against the bright, sunlit city is a later medium shot of Jane in her full white dress sitting on her bed amid the dark grey and brown furnishings of the room, posed contemplatively like a Vermeer figure [**frame 62**],

[**frame 62**]

a pose reinforced with the added dimension of the scrape of slippers on the floor, the distant clanging of a single bell, and the canal water lapping against wooden hulls outside—selected sounds of isolation. The scene of Jane alone on the terrace—pacing back and forth, listening to the street singers and the lovers laughing, throwing a rock into the water to break the tension only to retreat in embarrassment when a gondolier mistakes it for a summons— is most subjectively expressive and made to seem genuinely poignant rather than heavy-handed when she is brought to the brink of tears. It is less manipulative than a later scene with the Jaegers when Jane, after failing in earlier exhortations to have them join her in a drink ("Prego, pretty prego"), asks to accompany them on their evening out: by holding on the couple in the boat after Jane has given up and withdrawn back onto the terrace out of sight, Lean reveals their hesitation to the audience but not to her, slipping momentarily and effectively into the ironic mode and diminishing identification with her subjective emotion when he cuts back to her.

Throughout Lean drives the picture forward from these small, climactic moments when Jane is flustered or embarrassed. By restructuring in this fashion, he not only moves away from the rhetorical explicitness of the play but also creates a visual flow between what were originally static acts and scenes. In fact, all of the play's action was confined to the terrace and sitting room. The theatricality of **THIS HAPPY BREED** and **BLITHE SPIRIT** are not in evidence; and the reason is the nature of Jane Hudson, a nature not found in the Gibbons or Condomine households.

Although it is the key to Jane's emotional flux, her self-consciousness renders her a more physically expressive figure than Laura Jesson or Mary Justin. There is not really much comic effect derived from it in the sense of making her actions something to laugh at. In fact, there is little in **SUMMER MADNESS** to qualify it as a comedy either in the traditional sense of a "happy ending" or in an abundance of amusing scenes, little except wry asides, such as the gondola jam created by the weekend tourists while "Santa Lucia" plays and loudspeakers recommend a glance at "page 27 of your guidebooks." The terrace scenes have more an air of desperate pathos than comedy, and Jane's acute discomfort on discovering the other goblets flares out in anger rather

[frame 63]

than awkwardness, so that her tipping over her chair becomes intensely dramatic, particularly following the banter of the departing McIlhennys.

The fall into the canal is an example of a scene fulfilling several functions simultaneously [frame 63]. On a narrative level, it supplies the needed excuse for Di Rossi to call immediately upon Jane at the Hotel and politely inquire if she is all right; it is also comic action, a restatement of a stock gag: Jane losing her footing while backing up to get a picture of Di Rossi's shop. Lean also combines the subjective factor of having the audience share another disconcerting moment with Jane, perhaps the severest in the film, with the ironic presence of Mauro, unable to get a word in and resigned to watching helplessly. The pure comedy of the scene is prolonged by having an unidentified witness perform a replay for his friends, but in high angle shot rather than the more engaging, eye-level medium shot of Jane up to and including the tumble into the water. This both extends the laughter and, while Jane is off-screen, allows for a gradual dissipation of the viewer's empathetic embarrassment. Finally, the sequence links the camera to Jane's "loss of control"—a physical loss of equilibrium in the action itself and an implied emotional agitation underscored by her feeble quip about "trying out for the Olympics," as she slips through the crowd and hurries away fearful of Di Rossi coming out and seeing her.

That link begins in the very first scene with Di Rossi, where, characteristically, Lean provides a visual summary of the inner states of both protagonists. Jane sits at an outdoor table near San Marco: while idly photographing the passersby she inadvertently records a pickup. For the first time her selective control of the scene is disrupted; her personal view of Venice is intruded upon. Disturbed, she stops filming. While she rewinds (in medium close shot, foreground), a pan reveals Di Rossi seated behind her reading a paper (medium shot, background). Lean holds on the continuing action: as she raises the camera to her eye and resumes, the motor noise catches his attention [frame 64]. This motivates a shot seen through her viewfinder of some flags drifting languorously in the breeze. This, in turn, creates a segue,

[frame 64]

after a medium close shot of Di Rossi now intent on Jane, to a close point-of-view of the folds of her dress, fluttering over her legs, moving up to her waist. The intensity of his gaze is translated into a track to a closeup of the back of her head; she senses it, fumbles with her sunglasses in symbolic concealment, and the incident ends.

The conflicting impulses which Lean sets in motion here are not quite the same as those of **THE PASSIONATE FRIENDS**. An instructive contrast may be possible using Vittorio De Sica's **STAZIONE TERMINI [INDISCRETION OF AN AMERICAN WIFE]** (1952). Like **PASSIONATE FRIENDS** this film opposes impulsive physical attraction to the guilt of acting contrary to established morality by engaging in an adulterous affair. It is also analogous to **SUMMER MADNESS** in that it considers the same cultural differences which finally separate Jane and Di Rossi (American woman, Italian lover) and operates within the same restrictions of time and place—a few days in Venice; a few hours in a Roman train station. It differs because Jane is never guilty except in the most puritanical sense: she and Renato are never forced by society or by the Motion Picture Code to conclude that what they are doing is wrong.[1] The cause of her repression, as has been noted, is less from fear of social judgment than from personal insecurity and unwillingness to "be hurt," presumably again. De Sica's picture is shot almost completely in interiors, full of shadowy compositions and oppressively tight close two-shots with lonely figures framed against dark metallic objects and modern glass fixtures or caught in crowds. Lean, on the other hand, has no choice but to energetically open up the play. In order to discover the magic that Jane expects from the "City of Romance," to make the miracle possible, he must find architectural expanses for his long shots, must concentrate on daylit exteriors and fill the nights with fireworks or music by Rossini, must provide a landscape that encourages her free and instinctive responses.

The subsequent scenes between Jane and Di Rossi are increasingly stylized. The second encounter, where Jane's eye is caught by Di Rossi's red goblet in the shop window much as his ear was caught by the noise of her camera, is a partial reversal of the first—she doesn't look up and recognize him until after she has removed her sunglasses [frame 65]. Their interaction is still

[frame 65]

mannered, not spontaneous, with the artificiality on Jane's part emphasized when she returns to the cafe on the chance of seeing him again, pretends to be with someone, and unwittingly discourages him when he does pass by later. Later, Lean will exploit two long sections of theatrical dialogue. He adds dramatic tension by staging both not just in long takes but in medium close two shots subliminally accentuated by slow, almost imperceptible travelling movements [frames 66 and 67].This seems to bring the couple closer together in a diminishing frame and parallels the gradual movement in their dialogue from basic lines of commu-

[frame 66]

[frame 67]

nication to greater frankness and finally understanding. As Jane's emotional insulation is penetrated by Renato, Lean again changes pace through his composition and editing. The progression is from mostly medium shots in the discussion of gardenias during the evening concerts and Jane's hushed "I love you" after Di Rossi kisses her to an overhead extra long shot of her crossing a crowded square. Her tiny figure moves in such a way that the reading time for the shot is unusually short and reflects her growing animation. This reflection is sustained in the succeeding montage of buying accessories and visiting the beauty parlor and restated in the dance scenes that evening.

The last additional element is color. The framing of the red goblet in the window so that its color all but overwhelms the shot [frame 68] gives it both visual and thematic impact. In the latter sense, Jane mutely echoes the goblet's catalytic role with the red dress she wears in a later scene. But primarily color contributes greater pictorial expressiveness to Jane's passionate evolution. First it changes from the dull brown and trapped, hazy sunlight in the two shot in the parlor, when Jane's hair is still wet from her accident and wrapped in a towel, to the deep blue outside Renato's house, the only light when he pursues her down a dark alleyway. [frame 69] Then the explosions of fireworks bathe

[frame 68]

[frame 69]

them in multicolored flashes as they embrace on the balcony. The following day they pose against the immutable hues of the houses on the "Isle where the Rainbow fell" and against the fiery colorations of the setting sun in an open sky, like Wells' "glowing afternoon of passion." [frame 70] These colorations mark the completion of the cycle, the end of Jane's transformation and the

[frame 70]

resolution of her inner conflict.

The bursts from the skyrockets also function, almost exactly like the longer and better-known sequence in Hitchcock's **TO CATCH A THIEF** (1955), as sexual imagery which, until Adela Quested stumbled onto Hindu erotica in **A PASSAGE TO INDIA**, was Lean's most direct and explicit. He may have chosen to drive the point home with such literal explosiveness simply as part of the generally vivid scheme of imagery. It might also be impressionistically interpreted as a celebration of the fact that, to that point in his work, more than any other character adapted from play or novel, Jane Hudson is Lean's character. Lean alters not just the name but, with Katharine Hepburn, her whole way of being, her appearance (Laurents' Leona Samish was played on Broadway by Shirley Booth) and her attitude. From the first glimpse of her on the train crossing the lagoon, she is no longer a cynical, intemperate, slightly overweight, middle-aged woman running away from life, but one who somehow senses that she has missed something and is energetically running after it. Leona Samish loses because she can never accept life for what it is, never come to grips with the problem that, as Phyl Jaeger tells her, "everybody loves you," but no one loves her. Jane wins because she can.

In Renato Di Rossi and in the use of Rossano Brazzi, Lean creates a male lead distinctly different from the earlier Trevor Howard portrayals of Steven Stratton and Alec Harvey, whom

Laura Jesson herself characterized as "ordinary." Despite his protest, in character, about being an "ordinary man," there is no way to avoid, even in playing against Brazzi's "Latin lover" image, some connotation lodged in his physical aspect of storybook prince coming to fulfill schoolgirl dreams. Of course, it might be inappropriate, given the visual context Lean creates with Venice, for Jane Hudson to discover anyone else. It would definitely be incongruous for Howard's Alec Harvey to swab the salt spray from her eye while waiting for a gondola. The Di Rossi of "Time Of The Cuckoo" is something of a gigolo, careless with his money at best, unscrupulous at worst. Lean makes Di Rossi almost painfully sincere, for Lean's interest, obviously, is in the fantasy/ reality of Jane's world, in the way she, and no one else, deceives herself. Accordingly, Di Rossi becomes an honest, stable, and mature figure, not just in quantitative years of age but also in qualitative light of Lean's other pictures. Lean is still playing against both the anxieties of social codes of conduct and wearying worldly outlooks, as represented in Fiorina's remark about her former lover: "For several years now we've been . . . unexcited." Di Rossi is still an essentially realistic characterization and still some distance temporally and temperamentally from Andrew Doryan in **RYAN'S DAUGHTER**. Di Rossi is not, it turns out, Jane's storybook prince, just an antique dealer who speaks humorously imperfect English ("He is my niece") and challenges her more prudish romantic preconceptions with bizarre similes ("You are hungry . . . eat the ravioli"). Because he does, it becomes possible in the final scenes, in a way it never was before, for Jane to "eat the ravioli," for her to separate fantasy from reality, for her to realize happily as Renato runs after her train that the physical possession of the gardenia, the fulfillment of the dream, is less valuable than the unguarded emotional experience.

8
THE BRIDGE ON THE RIVER KWAI (1957)

When their sufferings, their tortures,
their deprivations under their masters in
the jungle grew so intolerable . . . they came
to the realization that is was better and
more worthy of their human dignity to
perish.

—B. Traven, *General from the Jungle*

"I love traveling, going to strange corners of the world."[1] Lean's affinity for exotic locations really began with **THE BRIDGE ON THE RIVER KWAI**. In Ceylon and later in the Jordanian desert, on the desolate West Coast of Ireland, and in Bangalore, Lean forged visual correlatives to his personal excitement. As he devoted himself more and more to such location shooting, his time in production also increased. The year spent on **BRIDGE ON THE RIVER KWAI** mushroomed into the even longer gestation periods for **LAWRENCE OF ARABIA** and **DOCTOR ZHIVAGO**. Admittedly these projects were of an epic scale that would justify if not demand such an expenditure of time; but there was always more to it than that. Lean himself admitted: "I do become obsessed by a movie, in a sort of maddening way, I must say."[2]

Whether this compulsive side of Lean's particular artistry stems from a desire to extend the experience of the film for as long as possible or merely to make the best possible film, Lean carried this reputation for obsessive filmmaking throughout his career. Early on partner Ronald Neame said publicly, "His mind is absolutely along one line. His only really passionate interest in life is films, because it's the one thing he knows backward."[3]

After three pictures for Korda, whose "relationship with David Lean was admiring but hardly warm, perhaps because Lean's personality was too cold, too precise, and too serious"[4] but who had like Rank left Lean mostly to his own devices, working with Sam Spiegel promised to be different. "If a producer is truly creative, if he generates a project, it is important for him to run the show," observed Fred Zinnemann of Spiegel, "the other 'creative producers' are ridiculous. It is vanity."[5] The Lean/Spiegel collaborations quickly became legend as the "Hollywood" epitomé of irresistable force Spiegel versus immovable object Lean. It was no secret that after a year of filming **LAWRENCE OF ARABIA**, Sam Spiegel had to "drag" Lean out of the Jordanian desert. Lean himself remarked after the fact that "a film like **LAWRENCE OF ARABIA** calls for a band of dedicated maniacs. My job was to be the chief maniac."[6] Whether Lean knew or cared about Spiegel's reputation or that the producer had considered hiring Howard Hawks or John Ford before entrusting him with **BRIDGE ON THE RIVER KWAI**, the motion picture that resulted unquestionably changed the course of Lean's career and the nature of his projects. If Lean's work had drifted towards becoming, as Strelnikov would say of Zhivago's poems, "absurdly personal," donning an "epic" mask would provide Lean with the time and technical support to make personal films in a much more expansive context, to "have tremendously intimate thoughts combined with a very rugged but also beautiful landscape."[7]

BRIDGE ON THE RIVER KWAI divided into two narrratives: the story of personal conflict in the Nicholson-Saito confrontation and an action piece in the Shears "adventure." For most of the film they are also divided geographically, coming together only in the first and final sequences. The film opens with a shot of a hawk soaring above the jungle. This archetypal image of a free spirit or "soul of man" provides an immediate contrast with the prisoner of war camp. There the men's spirits are far from free. In a crude graveyard, two men are burying a comrade. One of them is Shears: a cynical, arrogant American who masquerades as an officer, buys his way out of work with items taken from the corpses, and laments over his compatriots' graves like a parody of a Greek chorus: "Here lies Corporal Herbert Thompson, serial number 01234567, valiant member of the King's own, or Queen's own, or something." His stated goals are simply staying alive and, eventually, escaping the compound.

William Holden, who was offered the Shears role after Humphrey Bogart and Cary Grant could not be signed, was at home in this part. Throughout the late forties and early fifties, he was frequently cast, most notably in Billy Wilder's **STALAG 17**, as the ugly American. Typical of these characterizations was an exaggerated, sarcastic disregard for others, frequently nullified by a final, out-of-character act of mercy. **KWAI** is no exception: after carefully establishing his disenchantment with the world in general and his abhorrence of both war and heroics, Shears becomes a conventional hero at the end by sacrificing his life to complete his mission to destroy the bridge. Shears' "Why me?" is never satisfactorily answered; but to contemporary audiences the act of questioning made him the center of the film, the character most easily understood and discussed. Not only does he refuse to accept the half-death of the prison, where irony must have it that he is the chief gravedigger, but he speaks of following his instincts and the importance of living to the fullest. Visually, the colorful wreath of flowers given him by the natives or the yellow tie he dons when escaping the prison are Lean's familiar shorthand for dynamism.

If the film begins by underscoring Shears' manic will to survive, it is as a contrast rather than a segue to Nicholson, whom Shears believes has "the courage of a maniac." While Shears is still in the camp, Lean uses him for ironic cutaways. When he anticipates Saito's repetition of his worn-out motto "Be happy in your work," Shears pose is merely mocking. When it follows the low-angle shot of a defiant Nicholson standing in the sun, made with a wide lens and set so that the light flares across it with flies buzzing on the soundtrack, Shears' wry aside, "Into the valley of death rode the six hundred," is also an admonition to the viewer about the nature of Nicholson's bravery.

For Lean, the character focus of the piece is clearly on Nicholson and his aberrant sense of duty. As he noted: "I'm fascinated by these nuts . . . Nicholson was certainly a nut, and so was Lawrence, in a wonderful way."[8] The conflict of wills between Colonels Nicholson, the newly-arrived English POW, and Saito, the Japanese commandant, is constructed on a series of dualities. Thematically, the film derives its thrust from the first paragraph of Boulle's novel: "Perhaps the conduct of each of the two enemies, superficially so dissimilar, was in fact a different, though equally meaningless, manifestation of the same spiritual reality. Perhaps the mentality of the Japanese colonel, Saito, was essentially the same as that of his prisoner, Colonel Nicholson." Lean reinforces this concept by placing them visually within the same psychological and spiritual sphere. In many of the widescreen compositions of the two men, they are, though at opposite sides of the frame, in similar positions. Saito's first formal meeting with his officers is composed analogously to Nicholson's council with his own men. In the initial confrontation in the prison yard, each Colonel is placed in a military posture with his men behind him: the stiff-upper-lip Nicholson to the right of frame; the overbearing Saito to the left. At these men's two conferences over a table, this opposition continues but with Saito now on the right. Up to and including the final scene at the river, these visual parallels are continually redrawn.

Lean balances the imagery of the film on a succession of levels. From the title sequence, the colors that predominate in Jack Hildyard's photography are those of mud and jungle. Once Shears has escaped, the story-line is developed through parallel editing, alternating sequences at the prison camp with Shears' struggle to get down-river, his rescue, and finally his reluctant return.

Given the multiplicity of characters and viewpoints in **KWAI**, Lean seldom uses subjective shots; but these also are balanced. When Nicholson first arrives, there is a travelling point-of-view that moves forward to peer over the edge of a rise and reveal the shabby huts of camp below with jagged rocks in the foreground. Later when Nicholson rides a handcar to the construction site, another moving point-of-view comes around an embankment to reveal the bridge. From Nicholson's chauvinistic perspective the triumphant second shot dispels the dismay of the first. What he saw when he arrived were the feeble attempts of his captors to impose their will on nature. What he sees now is the success of the British in doing just that.

Perhaps the best example of balance is Lean's staging of two key sequences. In the first, when Saito has Nicholson taken from the sweatbox and brought to him in the middle of the night, Lean uses a long take to underscore the tension in the power struggle of the two men. Saito tries to cajole Nicholson, offering him food and drink and a compromise. The camera dollies and pans to follow both men as they move about the room. At last, Nicholson's refusal to acknowledge any inferiority in his position, his stolid composure, his ingenuous questions ("Do you or do you not agree that the first job of an officer is command?"), provoke Saito's outburst: "I hate the British. You are defeated but you have no shame. You are stubborn, but you have no pride. You endure, but you have no courage." Finally, as Saito plunges his dagger in the tabletop and shouts for his men, Lean cuts, using Saito's cue to release the unspoken visual tension.

The second long take occurs during a conversation between Shears and Warden. After Warden draws back some curtains to reveal a map of Siam, he surprises Shears by asking how he would feel about going back. As Warden calmly explains that they know about Shears' service record and that he has been impersonating an officer, as he peels away Shears' alternatives, the camera again pans and tightens and holds Shears in the frame, trapping him as effectively as Warden has. When Shears wryly accepts Warden's offer ("As long as I'm hooked, I may as well volunteer"), Lean again uses character emotion as an edit cue and cuts to a different angle.

For Boulle, the ultimate irony in the foolishness of war is

that, after failing to destroy the bridge, Warden defends his decision to train his mortars on Nicholson as "the only line of conduct possible. It was really the only proper action I could have taken." In so doing, Warden operates from the same rationale as Nicholson. The motion picture uses Shears to drive that point home several times in the dialogue with Warden: "This is a just a game, this war. You and that Col. Nicholson, you're two of a kind, crazy with courage. For what?" The ultimate irony for Lean in this film, as in so many others before and after, is madness itself. Early on each colonel speaks separately with Clipton, the British medical officer, and accuses the other of being deranged. Saito is rhetorical: "He is mad, your colonel. Quite mad!" Nicholson is off-handed: "Actually, I think he's mad." There is little surprise that the word which occurs repeatedly to Clipton, the last words uttered in the film after he has witnessed so much death and destruction, are simply "Madness! Madness!"

For both Boulle and the filmmakers the underpinnings of the madness are the obvious links between Nicholson and Saito, their profession, their rank, and their common attitude towards this occupation. Nicholson and Saito are servants of King (or Emperor) and Country who execute orders and follow "the book." For Saito duty resides in *giri*, the samurai's obligation to serve his lord, in this instance the imperial command to construct the bridge at any cost. For Nicholson, "ordered to surrender," all that remains is the Code of Military Conduct, for "without law there is no civilization." If at first impression, their dispute seems no deeper than that, a clash of rule books, it may seem that way at the end also. As Shears defines their conflict, it is "How to die like a gentleman. How to die by the rules." For Lean, it is more than that.

The initial glimpse of Saito is in his hut dressed in a kimono and framed by Japanese prints and cherry blossoms. When he goes out to meet Nicholson and his company, he puts on a modern uniform but retains the traditional samurai sword. Saito is very much a remnant of the feudal Tokugawa period and wants to behave as a traditional warrior. In the novel, Boulle explains about Saito's sense of humiliation at not having seen action and his drunkenness. In the picture, a few shots make the

Col. Saito (Sessue Hayakawa) tries to convince Col. Shears (Alec Guinness) to stop resisting his demands.

same point wordlessly. When he slaps Nicholson's book away, it is a would-be warrior ranting: "You speak to me of code. What code? The coward's code. What do you know of the soldier's code? Of *bushido*?" Based on a set of standards which has lasted generations, Saito's life derives a continuity with the past and a degree of meaning. It is his own "escape from reality," the very thing which he accuses the prisoners of doing in attempting to escape the camp. This code is even more important than the war and the Imperial orders. The real thrust of Clipton's argument to Saito, as he menaces the officers, is that gunning them down would violate these principles, although shooting the unarmed English officers might have eliminated the resistance to building the bridge. Everything about Saito, public and private, his expression, his carriage, the box he stands on to address assemblies in the yard, all are implements in what he understands to be a rigorous application of this code. Ultimately, it is *bushido* coupled with the loss of face after Nicholson has taken over and finished the bridge for him, which will demand Saito's ritual suicide. He fails even at that, because Joyce's knife preempts it.

Nicholson's situation is only slightly different. He has no ironclad, time-defying "way of the warrior" to guide him; but he follows the traditional standards of a professional soldier. His personal beliefs dictate discipline, strict obedience, and following the rules to such an extent that he will die rather than let his officers work in violation of those rules. As the film progresses, Nicholson gradually strays from an authoritarian outlook and chooses to indulge some of his own fancies. The vision of erecting a bridge which will endure for hundreds of years fascinates and takes hold of him. After the work is completed, he reflects with Saito on its "beauty":

> SAITO (agreeing)
> Yes, a beautiful creation.
>
> NICHOLSON
> (leaning over a guardrail as the sun sets)
> I've been thinking. Tomorrow it will be
> twenty-eight years to the day that I've been
> in the service, twenty-eight years in peace
> and war. I don't suppose I've been home
> more than ten months in all that time . . .
> (shifting position) Still, it's been a good life. I
> loved India. I wouldn't have had it any other
> way. But there are times when suddenly you
> realize you're nearer the end than the begin-
> ning. And you wonder . . . you ask
> yourself...what the sum total of your life
> represents. What difference your being there
> at any time made to anything. Hardly made
> any difference at all, really, particularly in
> comparison with other men's careers. I don't
> know whether that kind of thinking's very
> healthy; but I must admit I've had some
> thoughts on those lines from time to time.
> (joyfully) But tonight . . . tonight!

Col. Saito (Sessue Hayakawa) is killed by the commando, Lt. Joyce (Geoffrey Horne).

At length, Nicholson drops a stick into the river and his reverie is broken. For most of the monologue, Nicholson is seen roughly from Saito's point-of-view: a tight medium shot at an angle from the back. This staging may suggest Saito's empathy but not his understanding; for this lunacy is uniquely Nicholson's. To make his "being there" count for something, Nicholson forfeited the very rights he would not allow violated earlier. He puts his officers to work and presses the sick into service. Although the doctor may wonder whether building a bridge for the enemy is treasonous or not, Nicholson is beyond consideration of the war or treason, of anything except realizing his vision. It is his desperate attempt to contradict the doctor's earlier observation that "no one will ever know or care what happens to us." Like John Ridgefield, Nicholson is lost to his dream. The atonal chords that accompany a shot aboard a raft, as the colonel relates his plan to his officers, both echo moments from Malcolm Arnold's earlier score to **THE SOUND BARRIER** and anticipate the visions of Lawrence.

When the bridge is completed and a memorial plaque

Col. Saito (sessue Hayakawa) throws away Col. Nicholson's (Alec Guinness) copy of the uniform code of military conduct.

identifying the builders is attached, Nicholson walks proudly over his monument and lovingly inspects it pausing to pick up a stray nail which mars its aspect. Unknown to him, on the near shore are a group of more practical men, men who make a battlefield out of a botanical garden, men who have come with cordite and plastique to annihilate his dream, men who saw him putting up the plaque through their binoculars and were outraged to think the Japanese had "got a British officer working down there on his knees." With these destroyers also arrives Nicholson's final dilemma: which loyalty is greater? In one draft of Lean's script, the colonel consciously chose not to expose the commandoes and pushed the plunger which demolished the bridge himself. In Boulle's novel, Nicholson actually saved the bridge. For Spiegel, one thing was clear: "There is no story in **KWAI** without a bridge, and the bridge acquires meaning only when it is destroyed."[9] The compromise was an ambiguous conclusion in which Nicholson is hit by shrapnel and falls on the plunger thereby taking the decision out of his hands. In either case, Nicholson's flirtation with the Romantic myth of perpetuating a personal identity vanishes with his hundred-year bridge, floats away like the plaque down the river amid the debris.

In the end, Clipton's cry of "madness" is not just the madness of war but of men with distorted values, the madness of a distracted dreamer. It is the insanity not just of combat but of codes which make enemies of men with much in common, which compels tired and bleeding soldiers to march proudly into a prison camp, which can twist an ordinary, constructive act such as bridge-building into an abnormal one. Where **THE SOUND BARRIER** ended on a regenerative note with Ridgefield and his grandchild, the chronicle of waste and destruction in **BRIDGE ON THE RIVER KWAI** ends as it begins with a shot of a hawk flying over. Nature implaccably and detachedly reasserts itself over the shattered bodies and dreams of men.

The completed bridge.

9
LAWRENCE OF ARABIA (1962)

*All men dream: but not equally. Those who
dream by night in the dusty recesses of their
minds wake in the day to find that it was
vanity: but the dreamers of the day are
dangerous men, for they may act their dream
with open eyes, to make it possible.*
> —Thomas Edward Lawrence,
> *The Seven Pillars of Wisdom*

We live, as we dream—alone.
> —Joseph Conrad, *The Heart of Darkness*

If those who admire and those who cannot abide Lean's work
were asked to select his best motion picture, the consensus
would almost certainly be **LAWRENCE OF ARABIA. LAWRENCE**
epitomizes what Lean meant when he spoke of intimate thoughts
in a vast landscape, an "epic" film, in most senses of the word,
that turns on a detailed character study. While the title character
of **LAWRENCE OF ARABIA** may well be "a nut" as Lean described him, the figure is far from the self-professed "ordinary"
protagonists of Lean's earlier work.

   LAWRENCE is also Lean's first collaboration with Robert
Bolt, which would ultimately produce seven screenplays but only

three films.[1] In the Preface to his play, "A Man for All Seasons,"
Bolt expressed a fascination with the notion of cosmic destiny, a
notion already touched on by Lean in two earlier characters,
Ridgefield and Nicholson:

> We all inhabit . . . the terrifying cosmos. Terrifying
> because no laws, no sanctions, no mores apply there; it
> is either empty or occupied by God and Devil nakedly
> at war. The sensible man will seek to live his life with-
> out dealings with this larger environment, treating it as a
> fine spectacle on a clear night, or a subject for innocent
> curiosity. At the most he will allow himself an agreeable
> frisson when he contemplates his own relation to the
> cosmos, but he will not try to live in it.[2]

To express this relationship, Bolt also asserts that he
"tried then for a 'bold and beautiful verbal architecture,' a story
rather than a plot,"[3] something that might have been antithetical
with the desires of a director who believed people "remember
pictures not dialogue."

The portrait of T.E. Lawrence which Lean and Bolt create
is not based but only loosely modeled on the historical person
whom Bolt called "a Romantic Fascist."[4] The undersized bastard
son of an English peer who went from leading armies to repair-
ing airplanes for the R.A.F. is only of superficial concern for Lean
and Bolt. They focus instead on the spiritual dimensions of an
enigma; and, in this context, such wanderings from the historical
path as the casting of the tall, handsome O'Toole in the lead,
making him the spiritual rather than physical equivalent of
Lawrence, are understandable. Within the framework of factual
incident—World War I and the Arab-English drive against Axis
Turkey—is presented a man who has chosen to descend not
only into the primitive landscapes of the desert but also to
venture through the dark terrain of his own soul. His long treks
across endless expanses of sand parallel his recurrent withdraw-
als into Self in order to search out his course of action, his roots,
his primal identity. For the conflict between the blond, fair-

skinned "Arab" and the slightly affected English officer, between El Aurens and Lawrence, between deliverer and demon is only a particularization of a longstanding inner conflict. When General Murray notes that "I cannot make out whether you're bloody bad-mannered or just half-witted," Lawrence replies ingenuously "I have the same problem myself." What Lawrence ultimately aspires to be is never clear, not even to himself. He longs for the desert, for the catharsis of heat that he merely toys with by snuffing out matches with his fingers, for a blistering purgatory in the face of Dryden's warning that "only Bedouins and gods get fun out of the desert. And you are neither." So to free himself from the parlor games of the intelligence service, where "the trick is not minding it hurts," and his own psychological snares, he enters the desert.

Lawrence quickly adapts to the desert and the Arabs. Simultaneously he becomes a dreamer of the day. The "fact" that this Welshman is out of place here is never visualized. Rather Lean catches him reclining contemplatively in front of the bleached branches of a tangled, windswept bush. Already, with his dusty tan uniform and his sand-flecked hair and skin, he has begun to blend with the natural surroundings. Exteriorly his figure is camouflaged or lost in the panoramic long shots where Lawrence and his guide become specks in the desert tides. Internally he senses the beginning of something: "I am different," he assures Tafas. He discovers a destiny.

The first chance to test this is the encounter with Sherif Ali at the Harith well. Framed together at opposite edges of a medium shot, it is Ali, not Lawrence, who stands out from the background in his black robes and who dominates the frame. Yet it is Lawrence who seems to draw strength from the terrain, who despite the murder of his Masruh guide is confidently resilient, like the desert brush, against Ali's blustering threats: "You have no fear, English?" "My fear is my concern." It is the outsider who remains unperturbed before this dark, menacing figure who has slipped from the waves of a mirage to kill his friend, steal his compass, and perhaps leave him to perish. It is Ali who is a bit unnerved; and from the empty sky that remains when Ali has

Prince Feisal (Alec Guinness) tells Lawrence (Peter O'Toole) that his people need "a miracle."

ridden out of the shot, Lean tilts down to reveal Lawrence riding in the distance, tranquil and alone.

"I think you are another of these desert-loving English." There is justice in King Feisal's observation; but the desert seems to reciprocate that love, the elements fall into accord around Lawrence. In a meeting with Feisal, Lawrence demonstrates a knowledge of those elements and of Arab tradition ("I think your book is right; the desert is an ocean in which no oar is dipped.") and a sympathy for both. Feisal is direct and pragmatic: "We need what no man can provide, Mr. Lawrence. We need a miracle." While he speaks, a mysterious night wind arises and the masts of the tent creak in response. As if hearing a deific message, Lawrence goes among the dunes to contemplate. Again his position is visually understated: a high angle shot flattens him against a wall of rippling sand, the thin form of a minor British functionary arrayed against the currents of natural and historical force. Lawrence ponders this dilemma through a night of wind and dust, wandering in long shot, until morning lights his crouching silhouette, and a close-up as he breathes the decision to himself: "Akaba." Akaba, or Jerusalem, or Mecca—Lawrence pronounces it like a shrine. For in this scene of ordeal in the desert, in the creation of Feisal's "miracle," Lean and Bolt begin to extend the image of a mortal facing personal cataclysm to include messianic analogies and religious symbols. Lawrence is not just a man "who broke the bank at Monte Carlo," he is a man willfully aspiring like Moses or Christ or Mohammed to prophesy and to lead.

This deific equation is established in the initial cut from Dryden's office to the desert. In an instant, the artifacts—an alabaster Egyptian cat, a painting of a sunrise—and the artificial are left behind. That sentiment is echoed in Lawrence's action, in the more natural blowing out of the match rather than extinguishing it with his fingers. But beyond the obvious meanings of the cut as the painting is animated and another layer of reality is embodied in an expanded "frame," the timing of it to the match going out suggests that Lawrence no longer needs to sustain himself with match games when he has the limitless heat of the sun. That sun itself appears suddenly on the right of the frame exactly where Lawrence was standing. Whether it replaces him or he becomes it, the implications of a fiery inner rising or of a new Ra being born are unobtrusively added.

After the Apocalyptic image of the golden solar disc shimmering through the silent curtain of heat, Lawrence begins to assume dimensions that are larger than life. He does so literally when he clambers awkwardly up onto his camel and, in extension of the archetypal parallels, "Full of the Holy Spirit . . . [is] led by the Spirit about the desert for forty days." (Luke 4:1-2). Whether Lawrence resists or assimilates the power of the desert does not diminish the experience: it is his own ordeal, his own "forty days" gaining knowledge in the wilderness. Lawrence does assimilate, but Lean does not disguise his figure to the point of making him just an animated shrub or bit of rock—that would go counter to the direction already indicated. From the earliest scenes Lawrence is associated with wind, speed, fire, heat, and light. All these suggest a pantheistic union with the elements, but none erase the individuality of Lawrence.

Mentally, Lawrence's delusions are not of grandeur. Before entering Feisal's camp, he emerges purified. Although there may be a reflection of expanding self-esteem behind the comic relief of his singing "I'm the man who broke the bank at Monte Carlo" and listening for the echo, the principal connotations are of a kind of spiritual rapture. More importantly, Brighton's applause, which reverberates over shot like a series of distant gunshots, and the contrast to Lawrence he affords in his impeccable uniform reaffirm the ominous presence of a "real" world, a world at war which summons Lawrence back to his "public life." So when the despondent Feisal looks around in the midst of a Turkish air raid a point-of-view reveals Lawrence behind the black smoke, suddenly before him in medium close shot, as if risen from the earth in answer to his prayers.

Lawrence's second confrontation with Sherif Ali comes after his night of meditation, and this time he is clearly the victor. In a sustained close two shot, the dark and light faces contend within a restricted frame—separated in mind over the feasibility of crossing the Nefud desert and in body (in two dimensions) by the mast of the tent—until a cut back gives Lawrence room to raise his arm decisively and exclaim: "It's only a matter of going." Lawrence's fervor, which Ali, of course, calls madness, overwhelms any reluctance or apprehension. He acquires disciples: the gap-toothed Gasim; the eager Farraj and Daud who kiss his feet and receive blows for him, causing Ali to remark: "These are not servants. These are worshippers."

The incidents involving Gasim also exemplify the manner in which Lean and Bolt shift emphasis. The record of the occurrence in the Nefud in "The Seven Pillars of Wisdom:"

> . . . Gasim was my man and upon me lay the
> responsibility for him.
> I looked weakly at my trudging men, and
> wondered for a moment if I could change with
> one, sending him back on my camel to the
> rescue. My shirking the duty would be under-
> stood, because I was a foreigner: but that was
> precisely the plea I dare not set up . . .
> So without saying anything I turned my unwill-

ing camel round and forced her, grunting and
moaning for her camel friends, back past the
long line of men, and past the baggage into the
emptiness behind. My temper was very
unheroic, for I was furious with my other servants, with my own play acting as a Bedouin,
and most of all with Gasim . . . a man whose
engagement I regretted and of whom I had
promised to rid myself as soon as we reached a
discharging place. It seemed absurd that I
should peril my weight in the Arab adventure for
a single worthless man.[5]

differs markedly from the movie version. When the film Lawrence
is apprised of Gasim's disappearance, he does not hesitate over
going back personally nor question the "absurdity" of the venture.
Nor is his departure unnoticed:

> ALI (trying to stop Lawrence)
> Gasim's time is come, Aurens. It is written!
>
> LAWRENCE
> Nothing is written.
>
> ALI
> Go back then. What did you bring us here
> for with your blasphemous conceit? Eh,
> English blasphemer? Akaba? What is Akaba?
> You shall not be at Akaba.
> [a travelling medium close shot]
>
> LAWRENCE (turning to answer)
> I shall be at Akaba. That is written.
> (pointing at his head) In here!
> [He exits.]

The disparities in the two renderings are readily apparent; but
besides subverting the book's cynicism, the adaptors use Ali,
again, to clarify their Lawrence's growing sense of, if not deific

Lawrence (Peter O'Toole) executes his own wounded man, Farraj (Michael Ray), rather than leave him to be tortured by the Turks.

Actors Alec Guinness (left) as Prince Feisal and Jack Hawkins as General Allenby with producer Sam Spiegel (between them) and David Lean.

omnipotence, at least unimpeachable destiny. The subsequent recrossing of "the sun's anvil"—scorched earth that resembles cracked, white plaster baked to a hardness which the tread of the camels fails to disturb—becomes a matter of inner conviction rather than doubt, not a case of necessity (done to avoid losing face) but of willfulness. From an incident which occupies a single chapter out of fifteen in Book Four: "The Expedition Against Akaba," Lean and Bolt fashion a key episode in the "journeying" phase of **LAWRENCE OF ARABIA**. In the original memoir, Lawrence agrees with Auda who has ridden back to rescue the rescuer: "'For that thing, not worth a camel's price . . . ' I interrupted him with, 'Not worth a half-crown, Auda'." However, in an epic construction, the return for Gasim cannot be "unheroic": it must become a display of charismatic authority, culminating with Lawrence's unassisted (and unexpected by those who presumed him dead) ride back into camp. In a tight medium close shot, he levels his penetrating gaze at Ali and uncovers his face; but before drinking he defiantly reasserts that "Nothing is written." Or rather Lawrence will write; for that is the self-conscious purpose in this action, in finding the "lost sheep," in saving the "dead" as ostentatiously and dramatically as Christ raised Lazarus, in demonstrating that he is more god than blasphemer.

Characteristically from the fatalistic perpective in Lean's and Bolt's past work, Lawrence must ultimately lose in the question of "what is written." Lawrence's execution of Gasim is original to the film, and it provides a kind of anticline to the summit of Lawrence's success in traversing the Nefud and recruiting Auda abu Tayi, postponed from an earlier position in the book. After Lawrence murders to placate the rival factions, the Harith and Howeitat chieftains exchange words on his display of emotion:

AUDA
What ails the Englishman?

ALI
That that he killed was the man he brought
out of the Nefud.

AUDA
Ah, then it was written.

The conclusions are inevitable. Previously, Ali and Lawrence had casually discussed his "identity," ("Not El Aurens, just Lawrence") with Lawrence divulging his illegitimacy. For the Bedouin such a lack of heritage is tantamount to a lack of being; but Ali's recommendation ("It seems to me that you are free to choose your own name. El Aurens is best.") advances a cycle of rebirth. The contingent factor is that "He for whom nothing is written may write himself a clan." Lawrence is legitimized: he dons Harith robes and his uniform is ritualistically burned, then he goes off to marvel at his new apparel, his new being. In medium close shot he draws his knife and stares at the blade to adjust his headgear; he laughs, spreads his arms to the wind, and watches his outstretched shadow running over the sand. In this

Lawrence (Peter O'Toole) prepares to detonate a charge beneath a Turkish Military train.

scene, the first stage of Lawrence's "transfiguration" is completed—his godlike portion is grasped. But before the battle, lurching away from Gasim's body, it is the demonic half that is discovered. Despite Ali's reassurances ("You gave life and you took it. The writing is still yours."), Lawrence cannot come to grips with the full nature of "El Aurens." When he makes out a voucher for Auda's mercenary gold ("Signed in his Majesty's absence by . . . me."), there is a telling pause that suggests both a momentary uncertainty over his own name and a sudden, sobering realization of his "majestic" accomplishments.

The Akaba sequence ends with the fall of the "invincible" city. Lean's camera, in sweeping travelling shots, follows Lawrence's mounted Arab army as it overruns the Turkish garrison—to find, as El Aurens had predicted, that the guns were indeed fixed impotently towards the sea. After the fighting, Lawrence passes before a golden sunset at the edge of the sea. Here Lean extends his color metaphor, adding to the burning orange of the sun which seems to set fire to the water, the red of the wreath which Ali throws to the conqueror. Both characterize Lawrence's dynamism; but the wreath is also the color of blood. For as fearful as he is of killing and of the unanticipated pleasure he felt when he shot Gasim, it is too late for Lawrence to put off his heroic robes, to avert his fate. He prepares to return to Cairo to report the victory:

> AUDA
> You will cross the Sinai?

> LAWRENCE
> Why not? Moses did.

> AUDA
> And will you take the children?

> LAWRENCE
> Moses did.

> AUDA (shouting after him)
> Moses was a prophet and beloved of God . . .

Lawrence (Peter O'Toole) leads the assault on the Turkish train.

The return to Cairo traces a full circle, ending Lawrence's series of journeys and costing him another follower (Daud) in the process. It also confirms his rebaptism as El Aurens, invalidating Ali's doubts ("I see. In Cairo you will put off these funny clothes, tell stories of our ignorance and barbarity. Then they will believe you.") and ostracizing Lawrence in the officers' club from his own kind. This realization comes upon him like the ship looming up out of the dunes, hits him as tangibly as the water Farraj throws on his brooding visage, leaves him, as Allenby remarks, "riding the whirlwind."

Lawrence does not "grow in wisdom before God," only in confusion about his "calling" and alienation from his fellows, first English then Bedouin. While there is little doubt that Lean's and Bolt's sympathies are with Lawrence, they do remain aware of one man's limitations, of his fallibilities, and of society's repressive action against the nonconformist. He may have visions of a "pillar of fire," but his corporeal being can still sink in loose sand. Accordingly, Lawrence becomes more compulsive. Feisal sums up one aspect of it to the newsman, Bentley. "With Mr. Lawrence, mercy is a passion. With me it is merely good manners. You may judge which is the more reliable." Whether stepping out in front of the guns to fire a flare or watching as a scalded Turkish officer empties his revolver at him, Lawrence grows fascinated with his own recklessness, tests his own legend. When Auda warns, "You are using up your nine lives . . . " Lawrence glibly counters, "Didn't you know? They can only kill me with a golden bullet." When he parades atop the wrecked train, his arm and palms bloodied, framed against the sun, Lawrence still has, figuratively and literally, some self-control. Gradually it slips away from him, like the numbers of his men returning to their homes.

Lawrence's sardonic reply to Bentley's question, "What is it that attracts you personally to the desert?"—"It's clean"— is made bitter by the death of Farraj, for it cannot remain clean stained with the blood and littered with the bodies of his disciples. That fact is too hard to face up to. By the time Lawrence and Ali reconnoiter a Turkish-held town, he has insulated himself totally in his own myth—"Do you think I am just anybody, Ali?" He flaunts his presence before the street patrols, arms outstretched again, exultantly walking on water (a rain puddle). Ali raises his eyes anxiously: "Be patient with him, God." "Peace, Ali," Lawrence replies, smiling. "I am invisible."

He is not invisible. The pawing of the Turkish commandant and the beating—back bare, spread-eagled on a narrow bench with a grinning private holding him down—sober him, make him fearful of crucifixion. For within all the levels of allegory, the sting of the whip becomes the momentary truth, pain the proof of mortality. Discarded and groveling in the mud, he cannot dodge that realization, cannot keep terror from undermining his ill-defined inner strength, cannot avoid existing on a human level. El Aurens is arrogant, conceited, sadomasochistic, and possibly homosexual; or, as more directly stated by Auda, "He is not perfect." The pleasure violence and pain gave him, his unwillingness to be a subordinate, his frustrated fervor for Arab nationalism—all are human failings, and as such Lawrence admits to them with difficulty. But when he tries to back away, to retreat into this aspect of himself—"The truth is I'm just an ordinary man"—primal elements contradict him. If the scars on his back do not quite make him a scourged Christ, his ill-fitting tan uniform (the others now wear green) mutely affirms that he is no longer just another soldier. Lawrence protests ("All right, I'm extraordinary. So what of it?"), but Allenby has an answer for that also—the cup cannot pass away. In low angle medium close shot, Lawrence looks sadly skyward.

As Akaba was the messianic confirmation, the massacre of the retreating Turkish column is the fulfillment of the satanic Lawrence. Rushing frenziedly amid the gun bursts and the dying, revolver smoking, curved dagger red, Lawrence shoots holes in men already dead. The signs of obsessive madness that merely seeped out, like the lines of blood traced across his back, now flare out, like the purple flag that sweeps past his face prior to the attack. Soon Lawrence is bound back for England with Feisal mouthing the irony, "El Aurens is a sword with two edges. We are equally glad to be rid of him, are we not?."

Aurens and Lawrence, the two-edged sword, merciful and murderous, framed in painful halftone of light and dark before his betrayers, a man who could not be a god—one and both remain a paradox which Lean and Bolt choose not to unravel. There is pity for, but not penetration into, this character who has descended into the maelstrom and come up mortally touched. Lawrence's dream of an Arab state ends in ignominious tribal dissension. Auda drifts off; Ali disappears into the shadows. Lawrence leaves the conference with Allenby's promise of his own cabin on a boat home. As he moves distractedly through the hotel lobby towards a waiting car, the medical officer who called him a "filthy little wog" at the hospital and whom Lean and Bolt wryly selected to defend Lawrence's memory at the hero's funeral approaches him to ask a favor:

> OFFICER
> I say, it's Colonel Lawrence, isn't it?
> [Lawrence nods wearily]
> Well, may I shake your
> hand, sir?
> [He takes Lawrence's hand]
> Just want to be able to say I've done it, sir.

Lawrence walks off into his own darkness; but the officer's reactions indicate that he has failed to notice anything unusual. To him, Major T. E. Lawrence has already ceased to be. The myth has so completely concealed the man that the "true" Lawrence is gone, apotheosized into oblivion.

He drives one last time down a desert road; a motorcycle speeds past raising dust, a shuddering omen. His eyes glance up for a moment then fall back into an effete gaze, half-obscured by a dirty windshield, as the pillar of fire is quenched.

The logistics involved in a motion picture like **LAWRENCE OF ARABIA** could be enough to discourage the most energetic of filmmakers: over three years of scripting, shooting, and editing; thousands of extras and miscellaneous Moroccan armies, reconstruction of sections of Damascus, Cairo, Jerusalem, and Akaba, and months of isolation in the desert where temperatures reach 130 degrees. Through all of this, the end result can objectively be described as another example of Lean's economic and direct filmmaking. The editing, from the first, is a model of precision: the prologue moves from a foreboding overhead medium shot of the motorcycle under the titles to point-of-view travellings as red warning signs flash by intercut with broken sunlight coming through the trees and striking Lawrence's face and ends with a montage of his twisting body and the camera being subjectively hurled forward. Lean moves from Lawrence's precipitous death, from a close shot of the cycle's rear wheel spinning and, coincidentally, a fitting image for the thread of Lawrence's life, to a panning shot down the front of St. Paul's and the contentious mourners, establishing in less than five minutes an interpretive referent for the rest of the film. And every subsequent scene has a specific value in terms of narrative progression. No sunset or windstorm photographed by Freddie Young is extraneous. As Lean noted "It's contrast, you see, the violence of nature carrying on,"[6] a contrast which helps to develop character or clarify situations. Nor are the battle scenes ever gratuitously extended. The two principal encounters—at Akaba and with the Turkish column—are good examples of sequences helping to define the emotion of respective moments in Lawrence's life. The first with its extreme long shots and moving camera surges with the energy of Lawrence's promised "miracle." The second, with its claustrophobic and smoke-filled medium close and close shots, reflects the oppressive madness of the now bloody liberator.

While **LAWRENCE OF ARABIA** is as much a character study as **MADELEINE** or **GREAT EXPECTATIONS** or **BRIEF ENCOUNTER** or any of the "smaller" films, Lean does not subjectify the picture as in the past. Perhaps that is because Lawrence, unlike Pip or Henry Hobson or even Nicholson, is less a figure to urge identification with than to take the absolute measure of, one whose stature is genuinely larger than life and whose feelings can be externalized only to a limited degree. As with Ridgefield and **THE SOUND BARRIER**, the very core of **LAWRENCE OF ARABIA** is the lingering inscrutability of a hero with a vision, of one who cannot be fully empathized with but who must live as he dreams—alone.

10
DOCTOR ZHIVAGO (1965)

And what if all animated nature
Be but organic Harps diversely fram'd,
That tremble into thought, as o'er them sweeps
Plastic and vast, one intellectual breeze,
At once the Soul of each, and God of all?
 —Samuel Coleridge, "The Eolian Harp"

After the experience of making **KWAI** and **LAWRENCE** with Sam Spiegel, which resulted in two succesive Best Director Academy Awards, Lean was approached by Carlo Ponti, who owned the film rights, to adapt Boris Pasternak's *Doctor Zhivago*. This new project provided several immediate challenges. The first was its sprawling narrative line, spanning over four decades of Czarist/Soviet history and, in the process, introducing multifarious characters in the tradition of the great Russian novels. Like *The Brothers Karamazov* or *War and Peace*, the very complexity of *Doctor Zhivago* defied any attempt at rigorously "faithful" condensation for the screen, even in the approximately three hours running time which was originally planned.

Lean and Bolt realized at the start that the book's intricate interplay of characters against the social panorama of world war and revolution could not be encapsulated without doing serious damage to the characters themselves and the concepts they represented. After he and Bolt "spent ten weeks hammering out a

50-page line through the book," Lean recalled, "We provided dramatic construction where the book is not dramatic . . . If cut down too much, it might seem just another love story."[1] Working against a strong tradition, as evidenced in King Vidor's **WAR AND PEACE** or Richard Brooks' **THE BROTHERS KARAMAZOV**, of failing to bring the essence of the "epic" Russian novel to the screen, they eventually found their fulcrum: "The story of **DOCTOR ZHIVAGO** is very simple. A man is married to one woman and in love with another. The trick is not having the audience condemn the lovers."[2]

According to Bolt, "[**DOCTOR ZHIVAGO**] is an example of the impossibilty of ever seeing the 'film of the book.' The film of that book, if you took the novel as a shooting script, would take about a fortnight to show, fourteen days and nights of continuous running period. You can only show a hundredth of a novel in dramatic form—and that is an act of compression which is so radical it's not the original in another form. And if you don't make that pretense, you have to admit that you are giving something quite different."[3] Because of these problems, many of the novel's minor characters were cut and/or combined and the final section was excised. From the opening scene with the adult Yuri and his chance encounter with Lara on a streetcar, the "simple" story consisting of Zhivago, his wife Tonya, and his mistress Lara was the focus.

Even with this rigorous editing, the final screenplay and subsequent film disclose the limitations of another of Lean's thumbnail sketches: "The film is not the story of the revolution, but the story of what happens to a small group of people when the revolution crashes down on them."[4] In **LAWRENCE OF ARABIA** or **RYAN'S DAUGHTER**, this is indeed the case. Lean and Bolt effectively stylize and otherwise incorporate the historical elements, so that the more personal aspects of the story may develop unobstructed. **ZHIVAGO** is burdened with an excess of simplified history. The factions of the revolutionary struggle in Russia may be reduced to caricature with little more dimension than the recreated banners of Lenin, Trotsky, and Stalin. The Czarists and the bourgeois are exploitative, hedonistic, and arrogant, from Komarovsky to the Dragoon Colonel who is pommeled to death by the retreating army. The Bolsheviks such as Comrade Yelkin, Razin, and to a lesser degree Zhivago's own half-brother, are joyless, ruthless, and recalcitrant. These characters are never treated as distinctive human beings; yet they occupy a fair amount of screen time. This convenient stereotyping of the opposing political sides has a tendency to overlap into the major figures. There is, for instance, the potentially tragic but underdeveloped Pasha. This disappointed idealist begins as a naive radical, as an organizer of workers' rallies who loves Lara for her assumed innocence. Ultimately, he is disappointed in both and seeks to bury his emotions beneath a new persona, General Strelnikov, the merciless demagogue who can shell the city where his wife lives because "the private life is dead." His story, like the first impression he makes on Zhivago, is quite dramatic; but, as Lara and Yuri demand most of the screen time, it remains peripheral to the film's plot. Eventually Pasha is dropped completely; and his suicidal end is merely reported by Komarovsky. By using a framing device which flashes back from Zhivago's brother, Yevgraf, and his search for Yuri's daughter, Lean and Bolt could retain whatever portions of the novel they saw fit. Characters such as Pasha, who might have been expanded or explicated or dropped altogether, can easily appear merely half-formed and frustrate a viewer who anticipates more from the cues in the story-line.

The essential movement of all of Lean's motion pictures, no matter how deeply enmeshed in history, might be termed "antisocial." This is not to say that Lean is unconcerned with social issues. His choice of subjects, if anything, implies the opposite; but it should be clear by now that his interest centers on the individual and that person's plight during moments of emotional crisis or conflict with social conventions. Yuri Zhivago, the poet-doctor, is an apt hero for Lean. He is imbued with a strong but simple desire for life, as epitomized in his dialogue with Strelnikov: "And what will you do, with your wife and child, in Varykino?" "Just live." He can see beauty in even the ugliest moments, even in the stomach-pumping of Lara's mother. His poetry is extremely personal and introspective or "Petit-bourgeois and self-indulgent" according to the revolutionaries. For although he can sympathize with the revolution, Zhivago places personal creation and individual worth on a higher scale of values.

"The madding crowd" in Lean's work is always a fickle and frequently repressive conception. In **OLIVER TWIST**, **MADELEINE**, and **RYAN'S DAUGHTER** crowds violently obstruct the protagonists. Witness Oliver's capture after the theft of Brownlow's handkerchief or Madeleine's ride to the courthouse or Rosy's punishment. As the winds change course the mob may take the main character's part, as when the Londoners rescue Oliver from Sikes or the crowd cheers Madeleine after the trial. In **DOCTOR ZHIVAGO** the representation of this concept is fairly direct. Often Lara and Yuri are moving both literally and figuratively against the flow of history. Among Czarists and bourgeoisie, Yuri is a proponent of the workers' cause; yet when the revolution does begin, he has misgivings about the style of life advocated by the Bolsheviks. Contrary to their advice, he continues to compose what Strelnikov calls his "absurdly personal" poetry. For Yuri and his family the revolution and its revolutionaries, like the war and its warriors, are less beneficent than disruptive factors, as first the Imperial army and then the Red partisans press him into service as a medical officer. In the end, Yuri's own death by heart attack is indirectly brought on by the crowd of passengers in a streetcar who prevent him from reaching a woman he believes is Lara.

More than once, Lean expressed his admiration for the departure sequence in King Vidor's **THE BIG PARADE** for its placement of a solitary figure in counterflow to a mass of people and cited the scene in **ZHIVAGO** after the throng of deserters overpower a troop of reinforcements and massacre their officers as his version. At that point in the film, Yuri and Lara have encountered each other several times but never actually met. Now Lean frames both of them in successive moving shots going against the movement of the troops as they try to reach an injured man. The figurative values added in this staging are two-fold. It expresses the emotional situation of the two characters as discussed above; and it foredooms their relationship by bringing

Zhivago (Omar Sharif) and Lara (Julie Christie) are reunited at her house in Yuriatin.

them together at last in such a hostile context.

Even though the passion of Yuri and Lara is the avowed nucleus of the story for the filmmakers, that passion is not fulfilled physically until the second half of the picture. It is nearly the end, at Varykino with Lara, when their passion is so idealized that it almost becomes *amour fou*, which Luis Buñuel defined as "overpowering desire, self-contained, feeding on itself and blind to all others. This love walls the lovers off, makes them indifferent to the accepted ways of society, ruptures all family ties, and brings them to destruction."[5] The setting seems, at first sight, transposed from some medieval romance. The summer mansion is topped by frosted Byzantine cupolas and covered inside and out with artificial snow and cellophane, so that it resembles a fairy tale ice castle. As Lara and Yuri open the door, the chandelier tinkles and a breeze softly stirs the drifts. The couple wanders in hesitantly, in wonderment: in this otherworldly atmosphere their hope of one last idyll resides. Here, also, Yuri is able to write

**Zhivago (Omar Sharif), Lara (Julie Christie),
and her daughter, Katya (Lucy Westmore),
take refuge in the house at Varykino.**

again. He sits at a table in the sun room which is miraculously
stocked with blank paper, a new pen, and a full inkwell. As
wolves, emblematic of a hostile outer world slowly closing in,
howl outside, the balalaika sounds defiantly on the track. In this
magical place Yuri fashions his "Lara cycle" of sonnets; and the
act of artistic creation is given a mystical aura.

 Pantheism, Color, Symbolism. For the Romantics the
emotional and metaphysical was the soul of the poet and his art.
This attitude is less significant to Pasternak's character in that his
hero is both doctor and poet, a man of science and of letters. In
Lean and Bolt's adaptation, Zhivago's dual vocations might have
reflected the duality of human impulse. Instead they stripped
away much of the frailty and almost all the pettiness of Pasternak's
character; and despite the suffering and cruelty which he must
witness, they Romanticized his experiences as a doctor.

The flashbacks as a framing device for the entire story are original to the film. They begin with the funeral of Yuri's mother, a "simple woman" who had a talent for the balalaika. The birth-death cycle is fully expressed here: after a shot of the mother entombed in her casket, Lean cuts to a rush of wind blowing the leaves about Yuri and the strains of his mother's "enchanting" balalaika are heard, sounding like Coleridge's Eolian instrument as "if all animated nature be but organic harps." In this pantheistic imagery typical of Lean, there are also visual and aural correlatives to Shelley's "Ode to the West Wind":

> O wild West Wind, thou breath of
>   Autumn's being,
> Thou, from those unseen presence
>   the leaves dead
> Are driven, like ghosts from an
>   enchanter fleeing.

The gift of inspiration has been passed. Yuri, like his mother, will become an artist. The physical symbol of this gift, the balalaika, is left to Yuri, who in turn will give it to his and Lara's daughter. This becomes the closing note in the final scene, as Zhivago's half-brother tries to convince a young girl, Tonya, that she is Yuri and Lara's child:

GENERAL ZHIVAGO
Tonya!
    [Tonya and her companion, a
    Young Engineer turn towards him.]
Can you play the balalaika?

YOUNG ENGINEER
Can she play?
    (nudging Tonya, who does not answer)
She's an artist!

GENERAL ZHIVAGO
An artist . . . Who taught you?

YOUNG ENGINEER
No one taught her.

GENERAL ZHIVAGO
Ah. Then it's a gift.

The last shots are of water pouring through a huge dam, resuming its interrupted course. Despite the pride which Tonya has in her young man's accomplishment in controlling such a monumental structure as the dam, it is also symbolic, as in **BRIEF ENCOUNTER**, of the manmade world and its constraints. The continuity of life, natural forces, and the gift of artistic inspiration overcome the artificial obstructions. The gift which Tonya, in particular, receives has transcended the whole of the narrative. From the death of Yuri's mother, her grandmother, it has led to the presence of Tonya's vibrant sense of life at picture's end as she walks across the dam.

The scheme of nature analogies and color in **DOCTOR ZHIVAGO** is fairly systematic. White has a prominent position. In Tonya Gromeko it can connote a fundamental, if not actual, purity and innocence, as it did with Mary Justin in **THE PASSIONATE FRIENDS** or Jane Hudson in **SUMMER MADNESS**. The idyll at Varykino functions like the Alps for the lovers in **PASSIONATE FRIENDS**. It is a stark image of isolation and insulation. When Lean noted regarding the proposed decor in NOSTROMO, "I want it to be terribly stark,"[6] the same concept was in development. In escaping social structures, Lara and Yuri like Mary and Steven retreat to their own fortress of "silent, secret snow"; but only until the sun melts the protective layers and leaves them exposed.

In this film, the "life-force" is often associated with Lara, through symbol and color. Yellow is hers. When the panavision screen frames the gray interior of the field hospital, it has only one bright spot: the sunflowers which Lara has brought into it. It is the sunflowers to which Yuri is instinctively drawn when he first enters her rooms at Yuriatin, just as he was drawn to the field of yellow spring daffodils. Lean's typing of Lara is never more direct than in the dissolve from a close shot of such a daffodil to

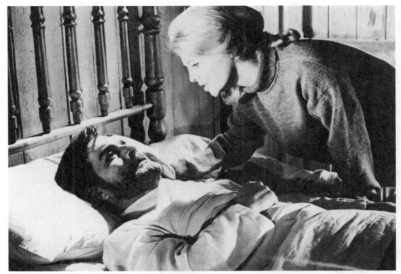

Lara (Julie Christie) nurses Zhivago (Omar Sharif) after his escape from the partisans.

Lara (Julie Christie) prepares to shoot her seducer, Komarovsky, at a Moscow Christmas Party.

**Mounted dragoons attack demonstrators
in a Moscow square.**

her face; but there are other implications of her presence including the sun which Zhivago follows through the forest near
Yuriatin. In fact, this sun leads him to Strelnikov's train where he
learns that Lara is in Yuriatin.

There are instances in **DOCTOR ZHIVAGO** where the
symbolic usage is more overt than in any other of Lean's pictures.
When Lara leaves the army hospital, Lean uses the sunflowers
again in a cut from wilting petals to a dejected Yuri walking past.
The very first physical contact of the lovers, on a streetcar, is
undercut with sparks from its electric power cable. Overt visual
similes like this make it clear to the viewer that Lara is an electric,
catalytic force in Zhivago's existence, the inspiring energy which
the life-seeking poet needs to create, even before he knows its
name or her name.

There are also frequent shots that suggest Zhivago's direct
relationship to nature. To escape Moscow, Yuri and his family

David Lean with cast members Rod Steiger (left) as Komarovsky, Julie Christie as Lara, and Tom Courteny as Pasha/Strelnikov.

must ride in a crowded cattle car. At every opportunity during the journey, Zhivago slides open a slat and stares out at the countryside. At night, he concentrates on the moon as he peers from the train. The moon is what he follows when he deserts the Red Guards and returns to Lara. By then it, too, has become more than a Keatsian ideal of "high romance," has become a white, symbolic "power" linking nature with life (Lara) and reanimating it. From **HOBSON'S CHOICE** to **A PASSAGE TO INDIA**, the moon entices Lean's characters, like the narrator in Dante Gabriel Rossetti's poem: "Weary already, weary miles to-night/I walked for bed: and so, to get some ease,/I dogged the flying moon with similes./And like a wisp she doubled on my sight/In ponds; and caught in treetops like a kite;/And in a globe of film all vapourish/Swam full-faced like a silly silver fish." ["A Match with the Moon"]

Lean and Bolt use the alternation of winter and summer both as a device indicating the passage of time and as a pantheistic extension of the ebb and flow of human emotion. On the one hand such an extension may subtly amplify the Bolshevik philosophy, for in the awesome natural changes that mark the turning of the season, in the vast, snow-covered plains that become endless fields of wheat or flowers, the human aspect can be lost. On the other hand, it matters not whether the human endeavor is individual or collective in the face of an overwhelming nature. The winter wolves which bay outside the house at Varykino are neither malevolent nor beneficent but part of the same life-force into which Yuri taps when he writes his poems. They are attuned to the same ebb and flow as he. How else could Yuri send them off with but a wave of his hands.

In **LAWRENCE**, Lean and Bolt have a hero who is both wolf and lamb. Despite Yuri's admonition to Lara, when she wonders what might have happened if they had met sooner ("If we think about all that, we may go mad"), despite the fact that the things which Yuri witnesses might easily have brought Clipton's final words in **KWAI** to his lips, the character madness of Nicholson and Lawrence is not a factor in **DOCTOR ZHIVAGO**. Instead the dark side of the life-force is personified in Komarovsky, the venal government official who introduces Lara to the world of exploitation and betrayal. The color red figures prominently in the early scenes with Komarovsky in the decor of his house, the walls of the restaurant where he takes Lara, and the dress he purchases for her. As vulgar and corrupt as he is, his fanatical loyalty, like Zhivago's, is to life, and to those "not high-minded, not pure, but alive." In moving Lara to attempt his murder, he is the first person who forces her to confront her own desires and needs.

Subjectification. Visual and Aural Imagery. In **DOCTOR ZHIVAGO**, Lean's direct and dialectical editing style may again reinforce the imagery without superseding it. Again Lean frequently combines figurative elements and montage to add further meaning. The cut from Lara and Yuri accidentally touching to a spark on the cables is an obvious example of an associational montage; but it simultaneously acts as an externalization of sensation and a dynamic trope that foreshadows Lara's future relation to Zhivago. There are many subtler instances as well.

The staging of the scene with young Yuri at the funeral is typical. He glances up as the wind shakes the branches and blows the dead leaves from the graveyard trees, much as the young Pip did in a similar setting in **GREAT EXPECTATIONS**. As he watches the coffin lowered into the earth, the sound of the dirt on the lid is amplified. There is even a shot of the woman lying inside it. When Lean cuts back to Yuri, his eyes open as if awakening from a dream. The implication is that he has projected himself mentally into the grave and that the shot of the corpse was somehow from his point-of-view. As has been noted, this initiates the film's frequent allusions to the concepts of inspiration and rebirth, and the added context is subjectivity. By focusing on the details that Yuri, the living child who promises perpetuation of the parent's spirit, sees, Lean personalizes the sequence and, by extension, the motif that will drive the entire narrative—for what other rationale is there for Yevgraf's search for his brother's daughter than the hope of finding a spark of Zhivago in her?

Since this motif also drives the pantheistic scheme of **DOCTOR ZHIVAGO**, Lean's compositions appropriately open with the opposition of the natural and artificial elements on a grand scale: at the dam, as already mentioned, and immediately after in the cut to the broad vista of the Urals which begins Yevgraf's flashback. In that shot, which Lean holds for several seconds, the distant, snow-covered mountains dwarf the procession of mourners but not the orthodox cross that is in the right foreground. Here the perspective is an objective one. Ostensibly, so is the sequence after the funeral. Having taken the viewer directly into Yuri's mind with both naturalistic (the trees) and expressionistic (the inside of the coffin) point-of-view shots, the sense of subjectivity carries over into Yuri's bedroom, where it is sustained as much by sounds as by images. These sounds are also naturalistic (the constant gusting of the wind outside; the branch tapping against the bedroom window) and expressionistic (the balalaika in the underscore).

Early in his career, Lean spoke of how a filmmaker "achieves the illusion of reality with a series of touches."[7] When Komarovsky first notices Lara ("How old are you now," he asks), he places a scarf around her head before examining her face. She removes it and he leaves. A few scenes later, as she ponders the prospect of a liaison with Komarovsky, Lean frames her before a mirror. Her head is scarved, tilted slightly in uncertainty. Then with a dissolve to a moving train, Lean expresses the surge of emotion within her, and her unstated decision is clear to the viewer.

Lara's sense of finding herself, while not central to **DOCTOR ZHIVAGO**, nonetheless relates as firmly back to Laura Jesson and Mary Justin as forward to Rosy Ryan and Adela Quested, to the other Lean heroines who are the emotional nexus of those films. In the beginning, when her self-image is poorly defined, Lean stages the scene where she wears Komarovsky's red dress so that as he sits watching her, she is a headless reflection in the mirror beside him at the right edge of the frame. It is her emotion which is externalized here, as her body, that which she assumes is all he desires, is all that is visible. In contrast, near the end of the film, when Lara is so moved by reading Zhivago's poem about her, she is at the shot's center; no bright color distracts the audience's attention from her face. Zhivago comes into the shot. Wearing a dark robe, he stands beside her as she sits, so that his head is not visible and his figure is indistinct. Even as she says, "This isn't me, Yuri," the visualization validates his reply, "Yes, it is."

In the series of cuts after her "rape" by Komarovsky, Lean creates another type of subjectivity out of the montage. For the sucession of shots: her tear-stained face, a gun, Lara at Komarovsky's door, etc., not only provide a quick summary of what could have been tedious exposition but do so in the impressionistic context of Lara's distraction. One of the most frequently cited sequences of the film, the massacre of the protestors reminiscent of Eisenstein's "Odessa Steps" in **BATTLESHIP POTEMKIN**, refers back in Lean's work to the hanging scene in **GREAT EXPECTATIONS**. In both instances, Lean shifts the emphasis from the horrifying event to the reactions of one individual—here, Zhivago—a shift from the "objective reality" and structural awareness of Eisenstein to the "subjective" and personal consciousness of Lean.

Despite his beginnings as an editor, if Lean had any side in the traditional montage versus mise-en-scene opposition, it

David Lean on location in Northern Spain.

would be with the latter. In all of Lean's work, the primary source of dramatic information is the individual character and the individual shot. This is not to say that Lean's narrative viewpoint is rigidly individualist rather than populist. Rather the stylistic manipulations which Lean imposed as metteur-en-scene, the choices of content, composition, angle, and duration, create the first level of meaning. From that basis Lean's cuts, dissolves, and cross-references to earlier shots create additional impact. Whether that meaning is subsidiary or superior depends to some extent on Lean's manipulation and to some extent on the viewer's perceptions. The sunflowers which Lara places in the field hospital, for instance, make a figurative statement in and of themselves. That same meaning is expanded in the later juxtapositions with Yuri as noted above. Less obvious is the relationship of that shot to a much earlier one: at night after her funeral, the boy Yuri awakens and sees his mother's balalaika. His perspective of the angular, yellow-painted soundbox of the instrument leaning against a gray brick wall makes the same impact in the panavision screen as the sunflowers. The metaphor is simply and unobtrusively made: Lara is the spiritual as well as physical bridge between Yuri's mother and their daughter, Tonya.

As previous examples have suggested, Lean's subjectification in **DOCTOR ZHIVAGO** is, as in **THE BRIDGE ON THE RIVER KWAI**, necessarily keyed to more than one character. Of course, strictly speaking almost the entire story is from Yevgraf's point-of-view. Lean occasionally reinforces this with the unusual choice of having Yevgraf mouth his lines in the shot and speak them in voiceover whenever the character is in a flashback scene; but this aside the viewer is seldom reminded that the story is unfolding as a series of remembered past events.

Previous examples have also suggested that, as in all his work, Lean occasionally also subjectifies the soundtrack of **DOCTOR ZHIVAGO**. While the mode in which Yevgraf speaks dialogue is much more obvious and limited than the use of Rachmaninoff in **BRIEF ENCOUNTER**, Lean frequently combines visual and aural elements for a compound effect. Laura plays the music and then begins her flashback linking the two and expanding the figurative values of each subjective element. In **ZHIVAGO**, the underscore is keyed to the characters in a conventional way.

Maurice Jarre scored Lean's last four pictures. The "love" theme of Yuri and Lara, like that from Zeffirelli's **ROMEO AND JULIET** or the song from **THE WAY WE WERE**, long ago outpaced the film and became a standard for elevators and music boxes everywhere. As a result it may be difficult for a viewer to hear it today free of additional associations. Nonetheless Jarre's expressive combination of selected atonality and rich melodiousness follows in the traditions of the music of Lean's earlier films. The technique favored most with Jarre is the crescendo-diminuendo: in Zhivago it occurs most strikingly after a scene of love between Lara and Yuri followed by a travelling shot into Yuri and his wife's cottage at Varykino. The crescendo balalaika overlaps from the prior scene, but as the camera enters the house and frames Yuri lying guiltily by his wife's side, the music becomes atonal and diminishes abruptly. Similar juxtapositions of image and sound occur in **RYAN'S DAUGHTER** when Shaughnessy awakens to discover Rosy and her lover locked in an embrace outside and in **LAWRENCE OF ARABIA**, as the camera sweeps in to a vista of Auda's camp at Wadi Rhumm. A comparable effect in Malcom Arnold's work has already been noted in **HOBSON'S CHOICE**. Moments in **A BRIDGE ON THE RIVER KWAI**, such as moving from a victorious Colonel Nicholson being paraded on the shoulders of his men to the sobs of a beaten Saito, could also be cited. Lean frequently remarked to interviewers that, although he could not read music, he could tell a composer what he wanted. More than in any other film, Lean relies on motifs in **DOCTOR ZHIVAGO** for both recapitulation and even exposition. In two instances, when Zhivago watches Komarovsky tell Lara that her mother will live and when Lara confesses to Pasha why she shot Komarovsky, Lean places the camera on the other side of a window so that their words cannot be heard and opts entirely for music. Atypically, while the first is from Yuri's point-of-view, there is no one other than the camera outside the glass in the second.

11
RYAN'S DAUGHTER (1970)

Dance there upon the shore;
What need have you to care
For wind or water's roar?
What need have you to dread
The monstrous crying of the wind?
　　　　　　　　　　—W.B. Yeats,
　　　"To a Child Dancing in the Wind"

It was at present a place perfectly accordant with
man's nature—neither ghastly, hateful, not ugly:
neither common-place, unmeaning, nor tame;
but, like a man, slighted and enduring; and
withal singularly colossal and mysterious . . .
It had a lonely face, suggesting tragical possibilities.
　　　　　　　　　　—Thomas Hardy,
　　　　　　　　The Return of the Native

Black clouds and red-tinged mists fly from the face of the sun, as if an empyrean journey were beginning. Gliding back from this dark, preternatural world, green hillocks rolling past are gradually revealed. A sea-wind swirls up the cliff side, and Rosy Ryan perched on its edge helplessly watches her lost parasol fall to the waves. Father Hugh, fisher of flotsam and men and not apt to distinguish between the two, fetches it back. He shakes the salt water from his billowing cassock. Little enough, it seems, to begin with.

It seems; for Rosy Ryan, like Laura Jesson and Mary Justin, like Madeleine and Jane, is another vaguely yearning dreamer. It is a mental state unfathomable to Father Hugh, who can only ask, "What do you do with yourself, Rose?" She reads, but hers is the fictional fiction of youth: *The King's Mistress* by Raoul du Barry is the period equivalent of **BRIEF ENCOUNTER**'s *Flames of Passion.* At every opportunity she leaves the browns and drab greens of her village for the rougher symmetry of the coast, for the fragrant wild heather and the glistening blue and emerald of the sea with its sharp spray. As the film opens, it is to meet Charles Shaughnessy, the schoolmaster who taught her about "Byron, Beethoven and Captain Blood," and in whose footsteps, despite his caution that "I'm not one of those fellers myself," she would gladly walk. She does so, literally and figuratively; but even as close-ups catch her bare foot slipping into the imprints of his boots in the sand and her face smiling at this small accomplishment, Lean cuts back to an extra long shot: the relentless tide surges in all around, nearly throwing her off balance and erasing the tracks.

With deceptive ease, Lean brings these familiar elements into play. The conflict of the fanciful and the everyday, the pantheistic forces of wind and sea, empathy for a young girl given over to Romantic longings—all are contained in these first few minutes of the picture. As the dull "realities" of Rosy's situation are detailed—her ordinary, slightly tattered clothes; the coarse, meager abodes of the inhabitants of Kirrary; the vulgar manner of the village girls; even the craggy, sunbaked visage of the local priest— her desire for escape and adventure become more understandable. A tension is immediately introduced between the pristine "villageness" of Kirrary whose people congregate in the smoke-filled, common-house atmosphere of Ryan's pub and the isolated beach and woodlands. The conflicting spheres of influence are, again, artificial and natural. The emotional pull is as Hawthorne describes it in "Footprints on the Seashore": "At intervals and not infrequent ones, the forests and oceans summon me—one with the

roar of its waves, the other with the murmur of its boughs—forth
from the haunts of men."

Lean and scriptwriter Bolt are explicit. "You were meant for
a wide world, Rose," Charles tells her; and as Rosy widens her
search after life, after what Bolt calls "intenser modes of feeling,"
she strays closer to that "monstrous wind" which threatens more
than her parasol. But then the sun is what she seeks. She marries
Charles only to discover that he is no more than what he warned:
"You've mistaken a penny mirror for the sun." Wedlock is as
unelectric as Father Hugh had foretold:

FATHER COLLINS (reading)
Now "Marriage is a sacrament ordained by
God . . ." That means, Rosy, that once it's
done, it isn't up to me; nor Charles; it's done;
till one or the other of you is dead.

ROSY
I understand that, Father.

FATHER COLLINS
Hmph. Now God ordained it for three
reasons. First, that you an' Charles should be
a comfort to each other—in the long, dull
days an' weary evenin's. You understand
that?

ROSY
Yes.

FATHER COLLINS
Hmph. Well, second for the procreation of
good children an' to bring 'em up good
Catholics. D'you understand that?

ROSY
Yes.

FATHER COLLINS
And thirdly for the satisfaction of the flesh.

ROSY (quickly)
Yes.

FATHER COLLINS (gently)
Are you scared of that?

ROSY
Yes.

FATHER COLLINS
It's nothing to be scared of, Rosy. A function
of the body.

ROSY
I suppose all girls is a bit scared, before.

FATHER COLLINS
All fellers too.

**Rosy (Sarah Miles) listens shyly, but with keen interest as Father
Collins (Trevor Howard) talks of her forthcoming marriage and "the
satisfaction of the flesh."**

>   ROSY
> Yes?

>   FATHER COLLINS
> Oh, yes.

>   ROSY (quietly)
> It'll make me a different person . . .won't it?

>   FATHER COLLINS
> Marriage?

>   ROSY
> The . . . satisfaction of the flesh.

>   FATHER COLLINS
> Well, it's a gate I've not been through
> myself. (Reassuring, amused)
> No, it won't make you a different person.

>   ROSY
> I want it to.

>   FATHER COLLINS
> Child, what're you expectin'?
>   [She struggles for an answer. She
>   searches the sky. Father Hugh's gaze
>   follows hers. He sees a gull against the sky.]
> Wings, is it?

After her marriage, still without pinions, Rosy flees down the beach, disillusioned, despondent, and tearful, only to encounter the grizzled old cleric. He offers nothing but rebuke. He tells her that there are no wings. "There must be something more, Father Hugh," she argues. "Why—Glory to God— why must there be? Because Rosy Ryan wants it?" He answers her defiant "Aye!" with a slap, like a crusty bishop simultaneously confirming her adulthood and admonishing against sinful wishes: "You can't help having 'em [wishes], but don't nurse 'em or sure to God you'll get what you're wishing!"

At this point, as if a visual nexus, there is a dissolve to a bus stopping at a lonely country crossroads. Someone gets off. As the vehicle rattles on its way, the shadowy figure of a tall young man dressed in a British Army uniform is revealed. A car arrives to meet him, and, as he slowly moves to board it, a close shot of his polished boots emphasizes a physical impediment: he limps, rather markedly. Major Doryan arrives like a hobbled Apollo gone to earth in a burned-out chariot. He arrives to answer Rosy's yearning in a flurry of sensual rapture, to sweep her up into a transcendent passion, set as Romantic love "should" be, as Laura Jesson might have envisioned it from her train compartment, against ruined medieval towers, in sea caves and sheltered groves. When Laura gets off the train at the end of her affair, she notices that it is "without wings, without any wings at all." Rosy is younger and more determined to fly.

Significantly, Doryan does not first encounter Rosy in such transitory settings as a tea room or sidewalk cafe or streetcar, but in the familiar (to her) front room of her father's tavern. Their second meeting takes place behind her husband's schoolhouse and is quickly followed by a tryst in a nearby forest. Their affair is both intense and isolated with the result that, unlike Laura or Mary Justin or Jane, Rosy does not have control over it, for she has no other place to which she may flee or return. Part of the reason for this is that Doryan is not just another English officer back from the front but very much a "creation" of the heroine, someone conjured up as Emile L'Angelier was by Madeleine in a moment of wishful thinking. This notion is reinforced directly by the dissolve from such a thought to Doryan's arrival and indirectly by his entry into the pub while Rosy reads a book of poems as if he has sprung from the pages of verse. Doryan intrudes powerfully, almost metaphysically, and Lean exploits this intrusion, much as he did in the first shot of L'Angelier and again unlike **BRIEF ENCOUNTER** or **SUMMER MADNESS**. By boldly interpolating the usual progression from initial acquaintance to love, Lean totally exploits audience expectation and literally throws Rosy and Doryan together.

Figurative Usage and Color. Andrew Doryan is not the "perfect" Byronic hero, not tailored to the imagination of his

Rosy (Sarah Miles) and Charles (Robert Mitchum) go to the beach during the final storm sequences.

Charles imagines that his wife, Rosy (Sarah Miles), and Major Doryan (Christopher Jones) find a shell as they walk along the beach.

Charles Shaughnessy (Robert Mitchum) is seized by a crowd of villagers who suspect him of collaborating with the British.

Major Doryan (Christopher Jones), wanders the dunes of an Irish Beach, followed by Michael (John Mills), a pathetic, mute creature whose limp is identical to Randolph's.

heroine as closely as L'Angelier was, but rather a genuinely imperfect one: sullen, vulnerable, too mysterious to penetrate, even limping as Byron himself did. If anyone, Doryan most resembles Lawrence, in his very appearance and manner, in his introspective attitude, even in his fixed, compulsive stares. As with Lawrence, Lean expresses Doryan's character through physical detail and associated imagery. His mien, from the spotlessness of his boots which conceal his deformity to the sallowness of his clean-shaven face, even to the methodical manner in which he taps cigarettes against his silver case, suggests a suppressed but lingering disquiet. Disquiet conveyed so strongly that when he flashes back to the trenches and a black shell burst fills the screen, it clearly reflects the explosive state of his own afflicted mind.

Doryan's character is also clarified by the basic but pliable arrangement of his figure in a landscape. He stands, at first appearance, leaning slightly, eyes fixed directly ahead, and behind him the dusky strip of sky that separates the brown earth from the blue-black clouds stretches narrowly. A close shot frames his head against this oppressive overcast with his face lit in a gray half-tone, exactly as Lawrence's was in his last meeting with Allenby, rendered almost impressionistically, as if reflected from the ground below him. He peers down painfully at his sole welcomer, Michael, the crippled village fool, then turns to move and drags his leg behind him. Later, in his rendezvous with Rosy, his figure hurrying awkwardly across the skyline in silhouette will alternate with high angle medium shots where he sits in his room, confined and motionless in the semidarkness.

Charles Shaughnessy's figure, in contrast, avoids the sky-line. He is framed instead against the solid though stained walls of his schoolhouse or the flat-painted green door of his parlor. In the beach scene where Charles discovers the footprints of Rosy and Doryan leading towards a tidal cave, he falls back from the realization and from the footprints on the right side of the frame against a massive gray rock. When he leaves Rosy in the middle of the night, he wanders towards a shelf in the cliff by the inlet and sits there among large gray stones. Against this background, he is as solid and permanent as Doryan is temporary and illusive, both physically and in Rosy's life; and he finds support in the terrain which seems so visually antipathetic to Doryan.

The use of color is also most clearly defined in terms of Rosy. Her garb when walking down the beach to meet Charles is fairly prosaic: beige and dark gray like the rocks, a straw hat with paper flowers, neat but threadbare, a drab costume at best, which she feebly tries to improve with a pendant watch and incongruous lace gloves. Even her parasol purchased at auction by her father from a dead woman's possessions, for all its frilliness, is a simple, unstartling black and white. Later, the prospects for her marriage are summed up in the colorations of two point-of-view shots as she lies in bed waiting for Charles: a stained brown ceiling and a glowing red window, which as in **MADELEINE** is both a sexual symbol and an opening to a less restricted world. Representations of the spoiled everyday and the unusually bright, of the dismal and the ecstatic, provide visual counterpoint. What Rosy gets are the stained walls of Charles' schoolhouse, the same walls the camera panned across slowly while she waited for him to emerge from his parlor and propose to her. The only deep, the only strongly felt color which is ever added to that parlor is the tiny fringe of red cloth which Rosy will later drape beneath a white plaster bust of Beethoven. Rosy contents herself with wearing beige and gray, but parts of the decor begin to embody her spirit, like the tarnished brass bedposts and the door to the bedroom which she paints a bright yellow and against which she is repeatedly framed. In her return home after riding with Doryan, Rosy retreats to that bedroom behind that yellow door. Lean frames Charles standing against his green door in medium shot behind her closeup, so that he is "held" at a distance from her between her door and the sill.

It is not until her meeting with Doryan in the pub that Rosy's color begins to blaze. A bright yellow spot reflects in the mirror behind her. As she serves him, a close shot catches yellow liquid swirling in a glass. After Doryan's seizure has passed and the lights have come up again, the brownish wall behind them is suddenly suffused with yellow. As the love affair intensifies, she assimilates other colors: the red petticoat, which Doryan saw hanging on the line as he rode past the school on the day of his arrival, and black shawl she wears to go riding are the hues of Doryan's dress uniform. In Charles' fantasy of Rosy and Doryan strolling like young lovers on the beach, she will wear a yellow dress; but only in fantasy is this possible for she does not own a yellow dress— another figurative mark of the affair's impermanence. When the two storms, of the sea and of her passion, have abated, Charles' words—"I'm going to leave you, Rose"—will drain the color from the door behind her, as a final trope of her position.

    Archetypal Imagery; Pantheism. As were Lara and to a lesser extent Nancy and Jane Hudson, Rose is ascribed, through repeated visual links and through color, the delicate traits of her namesake. The "wrong" of which Charles speaks when he tries to convince Rosy that he is not for her is that in taking their relation beyond that of pupil and teacher, beyond the sexual segregation of the schoolroom, which even has separate entrances for boys and girls, into the parlor and the bedroom, he is compelled literally to "deflower" her. Conscious of this and feeling guilty over it, Charles can no longer consider her a child; but he is incapable of responding to all her needs as a woman. Rather he idealizes her against her wishes: "You're a wonderful girl, Rose." "No! No, I'm not." He continues to treat her like the floral specimens which he gathers, presses between the pages of an atlas, mounts, and labels.

    Rosy also resembles the birds whose wings she envies. Like a gull she hovers over the sea and, rock-bred, follows Charles. She does so, as Father Collins' flock follow their faith, for want of any other mysteries. Accordingly, Charles' original image as teacher begins to assume wider, messianic dimensions. Like Mary Magdalene, Rosy walks in his footsteps. She becomes a disciple, the only one among the villagers who appreciates his tolerance towards the British, his self-effacement, and his aesthetic insulation. Charles himself is eventually "stigmatized" as the rough boots of the village men bloody his outstretched hands during Rosy's ordeal, fulfilling her conception of him as a long-suffering, "rare man." He will even wear a flowing robe and be seen walking by the water's edge.

    It is Doryan's character, of the three, that is the most archetypal and the most enigmatic. From the first shot of him and the revelation of his agonized expression, Doryan is marked as one possessed of and by hellfire. Psychologically and realistically he is shell-shocked; but the traits of his illness are satanic, from the fits of shaking and his injury ("Pegleg!") to his dusky uniform and his black horse. His stare can wither, as it does the taunting Moureen. His disturbed and disturbing presence sends Michael fleeing from the room in terror. To Rosy, Doryan is not just another penny mirror, not just someone who sensually ignites her, but the sun she has been seeking all along. Such an identification was previously made with Lawrence. Lean graphically reinforces it here in a medium close shot of Doryan seen through the windshield of a lorry and seated so that the sun is reflected squarely over his face. Later, in Michael's eyes, Doryan will even wield thunder, when he throws a detonator cap against an old boiler. He is driven by a primitive energy, surging up like the sputtering generator and driving his unearthly silhouette out across the countryside. In a sense, when Doryan arrives at Kirrary, he has already perished, mentally and physically, adding irony to the former post-commander's off-hand observation: "You look about finished, sir." Doryan is about finished, an "alien" waiting in a strange place for bodily death. Because of this state of mind, Doryan shuns the company of his wife as he would familiar places and things. The black-and-white snapshots which the corporal unpacks and puts by Doryan's bed are of her and of a group of riders by a towered manor. So he rides with Rosy to a dark tower and for a few moments is "normal" again. With her he can escape into a primeval world which is simpler, more passionate, and protected by the deep shade where the moss grows on fallen trees. Even as he lies serene and sequestered in her arms, the sound of machine guns comes up on the soundtrack like a sigh, and he trembles again.

Lean again incorporates the wind and land and sea—air, earth, and water to match the human fire—into his pantheistic scheme. Like the wind which skims over the cobblestones in **MADELEINE** or introduces **HOBSON'S CHOICE**, Lean may use a sudden gust to snatch at Rosy's parasol or hat. More seriously, a colder current may cut at the viscera and frighten her on the footpath and send her scurrying back inside to Charles after a clandestine moment with Doryan. The same sort of wind moans and whistles through the trees in the glade, threatens to tear apart and destroy Rosy, the flower, as surely as Charles crushes her. It is also the demonic variant which haunts Doryan, which will neither die down nor dispel the black shadows, the black clouds, the black phantasms of shells exploding, over his soul.

The rugged terrain of Western Ireland is reminiscent of the moors of Emily Brontë or Thomas Hardy. Indeed, Lean was no stranger to that Hardy country "suggesting tragical possibilities." Both men consistently placed their heroines, major and minor, in such environments: the prologue to **OLIVER TWIST** where Oliver's mother struggled across a hostile landscape to the workhouse to give birth, strongly recalls a similar effort made by Fanny in *Far From the Madding Crowd*. Bathsheba, entranced by the Byronic Troy in that novel, *Tess of the D'Urbervilles*, and Eustacia Vye, longing for Paris in *The Return of the Native*, are all markedly related to Rosy Ryan in their innocent beauty, their willfulness, and their desire for something more than the bleak surroundings offer. Kirrary invokes Hardy's moody "Wessex." Both are populated by a society that reflects a natural harshness, simple traditionalism, and intolerance of independent thought or action

Perhaps the most telling comparison between Hardy and Lean is their fatalism in regarding attempts to break from these confines or conventions. Tess ends her wanderings in illness; Eustacia in death. Bathsheba after experiencing passion with Sergeant Troy resigns herself to the solidity of Gabriel Oak, character names for which Rosy, Major Doryan, and Charles Shaughnessy could readily be substituted. Hardy's description of Eustacia Vye—whose "high gods were William the Conqueror, Stratford, and Napoleon Buonaparte," strikingly anticipates "Byron, Beethoven, and Captain Blood." Eustacia's "instincts [were] towards social non-conformity," which "seemed to long for the abstraction called passionate love more than for any particular lover" closely parallels the state of mind which Father Hugh reports to Tom Ryan as, "Your 'princess' has fellers enough (indicating his temple) . . . in here!"

Father Hugh's appraisal of Rosy is considerably more generous than his opinion of the village populace: "Devil take me if the whole lot of you is not possessed and damned." Short of that, Kirrary itself is an ambiguous place. Little is specified about it, its history, its industry, its prejudices, other than an abiding hatred of all things British. The young men and women seem to have nothing to do besides loiter in the high street, the only street, leering and giggling, taunting Michael and incurring the pastor's anger. At times, the villagers act as just another fixture in the background, adding relief or working up to a collective frenzy at the wedding party, which Lean intercuts with Charles and Rosy upstairs, as he did the highland dancers and the couple in **MADELEINE**. That group also anticipates the hostile gathering outside the school. The same faces, perhaps for many the same raucous expressions, are transformed into the kind of crowd that was a component of social repression in **DOCTOR ZHIVAGO**. Throughout the townspeople seem to be moving closer to Father Hugh's promise of perdition. Their one act of collective redemption, aiding O'Leary and the rebels, might offset the others, but for their obstinate, unregenerate ostracism of Rosy at the end. It could not be said that the villagers are evil. They lack sufficient dimension for that qualitative a judgment to be passed, as do the English soldiers, as does the constable whom O'Leary executes on the road. Nor is Kirrary merely a representation of the traits of society in general. Unlike the dark corners of the cities in Lean's black-and-white period films, it is too remote, too cut off from general society for that. Rather it becomes another outcropping of an already animated universe and another catalyst in Rosy's transformation.

The storm sequence spans and sets in opposition all these divergent natural forces. Its overtones range from the simple sight of the ammo boxes pitching like coffins in the surf to the broader implications of the contest of sea and land, of proverbial irresistible force and immovable object. It "clears" the air not just in the sky but around Doryan, Rosy, and Charles, bringing secrets to the surface as it does. It is also a manifestation of some great, fateful cycle, confirming and sustaining the sense of something impending which begins with Father Hugh's remark on the clouding sky: "You'd think they was announcing the coming of Christ."

If the storm, with its feathery fingers of trailing mist and its

David Lean demonstrating how he wants Sarah Miles and Christopher Jones to play a scene.

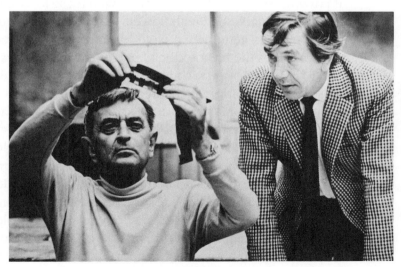

David Lean examines a piece of film while Robert Bolt looks on.

crashing fistlike sheets, is the most literal, preternatural intervention of the hand of God, there are subtler traces of such workings
throughout the film. Doryan, for example, could easily fill a kind
of reincarnative role. There are only three rifle shots fired in Ryan's
Daughter: two when Tim O'Leary kills the constable who has
recognized him; one when Doryan shoots O'Leary. In a sequence
where unseen crows caw ominously over shot, the constable's
body is thrown into a deep pit, yawning like the mouth of hell itself
and coughing up a cloud of dust. Doryan's arrival shortly after this
sequence, is never really seen. The bus pulls away and he is
standing there. He might as well have sprung from the ground, like
Lawrence before Feisal or Magwitch to grab Pip. The clear visual
link is with that black pit, as in **THE SOUND BARRIER** where the
smoldering crater from Tony's crash cedes to the birth of his son.
Inexorably, Doryan is led to avenge the policeman's death and, in
part, his own tropistic "death." When he shoots O'Leary in the leg
and cripples him, as he was shot and crippled at the front, it is as
if he had been dispatched to do so, as if—and this seems
particularly true in light of his uncontrollable seizure immediately
after the act—he were brought to it by some overwhelming
elemental drive.

   If anyone appears to be in harmony with these forces, it is
Michael, who, even garlanded with flowers in a grotesque parody
of a grinning satyr, is genuinely a child of nature. It is Michael,
finally, who provides the means albeit inadvertently for Doryan's
death. It is Michael who, by mimicking Doryan in the village, makes
possible the understanding which precipitates violence against
Rosy, who physically by his very presence and spiritually by this
promulgation of guilt compels Doryan's last, inward look at
himself. Among the skeletal ribs of a bleached ship in the red glow
of the setting sun, Doryan ultimately perishes in his own inferno.
It is to Michael that he passes some measure of his animation:
Michael is the first and last to see him and limps after him like a
shadow a few moments before he dies. Afterwards there is a low
angle shot of Michael leaping over a rise while Doryan's music
surges on the soundtrack. As surely as he passes on his cigarette
case, Doryan transfers a residue of his spirit to Michael, a "fact"

which Rosy's facial expression in the final scene where she kisses Michael goodbye clearly underscores. With Doryan's extinction, blown back to atoms as he sits, almost in visual pun, by a rusty old boiler or furnace, the final element—fire—merges figuratively back into the other three. He waits for the sun to go below the horizon and disappears with it. The sound of the match striking, which flares on the track when he arrives and which flashes in the screen darkness just before his suicide, foreshadows aurally the distant explosion that announces the cataclysmic release of his soul. Doryan expires in a flame or as Yeats expressed it: "flames begotten of flame, where the blood-begotten spirits come and all complexities of fury leave, dying into a dance, an agony of trance, an agony of flame . . ."

Subjectivity and Irony. **RYAN'S DAUGHTER** belongs more to the title character than any other. As with **THE SOUND BARRIER** or **HOBSON'S CHOICE**, Lean also has a number of major figures and, in the revolutionary sub-plot, a large section of narrative of which Rosy cannot be part to develop. Consequently, the structure of **BRIEF ENCOUNTER** or **SUMMER MADNESS**, with the narrative wholly bracketed by the woman's viewpoint, is not possible. Instead, Lean distributes the incidents of subjective perception, fixing momentarily on the person or persons most appropriate. The discussion between Charles and Rosy in the schoolhouse, for instance, operates within a kind of dual point-of-view manifested in the scene of Pip and Estella on the stairs in **GREAT EXPECTATIONS**. In the early stages, a slight high angle over Charles' shoulder in the medium and medium close two shots causes him to tower over Rosy. This visually approximates both her initial disadvantage in the argument and the very conception she is consciously fighting against in the dialogue: "I feel like a child in this place—and I'm not a child, d'you know that?" The music on the track, a record of Beethoven's "Fifth Symphony" playing in the parlor, "belongs" to Charles in that he admires and has chosen to play it; but it gives voice equally to Rosy's idealized notions of Charles, to her perception of him as a heroic, Romantic personality. For her, it suitably accompanies his presence, just as Rachmaninoff provided the right mood for Laura's wistful memories of Alec. As

Rosy's ardor begins to convince Charles, Lean alters the angle and, at intervals, enters totally into her frame of reference, as in the medium close shot of her with Charles' hand on her shoulder. The camera is at Rosy's eye level, "face to face" with her, so that with Charles' upper body unseen, she now dominates the scene. A further effect of the pose, which recreates Alec's parting gesture in **BRIEF ENCOUNTER**, is the empathetic sense of urgency which it instills in the audience. It leads them, despite whatever detached observations they may have previously made on Charles' "Romantic" aspects, to side with Rosy and emotionally ratify her quest of him as a husband.

Doryan's acutely disturbed state of mind is, of course, conveyed by a more startling and extreme method. The split-second inserts of shells bursting into black clouds of smoke and the whine of falling bombs take the spectator inside Doryan's brain to participate in his affliction. As with Pip's collapse in **GREAT EXPECTATIONS**, Lean gradually extends this visual and aural metaphor over the entire sequence of his fit of shaking in the pub: shuddering so intensely as he grips the bar that his drink tips over; an increasingly dense soundtrack full of discordant music and the noise of battle; the pounding, distorted sensory awareness translated into a wide-angle lens close shot of Michael's foot thumping against a bench. Finally the withdrawal into a self-created world becomes so complete that when Doryan falls back mentally into the trenches, Lean records the inner event as if it were a real occurrence, and he is literally transported from the pub back to the field of battle as his hallucination fills the screen.

Part of what attracts Rosy to Doryan is his so obvious distress. Even though the flashback images clearly emanate from Doryan's pain, because they are intercut with shots of the pub in which Rosy is also present, these images are "de-localized." Just as the sparks from the electric cable when Zhivago and Lara brush together might be taken as a visualization of either or both persons' sensation, there is a suggestion in the intercutting that Rosy participates in Doryan's anguish as more than a spectator. Another consequence of having them meet in such a heavily stylized scene, of bringing down the lights on the set so that she literally reaches

After riding deep into the secluded woods, Rosy (Sarah Miles) and Randolph (Christopher Jones) make love and for the first time Rosy experiences true passion.

out to him in the dark, allows her adultery to become, in context, an act of charity as well as of personal gratification and allows her to retain to some degree the audience's sympathy and approval.

The other aspect, the sexual fulfillment in Rosy's subsequent liaison with Doryan, is through her eyes. The sexual interlude in the forest becomes a stylized externalization of her total experience, in body and thought. In her first glance of Doryan that day—a long shot of him on horseback—he is, like a knight errant before a castle or Childe Roland come to a dark tower, the graphic embodiment of all her past Romantic dreams. Similarly, the images intercut with the lovemaking in the arbor both emerge from and are selected by Rosy to form a montage of attraction not with the event per se but with her rapturous consciousness. The dandelion is Rose, the flower, ecstatically rent not by wind but by passion. The two silken strands of cobweb intertwining are Rosy's imagined out-of-the-body view of her form united with Doryan's. The shot of the sun, Doryan's emblem, hazily diffracted as the branches sway rhythmically overhead is multi-subjective: what Rosy sees as she lies on the ground below and what she feels at orgasm, the whole earth suddenly pulsing with her, swelling with her breath, heaving up with her cries, then slowly, tranquilly restoring itself. As in past films from **BRIEF ENCOUNTER** to **LAWRENCE**, Lean's shot selection and imagery are intensely keyed to a particular character's emotions.

Eventually, in Charles' personal vision of Rosy and Doryan on the beach, reality and illusion overlap completely. Charles projects their figures out of his imagination into the confines of his own concrete world, that is into the same two-dimensional frame he occupies. Unlike Doryan's flashback to the war zone, this manifestation is not part of any psychological disorder but arises purely from anxiety and suspicion. Neither is it a memory of something which has been witnessed or felt. It visualizes what, to Charles, can only be a conjecture. At this point, the audience has a fuller grasp of the situation than he does, knows that Rosy's affair is a fact and that it was probably she and Doryan walking on the sand. Their narrative awareness is not advanced here; but by implementing Charles' viewpoint their knowledge of other factors is. Primarily information is conveyed about Charles' character. This was also an effect of Rosy's experience in the forest, but more was already known about her character at that point than about Charles' at this moment. The degree of mental anguish which he feels is graphically implied in the clarity of the images which he creates. At the same time, the style which he imposes on the sequence reveals his own romanticizing nature from the iris of gauze he places over Rosy's and Doryan's graceful motion across the open ground to the light breeze he expects would rustle her dress. He may magnify the incidents slightly as the score, a stately mock-Beethoven, is his idea of "Romantic" music. He may even discover his own exaggeration later, when he actually finds the shell that he pictured Doryan digging out for Rosy by the tide pool in her drawer, but it is smaller than he envisioned it to be. Charles' general response, distressed but controlled, and not accusatory when he questions Rosy on her whereabouts, reaffirms his moral strength and his self-effacement, even under stress. By relating two of Rosy's "excursions" with Doryan in a subjective manner, first through her fervent perspective then through Charles', Lean departs from objective observation into an idealized, almost lyrical treatment of the affair, not merely to externalize a character point-of-view. He also makes the narrative point through his visuals that Rosy and Charles both tend to idealize and to "dream" events, which subtly suggests to the viewer that they may belong together after all.

RYAN'S DAUGHTER is among the least ironic of Lean's motion pictures, not necessarily in the sense of plot, where Rosy's concealment of her father's guilt is in this mode, but in terms of an enforced mood. There are some wry moments in the dialogue: the double-entendre in Rosy's explanation of why her skirt is soiled after riding with Doryan: "Princess [meaning her horse] took a fall;" or Moureen's jibe at the masquerading Michael, "Oh, Major darling, let me touch your V.C. You see my husband hasn't got one." While these make no thematic impression, what is probably the most ironically revealing remark comes at the very end, in Father Hugh's parting words to Charles and Rosy, when he offers them a relic for a keepsake, "It's supposed to be a fragment of St. Patrick's staff. I don't suppose it is, though." Generally, Lean limits ironic usage to certain devices in his editing. In the first scene between Charles and Rosy, for example, he injects dramatic apprehension fairly directly. Rosy's infatuation is as painfully obvious from her cosmetic preparations, even when she discards her old shawl in her attempt at striking a most sophisticated air, as it is in her agitation when Charles recounts that he met a "stimulatin' woman" on his trip. By holding on a travelling two-shot as they walk, then tightening on Rosy as Charles describes how he and his woman attended a concert in Dublin ("She had the score"), and delaying the expected cut-away to Charles until he also mentions that "she'd been at the teachin' for over fifty years," Lean heightens and releases tension in empathy with Rosy.

The first close look at Doryan is more complex. The cutting reasserts the importance, which is already suggested by its position in the continuity, of his arrival. Staggered medium long, medium, medium close, and close shots draw the audience in to him, spatially and meditatively. They are manipulated into an anticipation of his face, made to scrutinize it as if there were something unusually noteworthy about it. Doryan just stares. His expression does not change or show surprise; and after setting up the scene in this manner, the close shot of his gait does not elicit the pity it might have because of the viewer's subliminal resentment at being misled. Reflectively, the series of cuts prevent the audience from feeling pathos which might have worked against their acceptance of Doryan as larger-than-life. As it will be an heroic not pathetic aspect which attracts Rosy to him, this also anticipates her point-of-view. The rapid, dramatic succession of shots does not allow the audience time to adjust, to observe Doryan and gradually build up an empathy with him which might subvert their identification with Rosy.

While Lean may appear, on occasion, to be superficially detached from the action, his images, intercut and overlaid, constantly underscore the picture's directions and conflicts. One short sequence of two shots, such as that which occurs late in the film after Charles' disappearance, can summarize almost all of them: Father Hugh has just left Rosy after promising an apostolic search for Charles the following day. A close shot captures Rosy's uncertainty for she doesn't know if she wants Charles to return; and yet he is so basically a part of her, she cannot think beyond his being there. Her face is side-lit: the left, dark as if favoring the more sinister colorations of Doryan; the right side is a soft gray as if gently radiant in Charles' presence. Still characterizing in this way Rosy's inner dilemma, her whole face is suddenly illuminated by a dissolve to the shore, the bright sand coalescing with her features, as if she were in free flight over it, searching anew for her destiny. Receding at the tide's edge are Charles' footprints, which she walked in once and which, it is inferred for an instant, she will choose to follow again. But after a moment, a shadow falls across them, Doryan's shadow, and nothing is resolved.

When it was released, the distributor, mindful of the impressive amounts of money grossed by **DOCTOR ZHIVAGO**, advertised **RYAN'S DAUGHTER** as a "story of love filmed by David Lean." Perhaps the final irony is that this tag line from the ad copy transcends its origins and becomes entirely accurate. There may be resonances in the film from Flaubert's Bovary to Yeats' concept that "girls at puberty may find, the first Adam in their thought" does not fulfill their flesh. Its imagery may refer back to Thomas Hardy or even in its flash cuts "past Eve and Adam's from swerve of shore to bend of bay brings us by a commodius vicus of recirculation back to" James Joyce. Whatever vestiges of the Anglo-Irish literary tradition Lean and Bolt may have brought to the conception, **RYAN'S DAUGHTER** is a motion picture. It expresses itself and its characters with a visual style that can be at once powerfully direct and immensely subtle. Because it was directed by someone who felt that "movies have been my life, I love putting images on screen,"[1] it is truly a work of love from David Lean.

12
A PASSAGE TO INDIA (1984)

They are older than anything in the world.
No water has ever covered them, and the sun
who has watched them for countless eons
may still discern in their outline forms that
were his before our globe was torn from his
bosom. If flesh of the sun's flesh is to be
touched anywhere, it is here . . .
—E.M. Forster, *A Passage to India*

After several aborted projects, Lean's first film in fourteen years was also his first sole screen credit as scenarist. While his adaptation of E.M. Forster's ironic chronicle of the emptiness of stereotypes based on race or class is for the most part straightforward and uncomplicated, Lean's own preoccupations are as always present. Lean adds only a few original scenes in his screenplay, but those few result in telling images from the first sequence where Adela Quested gazes through a rain-spattered window at the model of a steamship to the last one which echoes it so poignantly. While Forster's novel belongs to no particular character, maintaining its objective perspective even as it describes the inner thoughts of its diverse cast, Lean focuses from the first on Adela and fashions from her the last in a line of heroines searching for fulfillment stretching back forty years to Laura

Jesson.

The ineluctable apprehension that hangs over Adela throughout **A PASSAGE TO INDIA** recalls equally the atmosphere of **GREAT EXPECTATIONS** and its undertones of social malaise, as she confronts her "destiny" with the same uncertainty as Pip before Satis House. The images of the opening—a welter of dark umbrellas parting to reveal the window of the steamship line; the camera slowly moving to the right in a reverse angle as Adela appears—reinforce her isolation in a sea of objects. An insert of the clerk's pen reveals her name, then her conversation with him recalls that of Jane Hudson and the man sharing her train compartment on the ride into Venice. While the clerk smilingly remarks, "I envy you—new horizons," Adela lowers her head to reply, "I'll be staying on . . . probably." Her only glances up are at the prints on the wall which depict the ship, the Taj Mahal, and the Marabar Caves. From her indecision, Lean cuts directly to an actual monument at the edge of the Indian ocean, and a few shots later reveals Adela and her companion, Mrs. Moore, on the deck of the just-arrived packet ship.

In devising this opening, Lean imbues Adela with the same conflicting impulses of all his previous heroines. The prints on the wall represent once more an unknown filled with promise of "new horizons," of adventure, but far from the security of familiar surroundings. There is little spoken information about Adela's past, her upbringing, her previous travels ("First time out of England."); but little is needed. Dressed in a plain tweed coat buttoned high around her neck, a brown hat, and still wearing gloves of the same color as she nervously taps her fingers together, everything in Adela's demeanor suggests that, like Laura Jesson or Rosy Ryan, she has never left home. As the narrative develops, so does the depth of her conflict, for like Laura and Rosy, Madeleine and Mary Justin, she will try to balance her needs for personal independence, social enfranchisement through marriage, and sexual fulfillment.

These aspects are most dramatically underlined in another sequence entirely devised by Lean: Adela's visit to the decrepit shrine. In the preceding scenes, after Adela breaks her engagement to Ronny Heaslop, the son of Mrs. Moore, the older woman makes the concluding remark at dinner: "Sometimes I think too much fuss is made about marriage. Century after century of carnal embracement and we're still no nearer to understanding one another." Again Lean cuts abruptly to a brightly-lit day scene as Adela tours the countryside alone on a bicycle. As she takes a side path, the camera pans with her through the high grass and Maurice Jarre's music unmistakably echoes **RYAN'S DAUGHTER**. After going through a small gate in a wall, Adela reaches a darkened grove. At first, only the top of something is visible, a brick roof reaching skyward out of the tall grass. As she draws nearer a breeze sweeps through, and she can see stone figures draped in vines and behind the swaying tree trunks: a man and woman locked in an embrace; another couple fondling each other; a woman straddling her partner. As her gaze moves from one statue to another, the camera dollies into her face; and then she notices the monkeys on the shrine roof. Their shrieks startle her. Then for some unknown reason they cascade down the stones and carvings, and Adela flees in terror. Even as every image in the sequence both frightens and fascinates Adela, every sound, both music and the noises of nature, externalizes her turbulent state of mind.

In both novel and film, Adela breaks off her engagement at a polo match. In the former, she and Ronny then accept a ride back from a wealthy local and are involved in a minor car accident. After the excitement of that experience in which they "felt adventurous as they muddled about in the dust," their hands touch inadvertently; and Adela renews the engagement by re-marking, "Ronny, I should like to take back what I said on the Maidan." In the film, when Adela returns on her bicycle and encounters Ronny, she says exactly the same thing. Obviously, Lean has interposed quite a different adventure than Forster, one which Adela shares with no one and which addresses much more directly her sexual fears and desires, the emotions which are at the center not just of her character but also of the narrative itself.

Subjectification and Irony. Lean not only adds scenes to Forster's narrative scheme, he relocates and rearranges others.

Forster's first section, which is entitled "Mosque," takes its title from Chapter Two where Aziz and Mrs. Moore meet. That scene does not begin until the film's 22nd minute. Forster does not introduce Adela, "that queer cautious girl," until Chapter Three. In contrast, Lean does not introduce Aziz until the 12th minute. Coincidentally, these points are both 1/15th of the way into the novel and film respectively. Moreover, Lean takes discussions between Mrs. Moore and Adela and various of the colonials and places them at the film's beginning in the scenes with the Turtons on the train.

It is in these early scenes that Lean refines the focus on Adela. Having opened the motion picture with her, he now remains almost entirely in her point-of-view until Aziz's introduction. Sometimes this is literally so, as when Mrs. Turton remarks about Ronny that "he's become a proper sahib," which disturbs Adela. In Forster's exposition this revelation takes place at the club: "Miss Quested learnt it with anxiety, for she had not decided whether she liked dignified men." Lean, the filmmaker, makes the same point wordlessly with a reaction shot of Adela, then underscores it aurally and visually, as the sound of wheels on the track is suddenly louder and she turns to look out the window, which motivates a subjective shot of the dark river waters and bridge structures flashing by below. Most of the time, Adela is merely present and hence aware of the events in a given sequence. Yet even in the scene when Mrs. Turton comes into their compartment to introduce herself and speaks mostly to Mrs. Moore, Lean's staging traps Adela behind the door, where it draws attention to her and keeps her the center of visual interest.

There are several ironic shots in the opening sequences as well. At the arrival in India, Lean intercuts the Viceroy and his wife, posed in profile like heads on a coin, with Indian lancers at attention in their red uniforms and then with a crowd of lower caste persons waving and murmuring aimlessly on the dock. As Adela and Mrs. Moore cross the teeming dock, an as-yet-unidentified passenger (Mrs. Turton) holds her nose in disgust. Like the wide angle view of Jane's train traversing the lagoon in **SUMMER MADNESS**, there are also several establishing shots of the train to Chandrapore, crossing the countryside at night and seen in the distance with Indian sculpture in the foreground, as if the perspective were from the roof of a temple. With these monumental silhouettes, which in their static mass dwarf but fail to impede the "tiny" colonial train, Lean metaphorically restates the social context of the narrative. With regard to the passenger, Adela, he foreshadows the "adventure" to come. The last cutaway is the least subtle and most akin to Forster's viewpoint: a mass of Indians sleep under a railway bridge and, as the train passes in the rear ground, a single man coughs.

When the travelers arrive at their destination, Lean ends the introductory sequences with a final metaphor. Adela pulls back from a window through which Mrs. Moore leans as the train pulls in. A reverse angle reveals Ronny Heaslop, who steps forward and asks his mother, "Where's Adela?" As if from nowhere, Adela pops up beside him, taps him on the shoulder, and smiles. If the suggestion is as in earlier films that one character (Adela) has magically appeared in another's (Heaslop's) world, Lean's staging subtly elaborates on it. As Lean holds the two people in one medium close shot, Adela removes her hat and Ronny awkwardly hands her a small bouquet and kisses her on each cheek. Then after asking his servant to fetch the luggage, Ronny excuses himself to take part in the formal greeting of the returning senior official, Turton. As he crosses out of shot, the camera pans, as if to follow, then stops, leaving Adela alone and slightly confused. The figurative values in the shot clarify the emotions at play within it. Adela's open gestures, smiling, removing her hat, cannot overcome Ronny's stiffness. Even as she reaches out tentatively to squeeze his arm, he invites a third person (the servant) into the shot, breaking the intimacy between them and forces her to step back. Then he abandons her. As the camera pivots then hangs on Adela, she takes Ronny's place at the left of the frame, as if thrown into his position ("I'm part of the reception committee") and already uncomfortable in it.

In the next few minutes, which are intercut with the introduction of Aziz, Adela's feeling of alienation is exacerbated. The culminating metaphor comes that evening, as Adela sits on the bed thinking about tomorrow. She looks at herself in the mirror of the armoire, and her expression unmistakably suggests that she is wondering why she is there. At that moment, Lean dissolves to the next day, dissolves from her point-of-view of her reflection, or literally how she sees herself, to a close up of a brass plate which reads, "Court of the Magistrate," so that the polished metal emblem of Ronny's office visually seems first to envelop and then to obliterate her figure.

In these introductory scenes, Lean transmutes Forster's "queer" character into one which combines Rosy Ryan's yearnings with Mary Justin's need to remain her own person. Compare Rosy's conversation with Father Hugh with the dialogue between Mrs. Moore and Adela as they take tea outdoors:

ADELA
(disdainfully examining a small sandwich)
Cucumber.

MRS. MOORE
My dear, life rarely gives us what we want
at the moment we consider appropriate.
Adventures do occur but not punctually.

Or later, during Adela and Ronny's engagement party:

ADELA
It's a funny thing. I don't feel a bit excited.
Nothing's really changed has it? I feel
perfectly ordinary.

MRS. MOORE
Much the best feeling to have.

ADELA
I suppose so. . . . Do you mean that my. . .
my "bothers" are to do with India?

MRS. MOORE (evasive)
India forces one to come face to face with
one's self. It can be very disturbing.

Like Rosy, Adela anticipated that sexual passion would change her. Unlike Rosy, who expected "wings," Adela also sees the threat to her freedom. More than once, Lean photographs her sitting on or lying in bed at night, as he did with Mary Justin in **PASSIONATE FRIENDS** before her flashback to telling her lover that she did not want "to be possessed" by him. With Adela, whose "bothers" are less well-defined, Lean uses flashcuts and these cuts are not to a shared experience or real people but to the statues of lovers at the monkey shrine.

If, like Jane Hudson, Adela is the "independent sort," it is in the context of colonial India in the 1920s, neither a time nor a place much receptive to women with minds of their own. Clearly Adela has come to India searching, as Jane did in Venice, for "a magical, mystical miracle." Surrounded by the exotic locales she saw pictured when she booked her passage, she finds herself still eating cucumber sandwiches. In **SUMMER MADNESS**, Lean used Jane's camera as a simple, realistic shorthand for her frame of reference. In **A PASSAGE TO INDIA**, Adela's inner feelings, her repressed emotions, emerge on screen almost as violently as Major Doryan's flashbacks of bomb bursts. While Lean does preserve some of Forster's enigmatic treatment of the incident between Adela and Aziz at the Marabar Caves, he keys on the "echo" which torments Adela in the novel. Like the rush of sound in the train compartment and at the monkey shrine, the echo in the caves, which merely unnerved Mrs. Moore, rushes violently over the soundtrack, slams into Adela, and drives her mad. In that sense, despite the madness implicit in contemplation of suicide by Laura Jesson or Mary Justin, despite the overwhelming passions of Rosy or Madeleine which cause them to abandon their society's moral values, despite the very title **SUMMER MADNESS**, Adela is literally the maddest of Lean's heroines. In that sense also, she is closer to Doryan or Lawrence, disturbed, desperate, and finally incapable of controlling her actions as she scurries down the hillside away from the caves. Doryan's flashbacks to the trenches at once evoked the memory of the past and the mental anguish of the present. Adela's flashbacks in the courtroom are an exorcism, or a shock treatment, for her. The ultimate irony is that by the time Fielding asks her, "Are you mad?" outside the courthouse in the rain, her demons, like the echoes, have receded and she can truthfully answer, "No."

In the concluding section of the novel, Adela is gone. Forster posits a partial reconciliation between Fielding and Aziz, who learns that Fielding did not marry Adela, his "enemy," but Mrs. Moore's daughter; but each man is now aware that they can never overcome the ethnic barriers between them and simply be friends. Lean recreates this part of the book but with considerably less detail than might have been expected. After all, Fielding's desire to discover India through the Indians is strongly reminiscent of Lawrence's outlook on Arabia. There is no direct information about it, but the photograph of a tank in a battle scene, which Aziz noticed in Fielding's parlor, indicated some military background. Fielding's treatment by his fellow club members when he takes Aziz's side has the tone of the experience of Lawrence with Farraj at the officers' bar in Cairo. Despite all the other potential parallels to Lawrence in Forster's original, Lean ends the film as it began, on Adela. As she finishes Aziz's letter and turns to look through the rain-streaked window, the visual allusion is not to Laura or Rosy or Jane but to Lawrence behind the dirty windshield.

Pantheism and Supernaturalism. "What a terrible river. What a wonderful river." Mrs. Moore's impulsive remarks on the Ganges when she speaks with Aziz in the mosque summarize the conflicting qualities of the environment in which Lean situates his characters. Lean's film, extrapolating on Forster's lines and his suggestion that Mrs. Moore has gone to "catch the moon in the Ganges," creates an atmosphere of otherworldliness in the mosque. In the first shot Aziz dips his hand in a pool, and the ripples eradicate the moon's reflection. Then after he crosses to the other side to sit, as the high melodic line of the underscore blends with the distant natural sounds of dogs barking and men drumming, two slow travelling shots move in behind Aziz. He turns and a point-of-view shot reveals only the wind blowing leaves. The sequence is repeated, but this time Aziz sees a ghost and rises up with a start. The "ghost" is immediately revealed to be merely an old woman, Mrs. Moore; but the initial effect is

Peggy Ashcroft as Mrs. Moore.

undiminished.

The previous shot selection and staging, which has Mrs. Moore crossing the frame slowly in a wide shot, dressed and veiled in white, her feet not visible behind the low wall of the pool so that she seems to float, has created a visual simile: "Mrs. Moore enters the mosque like a ghost and startles Aziz." There is no question of the meaning in Lean's staging; but if there were, Aziz's later admission to Adela and Prof. Godbole that "when I first saw Mrs. Moore, I thought she was a ghost" would answer it. The fact that it is conveyed visually and not verbally leaves it open to further exploration. The sequence is built on visual motifs—the moon, the wind, the glistening river below them—that suggest the power of the natural forces all around them. The mosque itself testifies silently to that: roofless, several windows shattered, its floor and columns overgrown with grass and vines, the crumbling wall where Aziz sits. Unlike Forster's version of the events ("I went to the mosque, but I did not catch the moon"),

Lean lets Mrs. Moore see the moon in the Ganges. Small wonder in such surroundings that her glimpse of the river, moving impassively to the sea and sometimes, as Aziz observes, carrying bodies from Benares, should make such a powerful impression and provoke her contradictory exclamations about it.

If Mrs. Moore is not a ghost, she is, at least, as Prof. Godbole relates, "A very old soul." While that character's perspective for his statement may be, as Aziz explains, "in the Hindu sense," Lean's is not. While Lean invents entirely the conversation between Adela, Aziz, and Godbole by the pool at Fielding's house, Forster is not without comment on the matter of ghosts. It is a ghost which his Mrs. Moore assumes startled Adela and Ronny after their car accident, a ghost which intruded in the natural order and precipitated their engagement. After enduring the trial but before learning of Mrs. Moore's death, Forster's Adela discusses ghosts with Fielding:

> "People whom I respect very much believe
> in ghosts," she said rather sharply. "My
> friend Mrs. Moore does."
>
> "She's an old lady."
>
> "I think you need not be impolite to her . . ."
>
> "I did not mean to be rude. I only meant that
> it is difficult, as we get on in life, to resist the
> supernatural."[2]

Lean has seldom addressed the supernatural, or even paranormal, in his films (excepting, of course, the comedic scheme of **BLITHE SPIRIT**); nor is it treated directly in **A PASSAGE TO INDIA**. But where Forster's personage was an emblem of the ingenuous, unprejudiced, accepting state-of-mind which most colonials, in the end even Fielding, were incapable of achieving, Lean's Mrs. Moore, "the very old soul," traverses the narrative like a *bodhisattva*, trying to place her affairs in order before the current cycle of life ends. Lean fully reveals her "enlightened" state of mind less in her stated beliefs ("God has put us on earth

Dr. Aziz (Victor Banerjee) helps Adela Quested (Judy Davis) climb to the upper Marabar caves.

to love and help our fellow man.") than in her occasional ironies ("Love in a church, love in a cave, I am held up from my business over all these trifles."). In that context, her decision to leave is not an abandonment of Adela, Aziz, or her own son, but a necessary last step, a shedding off of worldly things. Clearly in the scene where she watches a breeze stir the weeds around two headstones in the local cemetery, the second of which reads "Only good night dear mother," Mrs. Moore knows that she will soon die. But only Godbole, whom she sees as her train leaves coming out onto the platform to gesture in profound respect to her, understands the "true" nature of her imminent transcendence.

That sequence is the fulcrum in the entire narrative's probing of the nature of life and death. Just before leaving, Mrs. Moore explains to Ronny that she must go to "settles things up . . . get away from all this muddle and fuss to some cave of my own, some shelf." In bringing Mrs. Moore to this point, Lean's visualization has counterbalanced the melodramatic human events with

The expedition to the Marabar caves.

markers of the natural forces all around, markers which link otherwise unrelated scenes. Mrs. Moore herself seeks the river, but it is the ominous wind, which blows so subtly at the mosque, that erupts first while Aziz eats at Hamidullah's and then in Heaslop's dining room. The vines which cover the bricks of the mosque also cling to the statues of the monkey temple. The moon reflected in the mosque's pool reappears in the daytime sky when Mrs. Moore flees the first cave. In fact, it is seen in two point-of-view shots as Mrs. Moore puts on her sunglasses and looks up at the sky. The first shot as she catches her breath is wide to include the full moon hovering above the outline of the caves, which Forster described in the excerpt at the beginning of this chapter as "flesh of the sun's flesh." The second shot is part of a typically pantheistic trope, which Lean creates from word and image. For as Mrs. Moore remarks that "like many old people, I sometimes think we are merely passing figures in a godless universe," Lean fills the frame with a close up of the lunar landscape as she says the last four words. Whatever her fears about death, it is in the natural world all around her, in the moon, in the sky, or reflected in the mosque's pool, that Mrs. Moore learns, as she tells Aziz, that "God is here."

If what happens at the caves shakes Mrs. Moore's beliefs, it is because they expose her to nature's darker, more secret and unsettling side. In the novel, Forster objectively describes Mrs. Moore's thoughts outside the first cave, as she "looked at the queer valley and their invasion of it. Even the elephant had become a nobody . . . but no one could romanticize the Marabar because it robbed infinity and eternity of their vastness." Forster abandons her sitting "motionless with horror," as Adela and Aziz proceed to the Kawa Dol caves. Lean's shot selection and cutting draw a different meaning from the valley, the sky, the moon, and tie Mrs. Moore into the events at Kawa Dol. Just as the moon filling the frame was an unnatural point-of-view shot, in that Mrs. Moore could not possible have seen such details of the lunar surface with the naked eye, Lean's techniques of editing picture and sound express the emotional rather than the literal truth. As was mentioned earlier, the clearest example is the explosion of sound that comes from the match which Adela strikes, the echo that fills the cave, an unfathomable sensation that her mind turns into an assault by Aziz. His perspective is also captured, as he staggers to the edge of the escarpment, where a slightly tilted low angle externalizes his own disequilibrium. In the midst of it all, Lean cuts from a tear on Adela's face to a splash in the tank below, which awakens Mrs. Moore, who asks, "What happened."

If the suggestion in that cut is that Mrs. Moore can "hear" Adela's panicked tears falling, that she can sense something she does not see, the scene of her departure is even more explicit. In the train compartment, Mrs. Moore is again wearing the white shawl, visible through a closed, dust-speckled window. As the train leaves, the sound of the engine becomes unusually loud, as if in an allusion to the cave echo that still torments both her and Adela in different ways. She reacts, perhaps to the sound at first but ultimately to something else. She peers out then opens the window so that she can lean through it. What she sees is Godbole, palms joined above his head, silhouetted until he steps out further onto the platform. In this sequence, which ends with the white figure of the woman barely distinguishable as the train accelerates into the night, two "old souls," two "ghosts," bid each

**Fielding (Edward Fox) consults with Godbole (Alec Guinness)
after they have missed the train to the Marabar.**

other a wordless but eloquent farewell.

> *Films are about people and their emotions.*
> —David Lean, *The Film Director*

It is no easier at this point than it was at the beginning of this study to classify Lean's directorial style. In his essay on "The Film Director," Lean wrote: "By watching the actor's mistakes, you will see what *not* to do. You will also see *what* to do, but that always looks so very, very easy when done properly and believe me it is very, very difficult."[3] As regards his handling of actors, the performances he guides in **RYAN'S DAUGHTER** and **A PASSAGE TO INDIA** are typical: carefully molded, pared of unnecessary outbursts, more given to understatement, to reaction shots and the impact of looks rather than words. Typical of this, in **A PASSAGE TO INDIA**, is Peggy Ashcroft's portrayal of Mrs. Moore, which won a supporting actress Academy Award and was the latest of a score of nominations, including Judy Davis as Adela, for performers in Lean's films. In **RYAN'S DAUGHTER**, John Mills as Michael, wandering poignantly about Kirrary, a long way from Pip, was the Academy Award winner. The other actors—Trevor Howard, the romantic lead of **BRIEF ENCOUNTER** and **PASSIONATE FRIENDS**, as the crusty Father Hugh; Leo McKern as the guilt-ridden publican, Ryan; Robert Mitchum cast against type as the solid but unexciting school teacher; Sarah Miles, ranging from innocent expectation to womanly passion; even Christopher Jones as the spectral Major Doryan—all become exceptionally drawn characters under Lean's direction.

Lean was widely criticized for using Christopher Jones in **RYAN'S DAUGHTER**, particularly by those aware that Marlon Brando spent months preparing to play the part. If, in fact, Lean did have to put extra effort in creating "Doryan," by using silent, brooding close-ups and even replacing Jones's voice in the dialogue scenes, the resulting portrayal is exactly what the narrative calls for: a disturbed, ambiguous character made into an emblem of tragic romanticism by Rosy. More recently, Lean's casting of Alec Guinness as the brahmin, Godbole, was re-proached by those who thought an Indian actor should have been used. "But I wanted a great character actor in a great character-actor part," was Lean's simple reply.[4]

Throughout his career, Lean displayed a penchant in his casting for using the faces of young, relative unknowns like Christopher Jones as often as those of old veterans like Mitchum. The list of current star performers to whom Lean gave the "first break" is a long one, which includes names such as Richard Attenborough, Peter O'Toole, Alec Guinness, Trevor Howard, and Omar Sharif. Lean's insistence on using Sharif over Paul Newman for the title role in **DOCTOR ZHIVAGO** is typical of his casting method. The actor problem for Lean was that "when the script's finished, it's in my head. And there are the actors, and I've got to try and make them measure up to the imagination I had of their part."[5] In anticipation of this, he tried to find those with whom he could work to create characters rather than bolstering the box-office with stars.

Technically, Lean's last pictures continually reapplied the early lessons of the cutting room: his narrative remained direct, his exposition visual rather than verbal, his work proceeded without false starts and avoided needless interludes even with longer-than-average running times. Like Griffith, Ford, or Renoir, his compositions were often static, fields aligned geometrically and movement confined to objects within the frame, as in the arrival of the Viceroy in **A PASSAGE TO INDIA**. Other usages, like the succeeding camera moves towards Aziz's back as he sits in the mosque or the two cross-cut travelling shots when Adela approaches the shrine, may recall Hitchcock's typical method of drawing the viewer in and creating suspense. But these quickly cede to a more direct juxtaposition of close-ups and point-of-view shots. His particular pantheistic symbolism, his protagonists, whether determined visionaries or emotional dreamers, and his figurative images place Lean's films in the Romantic tradition, which his thematic choices from **BRIEF ENCOUNTER** to **A PAS-SAGE TO INDIA** reconfirm. If Lean's work has any stylistic trademark, beyond this tradition, it is in his concentration on the subjective aspects of film, in his exploitation of audience empathy and externalization of his characters' thoughts or feelings for dramatic effect.

Despite the resurgence of acclaim for Lean's motion pictures in the past ten years, evidenced critically by awards from the American Film Institute and the Directors Guild of America and commercially by the restoration and reissue of his version of **LAWRENCE OF ARABIA**, even proponents of his work still find it necessary to make excuses for what they consider his failings or his lesser films. Occasionally, Lean's own words have been cited to support the assertion that he is more *metteur en scene* than *auteur.*[6] If there are any doubts about Lean's *auteurist* mind-set, long before the *Cahiers'* critics applied the concept to filmmaking, his 1947 essay quickly dispels them: "You must be a pretty big egotist. How can you be anything else if you are to make everyone see the film your way. The best film's are generally those that have the stamp of one man's personality."[7]

A more fundamental error with Lean or any other creator would be to pay greater attention to what he or she says than to what he or she does. Lean often cited in retrospect his great "failure" in **RYAN'S DAUGHTER**: "I made a fatal mistake. When the love affair started . . . I told Freddie [Young] 'make it as romantic as possible.' And we did, because I wanted to give the impression of somebody being madly, hopelessly in love . . . The fault was that I didn't tell the audience that's what I was doing. And the critics all thought I was being a wildly romantic filmmaker. I should have had the priest or somebody say, 'Rosy, you are seeing everything through rose-colored glasses'."[8] Certainly a critic as well as a casual viewer can overlook all the visual cues in **RYAN'S DAUGHTER**, can read nothing into Father Hugh's actual admonitions, can react to the film as nothing more than an overblown romance. Or they can see more. Admittedly, Lean does not bracket the influence which Rosy's state of mind will have over the staging as overtly as he did in **BRIEF ENCOUN-TER**. Nor should he have to, given the development of the way an audience perceives visual cues in the quarter century between the two films. If Lean made any mistake, it was in thinking, after the fact, that being more verbally explicit or trying to restrict the reading of the film would have necessarily altered anyone's perception of his already explicit imagery.

If Truffaut, Godard, Charbrol, Rohmer et al. in establishing *la politique des auteurs*, sought to interview filmmakers, it was not to discover a "world view" in their responses but to have that view further elucidated. Whatever the odd radical assessments made in the name of "auteurism,"[9] its most significant focus like that of any critical method must be on the films themselves; or as I.A. Richards observes, "What concerns criticism is not the avowed or unavowed motives of the artist."[10] The films examined here have one thing in common—David Lean the director, not David Lean the producer, David Lean the editor, David Lean the writer, David Lean the reader of books, nor any other persona of Lean other than director. If there is an underlying assumption by the authors of this study, it is simply that David Lean, the director, is an artist whose work merits critical examination. Whatever other work Lean may have done as producer, editor etc. is important only insofar as it affects and supports the work as director and as artist.

Clearly aspects of Lean the person can inform and guide those who seek to understand Lean the artist, but in the end that artist like any other can only be fully discovered through the work. To us, that work speaks for itself. If we were pressed to define Lean the "auteur," the only valid answer would be the intentionality that created the films examined here. Clearly that intentionality is much more than David Lean the person. From Noel Coward to Robert Bolt it spans and encompasses numerous collaborators. From shooting schedules to Sam Spiegel it overcomes and works around countless obstacles, both physical and mental, to guide each motion picture to its conclusion. It is clear also that some collaborators and some obstacles have a greater influence than others on the finished work. But in the end the finished work is just that, and in that work one discovers David Lean the artist and his world view.

Of course, neither **A PASSAGE TO INDIA** nor any of Lean's fifteen other motion pictures were fashioned either as objects for critical assessment or as chapters in testimony of a world view, but as singular works, communicating individual conceptions and demanding acceptance or rejection on that basis first. As has been suggested several times earlier, whatever insights formal analysis may offer, from a possible exegesis at best to glib value judgments at worst, it can never recreate a single moment or a single frame of the viewing experience. Nor can quoting dialogue, commentators, or the poetry and prose of other creators convey the effect of a given motion picture, of the other world which it may momentarily conjure up. As Lean often described his own early movie-going: "That beam of light travelling through the smoke, it had an immediate magic for me."[11] Given that our commentary in this study is limited to so many words and black-and-white images, the concept of a "poetical equivalent" to that magic has a certain appeal as a concluding statement; and, for that, Yeats will serve best:

> Come away, oh human child
> To the waters and the wild . . .
> For the world's more full of weeping
> than you can understand.

A PERSONAL AFTERWORD

David Lean the man is no more. His death just weeks before the oft-postponed commencement of filming of his last project NOSTROMO leaves us without what he intended to be his last film.

What remains of the man, beyond the sixteen films, are numerous interviews with Lean, in book, article and documentary form, and the reminiscences of those who knew him and worked with him. All found him brilliant, precise and more than occasionally difficult. Freddie Young, who won an Academy Award for all three films with Lean, "love(d) working with David because he's one hundred percent behind [you]."[1] Others like his most frequent collaborator actor Alec Guinness found Lean's talent and exactitude simultaneously inspiring and exasperating, "a man of genius cocooned in outrageous charm."[2] A few like his last leading lady Judy Davis still recalled only the worst the week after Lean's death.[3]

I met David Lean only twice. Once was in 1975, shortly after the first edition of this book was published, when he expressed dismay at the thought that someone had written at length about his work without his knowledge or permission. Lean was still angry at the mocking critical responses to both **ZHIVAGO** and **RYAN'S DAUGHTER**, still smarting from what he felt was an eviscerating personal attack at the National Society of Film Critics luncheon at New York's Algonquin Hotel in 1970. This displeasure had been well-documented and, knowing this, it was not without some trepidation that I agreed to be co-moderator with Ronald Neame of a "week-end" with Lean sponsored by the Directors Guild of America and the American Film Institute in

December of 1984.

That week-end began with a misstep, as the first public showing of A **PASSAGE TO INDIA** was delayed by more than an hour due to a techinical problem at the AFI theater. That Friday evening and the next day at the breakfast and lunch sessions, Lean's replies to questions from those attending were brief and occasionally impatient. Finally on Sunday, he began to feel more comfortable; and in the afternoon he agreed to spend a last hour or so with two dozen people crowded into a backroom of the commissary at the Burbank Studios. In that less formal setting, I could step out of my role as moderator, where I had spent hours sitting next to Lean but feeling constrained from asking but a few, general questions of my own. So I asked not just about **LAWRENCE** and **GREAT EXPECTATIONS** but about **MADELEINE** and **RYAN'S DAUGHTER**.

In thinking about that afternoon while preparing this second edition, while re-reading a copy of that first edition which Lean had ultimately offered to sign for me, while re-watching certain of the films and the interview programs on their making, and finally while reading the trade paper obituaries and seeing the video encapsulations of Lean's career immediately after his death, one of his answers kept returning to mind. I inquired whether it had been difficult to get the shot of Doryan through the windshield, with the same burnt-out expression on the actor's face as in the end of **LAWRENCE** but with the sun reflected in the glass. Lean raised an eyebrow, smiled, and said, "You noticed that, did you? It was bloody difficult, but I got what I wanted."

What to say then, in closing, about a director who mostly "got what he wanted"? In his last years, Lean often repeated his avowal that movies had been his life and that he loved putting images on screen. For those who, like Lean did, love motion pictures, those sixteen movies will always speak more eloquently than any observer for the artist who fashioned them.

—Alain Silver

BIOGRAPHY

For most of his career, David Lean was never very candid or voluble about his personal life or thoughts. Although he wrote two articles [annotated in detail in the Bibliography] and gave numerous interviews regarding his work, Lean the private individual was seldom mentioned and never probed in depth. This was true until 1987 when Lean granted a series of interviews to Stephen Silverman, which became the basis for his "official" biography. Another book, originally intended to be an "as-told-to" autobiography, is being completed by Kevin Brownlow and scheduled for release in 1993. Also forthcoming is a book on the making of **LAWRENCE OF ARABIA** by Adrian Turner. Lean did participate in several documentaries, including two with Melvyn Bragg, who worked with Lean on the "Bounty" project, produced by London Weekend Television which explore his working style in great detail.

David Lean was born in Croydon, England on March 25, 1908. His upbringing and education were in the strict Quaker tradition of his parents, so strict that Lean was not allowed to see movies or attend the theater until adulthood.

Lean was very devoted to his mother, Helena Annie Tangye, even more so after his father, Francis William le Blount Lean, separated from her and left the family. Lean's relationship to his mother remained close until her death, but there was always an emotional distance from his father which seemed to widen with the decades.

Ironically, it was Lean's father who helped him obtain his first job in the movies. After working for a short time in his father's accounting business, Lean determined at the age of nineteen that he would at least try to break into the industry that produced the silent movies which he had belatedly discovered. Inspired by the work of such early filmmakers as D.W. Griffith and Rex Ingram, Lean appealed to his father for assistance in finding a career to which he could wholeheartedly devote himself. "I said to my father, 'Dad, I'd like to go into the movies.' He was shocked."[1] Much to David Lean's surprise, his father used his influence and obtained an interview for him with the production manager at Gaumont Studios.

At Gaumont Lean's illustrious career began at rock bottom. He worked as a runner, a clapperboard boy, a camera assistant, a costumer, and then as a third assistant director. Within three years, he had worked his way into a regular position in the cutting room and, shortly after sound arrived, was made chief editor of Gaumont-British Sound News and, off and on, British Movietone News. He not only edited these newsreels but often wrote and narrated them as well.

In the early 1930s after a brief period of working in Paris, Lean began the transition as editor from newsreels to feature films. At British-Dominion Studios, Elstree, Lean worked with Merrill White, an American who had been Ernst Lubitsch's chief editor. During the day they cut A-pictures then "at six o'clock, we used to switch to the 'quickies,' and he'd take the first five reels and I'd taken the second five."[2] "Quota Quickies" were, as their name implies, cheaply-made films produced solely because of a protectionist British law requiring a minimum number of British films be exhibited in ratio to foreign-produced films.

Lean passed up opportunities to direct "quota-quickies," including two offers from future partner Anthony Havelock-Allan.[3] Instead, Lean prefered editing quality features involving celebrated actors such as Laurence Olivier, Leslie Howard, and Rex Harrison; writers such as George Bernard Shaw; and directors beginning with Paul Czinner in 1935 and continuing through collaboration with Michael Powell and Emeric Pressburger after the start of World War II. A large part of Lean's reputation as a first-class technician was because he sometimes "repaired" the work of a stage-minded director; and his experience editing these films and at times shooting inserts firmly established him as one of the most respected and highest paid editors in Britain by the end of the 1930s.

Before cutting down the eight hour rough cut of **49TH PARALLEL**, for which effort Michael Powell said of him, "I recognise that he is the best editor I ever worked with—or should I say worked for,"[4] Lean worked on **MAJOR BARBARA**. According to Lean, "Harold French was there for the dialogue because he was a stage director and I was there for the camera set-ups and did a fair amount of the direction. I was sort of *film* director; I was the camera end of it—but I've never had any credit for it."[5] Actually Lean received two credits. Part of the unusual arrangement with producer and novice director Gabriel Pascal, who had engaged Harold French and Lean as "Assistants in Direction" but not in the normal sense of the term (i.e. as "Assistant Directors"), was a prominent listing of their names on a separate card. Lean also received a credit for "Montage," and French, as "Dialogue Supervisor."

In 1940, Lean married actress Kay Walsh, who starred in a picture Lean edited in 1937 (**THE LAST ADVENTURERS**) and who would perform in **IN WHICH WE SERVE**, **THIS HAPPY BREED**, and as the doomed Nancy in **OLIVER TWIST**. In all, Lean was married six times: to Isabelle Lean, the mother of his only child, a son, Peter; to Walsh (1940-1949); to actress Ann Todd (1949-1957); to Leila Devi (1960-1978); to Sandra Hotz (1981-1985); and to Sandra Cooke (1990). On the strength of his experience with Pascal and directing inserts and second units for others, Walsh encouraged Lean to become a full-fledged director. What was still lacking was a chance to work with actors and direct performance.

That time came when West End luminary Noel Coward agreed to write, direct, and star in a film for Filippo del Giudice's Two Cities company about the sinking of the H.M.S. Kelly, a ship commanded by Coward's friend Lord Mountbatten. Much as Gabriel Pascal had, Coward felt he needed a cinema-wise "associate" director for his project, **IN WHICH WE SERVE**; and after many whom he queried had seconded Havelock-Allan's recommendation of Lean, Coward approached him. Lean's principal

condition was to be named co-director to which Coward acqui-
esced.[6] "Acting was a kind of mystery to me; and Noel, of course,
was simply wonderful with that, he was simply wonderful with
actors . . . When he wasn't acting in one of the scenes, he wasn't
there. So I handled the whole damn thing. Great piece of luck."[7]
For the first six weeks of shooting, **IN WHICH WE SERVE** had no
distributor, then del Guidice struck a deal with British Lion and
the film went on to be named "top moneymaker" for 1942.

The fortuitous association, having led to both fiscal and
critical success for Lean, became a long term opportunity with the
formation of Cineguild. Lean, associate producer Havelock-Allan,
and cinematographer Ronald Neame became partners with the
express purpose of making more films. Since Coward was very
satisfied with the result of the first collaboration, he offered
Cineguild more material, his two most recent plays which had
opened on successive evenings in September, 1942, the week
after **IN WHICH WE SERVE**, and which became films of the
same title: **THIS HAPPY BREED** and **BLITHE SPIRIT**.

In the final stages of World War II, Michael Powell and
Emeric Pressburger approached J. Arthur Rank with the proposal
for Independent Producers, an association of companies to be
underwritten by Rank which would keep the sound stages run by
D & P Studios Ltd. at Denham and Pinewood busy with production. According to Powell, "Rank had asked Emeric and me to
invite other creative producers to join our group and we had at
once invited Cineguild."[8] The films produced by Cineguild continued to be a joint effort in which all the principals of the
company performed various creative functions, sometimes
uncredited. With this pledge of on-going financial backing, Coward and Cineguild repurchased the rights to his one-act play, *Still
Life,* for 60,000 pounds, and in 1945, Lean co-produced, co-
scripted, and directed **BRIEF ENCOUNTER** which firmly established his reputation as a complete filmmaker. He was nominated
for an Academy Award in two categories (writer and director)
and the film won the Prix Internationale de Critique at Cannes.

Although the transition may not have been quite as
simple as Ronald Neame remembered it being ("I went to Arthur

Rank and said, 'Arthur, David and I want to make **GREAT EXPECTATIONS**' and he said, 'Okay, how much'?"⁹), Lean and Cineguild continued to be successful switching from Coward to Dickens with **GREAT EXPECTATIONS** and **OLIVER TWIST**. Then, however, they faltered with **PASSIONATE FRIENDS** and **MADELEINE**. Both pictures starred Lean's third wife, Ann Todd, whom Lean had met when he took over the direction of **PAS-SIONATE FRIENDS** from Ronald Neame.¹⁰ Lean himself had written an article for the *Penguin Film Review* extolling Rank's support of independent producers in 1947;¹¹ but by 1949, after **MADELEINE** and in anticipation that Rank would not be able to underwrite the Independent Producer companies such as Cineguild much longer, Neame and Havelock-Allan decided to part company with Lean.

The rift between the three had been building for some time, for as early as January, 1947, Noel Coward noted in his diary: "Dined with David Lean, who told me all about his marital problems and his professional problems with Ronnie and Tony."¹² In 1947, Ronald Neame directed his first picture, **TAKE MY LIFE**, for Cineguild, but Lean was not involved. Neame confirms the truth of Coward's diary entry for June 21, 1947 that it was his wanting to direct that had alienated Lean and adds that during **OLIVER TWIST**, Stanley Haynes—with whom both Lean and Neame had worked when he was "Assistant in Production" on **MAJOR BARBARA**—had become a kind of unofficial fourth partner and stayed on to work on developing scripts with and for Lean.¹³ By the time of **MADELEINE**, which Haynes produced, he and Lean were their own unit within the dissolving Cineguild.

With the break-up of Cineguild taking him somewhat by surprise, Lean found himself set adrift, separated for the first time since becoming a director from his partners of almost a decade. Dropping both Cineguild and Haynes, Lean made a new affilia-tion in August, 1950.¹⁴ His next two films were productions with Lean himself in the precarious position of producer and director for the redoubtable Alexander Korda and his London Films. The first, **THE SOUND BARRIER** in 1952, was a critical and financial hit and garnered the British Academy Award for Best Film. The second, **HOBSON'S CHOICE** (1954) with Charles Laughton in the title part, was an adaptation of a well-known 1915 stage comedy which had been filmed several times before. It, too, was a critical success and should have fully laid to rest any fears Lean might have had about working solo.

Lean's next film, **SUMMER MADNESS** (1955), is a pivotal one in his career for two reasons. It was his first true location film, made entirely outside of the studio and of England, which would set a pattern for his remaining films as well as his personal life. Secondly, the film incorporated a personal story into a broad, often Romantic, and visually striking setting, Venice in this case. These two elements would become fixtures of Lean's remaining films and projects. Katharine Hepburn, the star of the film, received an Oscar nomination, and Lean was named Best Director by the New York Film Critics.

BRIDGE ON THE RIVER KWAI (1957) is another watershed mark in Lean's career as it initiates his relationship with the "epic" film. Lean had been preparing another project for Korda when he died. After **SUMMER MADNESS**, Katharine Hepburn introduced him to producer Sam Spiegel, and together they began work on an adaptation of Pierre Boulle's sardonic novel, *Bridge over the River Kwai.* Shot on location in Ceylon at a cost of three million dollars—a sizeable budget for 1956—and running 161 minutes, **KWAI**'s World War II prisoner-of-war tale was considerably longer and more expensive to make than any film Lean had previously directed. Lean went over budget and schedule and quarreled both with Spiegel and star Alec Guinness, resentful of having been cast only after the services of Charles Laughton and Noel Coward could not be secured.[15] The story garnered more awards and journalistic coverage than all of Lean's preceding films combined. The film received seven Oscars, including Best Director, and was one of the top-grossing films of the next several years. It also sparked a controversy when novelist Pierre Boulle won the screenwriting Oscar, although almost all Hollywood insiders knew that blacklistees Michael Wilson and Carl Foreman had worked extensively on the script. If Lean needed any encouragement to continue in his epic style of filmmaking,

KWAI's domestic gross in its initial release of over $17 million on a negative cost of less than $3 million proved a positive reinforcement.

After **KWAI**, Lean remained in the Far East and worked with Emeric Pressburger on a possible biography of Gandhi for Spiegel.[16] After securing the rights which had been held by Rank, Spiegel proposed a different project to Lean, one based on the life of T.E. Lawrence, English adventurer and author, whose career has been a source of controversy and scandal ever since his death in 1935. Upon reading author Robert Bolt's treatment of Lawrence's life, Lean put aside a hoped-for biography of Gandhi for this new project which was to occupy the next three years of Lean's life. After extensive screen tests and a false start with Albert Finney in the lead and failing to sign Marlon Brando to replace him, Spiegel and Lean gave the newcomer Peter O'Toole the title role. With the release of **LAWRENCE OF ARABIA** in 1962, it was clear that Lean had expanded the horizons of the epic film even further. Incorporating a personal, psychological story into a realistically re-created historical context of Arab-British conflict surrounding World War I, the film became a landmark of its own.

Lean's next epic, **DOCTOR ZHIVAGO** (1965), was a return to the romantic triangle. Based on Boris Pasternak's tale of love and Revolution, Lean collaborated again with screenwriter Robert Bolt, cinematographer Fred Young, designer John Box, and composer Maurice Jarre. Shot in Spain with the unlikely Omar Sharif as the Russian protagonist, **ZHIVAGO**, like its two immediate predecessors, became one of the top-grossing films of the year and kept making money well into the following year. With over $50 million in domestic rentals and $200 million worldwide, Lean declared frequently that he earned more money from **ZHIVAGO** than all his other pictures combined. Despite its overwhelming box-office success and six Academy Awards, the picture was excoriated by the critics. It had been a long time since a Lean film received mostly poor notices.

After considering several projects, including THE BATTLE OF BERLIN for Carlo Ponti, Lean settled on **RYAN'S DAUGHTER** in 1968. Then called "Michael's Day," Lean worked on the script with Robert Bolt to transpose it from a rough adaptation of *Madame Bovary* to create a tale of "ordinary" characters a la **BRIEF ENCOUNTER** set in counterpoint to the Irish rebellion during World War I. The financial success of **ZHIVAGO** meant that no corners needed to be cut on the period recreation which saw an entire village built in the West of Ireland or on the epic elements such as a brilliantly-staged storm sequence that anchors the film, shot over several months on two continents, and of which Lean was particularly fond: "My favorite bits in my pictures would include things in **LAWRENCE** and a good bit of **DOCTOR ZHIVAGO**, but for one moment in a picture, I would say I was rather pleased with the storm sequence in **RYAN'S DAUGH-TER**."[17] The story of Rosy Ryan, the newly-married Irish woman who falls in love with a British soldier, is steadfastly in the foreground. However, at a budget of nearly $14 million and despite a yearlong roadshow engagement, **RYAN'S DAUGHTER** was slow to recoup it cost and grossed "only" $14.7 million domestically. Critically, **RYAN'S DAUGHTER** was an unmitigated bomb.

Lean often spoke about how he "lost heart" after **RYAN'S DAUGHTER**. For most of the decade following, he travelled the world with his fifth wife. He toyed with several epic projects. Joseph E. Levine had been underwriting development of a Gandhi script by Robert Bolt since 1967,[18] which Lean was to have directed but he dropped out in 1972 when Bolt delivered a draft that he thought disappointing.[19] Ten years later in 1982 Lean abandoned an adaptation of Dinesen's *Out of Africa*. Both were ultimately made by others. It was in 1977 that Lean began formal development of a project: a new version of the Bounty story with its infamous conflict between Captain Bligh and Fletcher Christian. He began work on the script with Bolt for what he initially hoped would be a two films to be called THE LAWBREAKERS and THE LONG ARM and even supervised construction of a replica of the Bounty. Bolt suffered a stroke in early 1978 and as the budget grew from $17 to $50 million, financial disagreements with a succession of producing companies from Warner Bros. to Dino de Laurentiis to Sam Spiegel finally forced Lean to abandon the project in 1980.[20] The film was finally made by de Laurentiis with Australian director Roger Donaldson and actors Anthony Hopkins and Mel Gibson.

1984 marked Lean's reemergence with a series of awards and honors, ranging from being knighted by Queen Elizabeth to the cover of *Time* magazine, and most importantly the release of a new film. Although Lean was compelled to write the script himself without compensation while the producers raised the $14 million budget from several different sources, this project, an adaptation of E. M. Forster's *A Passage to India*, had finally gone into production. Centering on a young English girl's passion in a context of festering Colonial British-Indian relations, the film was a final reiteration of Lean's fixation with interweaving historical events into a tapestry of personal passion.

In 1988, Lean was honored at Cannes for his "contributions to the British Cinema." From 1987 to 1989, he oversaw the restoration of **LAWRENCE OF ARABIA** to its original release length of 221 minutes and its subsequent world release. And in 1990 he joined former director honorees such as Alfred Hitchcock, Orson Welles, William Wyler, and John Ford as the recipient of the American Film Institute's Life Achievement Award. Lean was hobbled by a bad leg at the AFI reception, where he announced that shooting would soon begin on a new film based on Joseph Conrad's novel, *Nostromo*.

In 1986, Steven Spielberg had offered to produce a project for Lean, who considered *Empire of the Sun* and *Nostromo*. Disheartened by the prospect of working in China and the focus of the script, Lean abandoned *Empire* in early 1987. After five years of work, a succession of studios and executive producers including Spielberg, Lean, working again with Robert Bolt, had finished their screenplay of NOSTROMO based on the novel and an earlier draft script by Christopher Hampton. Tri-Star was funding a $44 million budget, John Box was the production designer, Serge Silberman the producer, and Dennis Quaid and Isabella Rossellini were to star beginning in March, 1991. One final hurdle, the reluctance of any company to insure the production because of Lean's advanced age and health problems, had been overcome by signing a "back-up" director, Guy Hamilton. In late January, pre-production was suspended due to Lean's illness. On April 16, 1991, Sir David Lean died.

FILMOGRAPHY

[NOTE: Technical credits given below are based wherever possible on actual prints supplemented by a variety of written sources. Running times for pre-1957 films are based wherever possible on actual timings of commercially available video tapes.]

EARLY WORK IN THE FILM INDUSTRY

Beginning in 1927 under an apprenticeship at Gaumont Studios, Lime Grove, Lean worked as a tea boy and clapperboy/assistant cameraman (on **QUINNEYS**, 1927, directed by Maurice Elvey). He next worked as assistant director on **SAILORS DON'T CARE** directed by W.P. Kellino; **THE PHYSICIAN** directed by George Jacoby; **HIGH TREASON** directed by Maurice Elvey; and **BALACLAVA**, directed by Maurice Elvey and Milton Rosmer, all 1928 releases. On **BALACLAVA**, Lean also served as set costumer, before switching to the cutting room and becoming an assistant editor. In 1930, Lean's ability to edit sound resulted in employment as Chief Editor for Gaumont-British News. From 1931-1935, Lean worked as Editor of (1) British Movietone News (also occasionally writing and speaking commentary); (2) Paramount-British News; and (3) Various "Quota-quickie" productions at British-Dominion Studios under Merrill White and reissues with synchronized effects for Paramount.

FEATURE FILMS AS EDITOR:

1930   **THE NIGHT PORTER** (Director: Sewell Collins)

1932   **INSULT** (Director: Harry Lachman)

1933   **MONEY FOR SPEED** (Director: Bernard Vorhaus)
        THE GHOST CAMERA (Director: Bernard Vorhaus)
        TIGER BAY (Director: J. Elder Wills; Editors: David Lean and Ian Thomson)

1934   **DANGEROUS GROUND** (Director: Norman Walker)

THE SECRET OF THE LOCH (Director: Milton Rosmer)
JAVA HEAD (Director: J. Walter Ruben; Editors:
Thorold Dickinson and David Lean)

1935 **ESCAPE ME NEVER** (Director: Paul Czinner; Editors:
Merrill White and David Lean)

1936 **BALL AT SAVOY** (Director: Victor Hanbury)
AS YOU LIKE IT (Director: Paul Czinner)

1937 **DREAMING LIPS** (Director: Paul Czinner)
THE WIFE OF GENERAL LING (Director: Ladislas Vajda)
THE LAST ADVEnTURERS (Director: Roy Kellino)

1938 **PYGMALION** (Directors: Anthony Asquith, Leslie
Howard)

1939 **SPIES OF THE AIR** (Director: David MacDonald)
FRENCH WITHOUT TEARS (Director: Anthony
Asquith)

1941 **49TH PARALLEL** (aka **THE INVADERS**) (Director:
Michael Powell)

1942 **ONE OF OUR AIRCRAFT IS MISSING** (Director:
Michael Powell)

FEATURE FILM AS ASSISTANT IN DIRECTION/ SUPERVISING EDITOR:

1941 **MAJOR BARBARA** (Director: Gabriel Pascal; Assistants in
Direction: Harold French and David Lean; Montage:David
Lean; Editor: Charles Frend)

FEATURE FILMS AS DIRECTOR

IN WHICH WE SERVE (1942, Two Cities Films)

Directors	Noel Coward, David Lean
Producer	Noel Coward
Associate Producer	Anthony Havelock-Allan
Screenplay	Noel Coward
Adaptation	[Uncredited] David Lean, Anthony Havelock-Allan, Ronald Neame

Director of Photography	Ronald Neame
Art Director	David Rawsley
Art Supervisor to Noel Coward	G.E. (Gladys) Calthrop
Music	Noel Coward
Editors	[David Lean], Thelma Myers
Production Sound	C.C. Stevens
Rerecording Mixer	Desmond Dew
Camera Operator	Guy Green
Production Manager	Sidney Streeter
Unit Manager	Michael Anderson
Make-up	Tony Sforzini

CAST   Noel Coward (Captain Kinross), Bernard Miles (Chief Petty Officer Walter Hardy), John Mills (Ordinary Seaman Shorty Blake), Celia Johnson (Mrs. Kinross), Kay Walsh (Freda Lewis), Joyce Carey (Mrs. Hardy), Derek Elphinstone (Number One), Robert Sansom ("Guns"), Philip Friend ("Torps"), Michael Wilding ("Flags"), Hubert Gregg (Pilot), Ballard Berkeley (Engineer Commander), James Donald (Doctor), Kenneth Carton (Sub-Lieutenant R.N.V.R.), Walter Fitzgerald (Colonel Lumsden), Gerald Case (Captain Jasper Fry), Ann Stephens (Lavinia), Kathleen Harrison (Mrs. Blake), George Carney (Mr. Blake), Richard Attenborough (Young Sailor), Juliet Mills (Freda's baby), Leslie Howard (Narrator [Uncredited]).

Running time	115 minutes

Distributed by British Lion (Great Britain) and United Artists (United States)

Released September 17, 1942 (G.B.); October 1, 1942 (U.S.)

Filmed from February to June, 1942 at Denham Studios and on location in Hertfordshire at a cost of 240,000 pounds

THIS HAPPY BREED (1944, A Two Cities Film. A Noel Coward/ Cineguild Production for Prestige/J. Arthur Rank)

Producer	Noel Coward
In Charge of Production	Anthony Havelock-Allan
Screenplay	Noel Coward, from his play
Adaptation	David Lean, Ronald Neame, Anthony Havelock-Allan

Director of Photography	Ronald Neame (Technicolor)
Art Director	C.P. Norman
Art Supervisor to Noel Coward	G.E. Calthrop
Conductor	Muir Matheson (London Symphony Orchestra)
Editor	Jack Harris
Sound	C.C. Stevens, John Cooke, Desmond Dew
Camera Operator	Guy Green
Color Directors	Natalie Kalmus, Joan Bridge (Associate), Harold Hayson (Technician)
Production Managers	Ken Horne, Jack Martin
Assistant Director	George Pollock
Dress Supervisor	Hilda Collins
Make-up	Tony Sforzini
Hairdressing	Vivienne Walker
Special Effects	Percy Day

Cast   Robert Newton (Frank Gibbons), Celia Johnson (Ethel Gibbons), John Mills (Billy Mitchell), Kay Walsh (Queenie Gibbons), Stanley Holloway (Bob Mitchell), Amy Veness (Mrs. Flint), Alison Leggatt (Aunt Sylvia), Eileen Erskine (Vi Gibbons), John Blythe (Reg Gibbons), Guy Verney (Sam Leadbitter), Merle Tottenham (Edie), Betty Fleetwood (Phyllis Blake).

Running time	107 minutes [Note: most other sources list 114 minutes; some trade reviews and the video release are 107]

Distributed by Eagle-Lion (G.B.) and Universal-International (U.S.)

Released June 1, 1944 (G.B.); April, 1947 (U.S.)

Filmed at Denham Studios from February to April, 1943

BLITHE SPIRIT (1945, Cineguild-Two Cities Films for J. Arthur Rank)

Producer	Noel Coward
Screenplay	Noel Coward, from his play
Adaptation	David Lean, Ronald Neame, Anthony Havelock-Allan

Director of Photography	Ronald Neame (Technicolor)
Art Director	C.P. Norman
Art Supervisor to Noel Coward	G.E. Calthrop
Music	Richard Addinsell
Conductor	Muir Matheson (London Symphony Orchestra)
Editor	Jack Harris
Production Sound	John Cooke
Rerecording Mixer	Desmond Dew
Camera Operator	W. McLeod
Special Effects	Tom Howard
Color Directors	Natalie Kalmus, Joan Bridge (Associate)
Unit Managers	Norman Spencer, S.S. Streeter
Assistant Director	George Pollock
Costumes	Rahvia
Dress Supervisor	Hilda Collins
Make-up	Tony Sforzini
Hairdressing	Vivienne Walker

Cast   Rex Harrison (Charles Condomine), Constance Cummings (Ruth), Kay Hammond (Elvira), Margaret Rutherford (Madame Arcati), Joyce Carey (Mrs. Bradman), Hugh Wakefield (Doctor Bradman), Jacqueline Clark (Edith).

Running time	96 minutes

Distributed by General Film Distributors (G.B.); United Artists (U.S.)

Released April 5, 1945 (G.B.); September, 1945 (U.S.)

Filmed at Denham Studios from February to May, 1944

BRIEF ENCOUNTER (1945, A Noel Coward/Cineguild Production for Prestige/J. Arthur Rank)

Producer	Noel Coward
In Charge of Production	Anthony Havelock-Allan, Ronald Neame
Screenplay	David Lean, Ronald Neame, Anthony Havelock-Allan, based on Noel Coward's play, *Still Life*

Adaptation	Noel Coward
Director of Photography	Robert Krasker
Art Director	L.P. Williams, A.R.I.B.A.
Art Supervisor to Noel Coward	G.E. Calthrop
Music	Rachmaninoff's "Second Piano Concerto" played by Eileen Joyce Conductor Muir Matheson (National Symphony Orchestra)
Editor	Jack Harris
Associate Editor	Margery Sanders
Sound	Stanley Lambourne, Desmond Dew
Sound Editor	Harry Miller
Camera Operator	B. Francke
Production Manager	E. Holding
Assistant Director	George Pollock
Continuity	Margaret Sibley

Cast   Celia Johnson (Laura Jesson), Trevor Howard (Dr. Alec Harvey), Cyril Raymond (Fred Jesson), Joyce Carey (Barmaid), Stanley Holloway (Station Guard), Valentine Dyall (Stephen Lynn), Everley Gregg (Dolly Messiter), Margaret Barton (Beryl), Dennis Harkin (Stanley), Majorie Mars (Mary Norton), Nuna Davey (Mrs. Rolandson), George V. Sheldon (Clergyman), Jack May (Boatman), Edward Hodge (Bill), Wilfred Babbage (Policeman), Henrietta Vincent (Margaret), Irene Handl (Organist), Sidney Bromley (Johnnie), Avis Scutt (Waitress), Richard Thomas (Bobbie), Wally Bosco (Doctor).

Running time	86 minutes

Distributed by Eagle-Lion (G.B.) and Universal (U.S.)

Released November 26, 1945 (G.B.); August, 1946 (U.S.)

Filmed at Denham Studios and on location in Carnforth on a ten week schedule from January to April, 1945 on a budget of 270,000 pounds

GREAT EXPECTATIONS (1946, A Cineguild Production for J. Arthur Rank)

Producer	Ronald Neame
Executive Producer	Anthony Havelock-Allan
Screenplay	David Lean, Ronald Neame, Anthony Havelock-Allan with Kay Walsh and Cecil McGivern, based on the novel by Charles Dickens
Director of Photography	Guy Green
Production Designer	John Bryan
Art Director	Wilfred Shingleton
Music	Walter Goehr (uncredited: Kenneth Pakeman, G. Linley)
Conductor	Walter Goehr (National Symphony Orchestra)
Editor	Jack Harris
Sound	Stanley Lambourne, Gordon K. McCallum
Rerecording Mixer	Desmond Dew
Sound Editor	Winston Ryder
Camera Operator	Nigel Huke
Production Manager	Norman Spencer
Assistant Director	George Pollock
Costume Design	Sophia Harris [of Motley], Margaret Furse (Assistant)
Continuity	Margaret Sibley
Choreography	Suria Magito

Cast   John Mills ("Pip"), Valerie Hobson (Estella), Bernard Miles (Joe Gargery), Francis L. Sullivan (Jaggers), Finlay Currie (Magwitch), Martita Hunt (Miss Havisham), Anthony Wager ("Pip" as a boy), Jean Simmons (Estella as a girl), Alec Guinness (Herbert Pocket), Ivor Barnard (Wemmick), Freda Jackson (Mrs. Joe Gargery), Torin Thatcher (Bentley Drummle), Eileen Erskine (Biddy), Hay Petrie (Uncle Pumblychook), George Hayes (Compeyson), Richard George (the Sergeant), Everley Gregg (Sarah Pocket), John Burch (Mr. Wopsle), Grace Denbigh-Russell (Mrs. Wopsle), O.B. Clarence (the

Aged Parent), John Forrest (the Pale Young Gentleman), Anne Holland (a Relation), Frank Atkinson (Mike), Gordon Begg (Night Porter), Edie Martin (Mrs. Whimple), Walford Hyden (the Dancing Master), Roy Arthur (Galley Steersman).

Running time   118 minutes

Distributed by General Film Distributors (G.B.); Universal-   Inter-national (U.S.)

Released December 26, 1946 (G.B.); April 24, 1947 (U.S.)

Filmed from September, 1945 to April, 1946 at Denham Studios and on location around London (Rochester and the Thames Estuary) at a cost of 385,000 pounds

OLIVER TWIST (1948, A Cineguild Production for Independent Producers Ltd./J. Arthur Rank)

Producer	Ronald Neame
Screenplay	David Lean and Stanley Haynes, from the novel by Charles Dickens
Director of Photography	Guy Green
Art Director	John Bryan
Music	Sir Arnold Bax, D. Mus.
Conductor	Muir Matheson (Philharmonic Orchestra of London); solo pianoforte, Harriet Cohen (the "Oliver" Themes)
Editor	Jack Harris
Sound	Stanley Lambourne, Gordon K. McCallum
Sound Editor	Winston Ryder
Camera Operator	Oswald Morris
Special Effects	Joan Suttie, Stanley Grant
Production Manager	Norman Spencer
Assistant Director	George Pollock
Costumes	Margaret Furse
Make-up	Stuart Freebourne
Continuity	Margaret Sibley

Cast   Robert Newton (Bill Sikes), Alec Guinness (Fagin), Kay Walsh

(Nancy), John Howard Davies (Oliver), Francis L. Sullivan (Mr. Bumble), Henry Stephenson (Mr. Brownlow), Mary Clare (the Matron), Anthony Newley (the Artful Dodger), Josephine Stuart (Oliver's mother), Ralph Truman (Monks), Gibb McLaughlin (Mr. Sowerberry), Amy Veness (Mrs. Bedwin), Frederick Lloyd (Mr. Grimwig), Henry Edwards (Police Official), Ivor Barnard (Chairman of the Board), Maurice Denham (Chief of Police), Michael Dear (Noah Claypole), Michael Ripper (Barney), Peter Bull (Landlord of the "Three Cripples"), Deirdre Doyle (Mrs. Thingummy), Diana Dors (Charlotte), Kenneth Downey (Workhouse Master), W.G. Fay (Bookseller), Edie Martin (Annie), Gravely Edwards (Mr. Fang), John Potter (Charley Bates), Maurice Jones (Workhouse Doctor), Hattie Jacques, Betty Paul (Singers at the "Three Cripples").

Running time   115 minutes (G.B.); 104 minutes (U.S.)

Distributed by Eagle-Lion (G.B.); United Artists (U.S.)

Released June 28, 1948 (G.B.); July, 1951 (U.S.)

Filmed at Pinewood Studios

THE PASSIONATE FRIENDS [ONE WOMAN'S STORY (U.S.)] (1949, Cineguild for J. Arthur Rank)

Producer	Ronald Neame[1]
Associate Producer	Norman Spencer
Screenplay	Eric Ambler, based on the novel by H.G. Wells
Adaptation	David Lean and Stanley Haynes
Director of Photography	Guy Green
Production Designer	John Bryan
Music	Richard Addinsell
Editors	Jack Harris (supervising), Geoffrey Foot
Sound	Stanley Lambourne, Gordon K. McCallum
Sound Editor	Winston Ryder
Rerecording Mixer	F.G. Hugheson
Camera Operator	Oswald Morris
Assistant Art Director	Tim Hopwell-Ashe

Set Decorator	Claude Manusey
Assistant Director	George Pollock
Costumes	Margaret Furse

Cast   Ann Todd (Mary Justin), Trevor Howard (Steven Stratton), Claude Rains (Howard Justin), Isabel Dean (Pat), Betty Ann Davies (Miss Layton), Arthur Howard (Manservant), Guido Lorraine (Hotel Manager), Marcel Poncin (Hall Porter), Natasha Sokolova (Chambermaid), Helen Buris (Flowerwoman), Jean Serrett (Emigration Official), Frances Waring (Charwoman), Wanda Rogerson (2nd Bridge Guest), Wilfred Hyde-White (Solicitor).

Running time	89 minutes [Trade reviews]; 91 or 95 minutes [other sources]

Distributed by General Film Distributors (G.B.); Universal-International (U.S.)

Released January 26, 1949 (G.B.); June, 1949 (U.S.)

Filmed at Pinewood Studios and on location in London and the Swiss Alps near Chamonix in 1948

MADELEINE (1950, A David Lean Production for Cineguild and J. Arthur Rank)

Producer	Stanley Haynes
Screenplay	Stanley Haynes and Nicholas Phipps (Dialogue) based on the actual case of Madeleine Hamilton Smith
Director of Photography	Guy Green, B.S.C.
Art Director	John Bryan
Music	William Alwyn
Conductor	Muir Matheson (Royal Philharmonic Orchestra)
Editor	Geoffrey Foot
Costumes	Margaret Furse
Assistant Director	George Pollock

Cast   Ann Todd (Madeleine Smith), Ivan Desny (Emile L'Angelier), Norman Woland (William Minnoch), Leslie Banks (Mr. Smith),

Barbara Everest (Mrs. Smith), Susan Stranks (Janet Smith), Patricia Raine (Bessie Smith), Elizabeth Sellars (Christina), Edward Chapman (Doctor Thompson), Jean Cadell (Mrs. Jenkins), Eugene Deckers (Monsieur Thuau), Ivor Barnard (Mr. Murdoch), David Horne (Lord Justice), Harry Jones (Lord Advocate), Andre Morell (Dean of Faculty), Henry Edwards (Clerk of the Court), Amy Veness (Miss Aiken), John Laurie (Scots Divine), Kynaston Reeves (Dr. Penny), Cameron Hall (Dr. Yeoman), Douglas Barr (William), Irene Brown (Mrs. Grant), Alfred Rodriguez, Moira Fraser (Highland Dancers), James McKechnie (Narrator).

Running time	102 minutes

Distributed by General Film Distributors (G.B.); Walter Reade and Universal-International (U.S.)

Released February 14, 1950 (G.B.); September, 1950 (U.S.)

Filmed at Pinewood Studios and on location in Cornwall in 1949

THE SOUND BARRIER [alternate titles **BREAKING THROUGH THE SOUND BARRIER** (G.B.); **BREAKING THE SOUND BARRIER** (U.S.)] (1952, London Films)

Producer	David Lean
Associate Producer	Norman Spencer
Screenplay	Terence Rattigan
Director of Photography	Jack Hildyard, B.S.C.
Production Design	Vincent Korda
Music	Malcolm Arnold
Conductor	Muir Matheson (London Philharmonic Orchestra)
Editor	Geoffrey Foot
Aerial Unit Director	Anthony Squire
Aerial Photography	John Wilcox, Peter Newbrook, Jo Jago
Art Directors	Joseph Bato, John Hawkesworth
Production Manager	John Palmer

Cast   Ralph Richardson (Sir John Ridgefield), Ann Todd (Susan Ridgefield Garthwaite), Nigel Patrick (Tony Garthwaite), John Justin (Philip Peel), Dinah Sheridan (Jess Peel), Joseph

(Will Sparks), Denholm Elliott (Chris Ridgefield), Jack Allen (Windy Williams), Ralph Michael (Fletcher), Douglas Muir, Leslie Philips (Controllers), Robert Brooks Turner (Test Bed Operator), Anthony Snell (Peter Makepeace), Jolyon Jackley (John), Vincent Holman (A.T.A. Officer); and the de Havilland Comet and Vampire; the Vickers-Supermarine Attacker.

Running time   118 minutes (G.B.);
                                  115 minutes (U.S.)

Distributed by British Lion (G.B.); Lopert Films/United Artists (U.S.)

Released July 22, 1952 (G.B.); November, 1952 (U.S.)

Filmed on a budget of 250,000 pounds

HOBSON'S CHOICE (1954, A David Lean Production for London Films in Association with British Lion)

Producer	David Lean
Associate Producer	Norman Spencer
Screenplay	David Lean, Norman Spencer, and Wynyard Browne, based on the play by Harold Brighouse
Director of Photography	Jack Hildyard, B.S.C.
Art Director	Wilfred Shingleton
Music	Malcolm Arnold
Conductor	Muir Matheson (Royal Philharmonic Orchestra)
Editor	Peter Taylor
Sound	John Cox (supervising), Buster Ambler, Red Law
Camera Operator	Peter Newbrook
Assistant Art Director	Bill Hutchinson
Production Manager	John Palmer
Assistant Director	Adrian Pryce-Jones
Costume Design	John Armstrong
Costume Supervisor	Julia Squire
Make-up	Tony Sforzini, George Parleton
Hairdressing	Gladys Atkinson
Continuity	Margaret Shipway

Cast   Charles Laughton (Henry Hobson), Brenda de Banzie (Maggie),
         John Mills (Will Mossop), Daphne Anderson (Alice Hobson),
         Prunella Scales (Vicky Hobson), Richard Wattis (Albert Prosser),
         Derek Blomfield (Freddy Beenstock), Helen Haye (Mrs.
         Hepworth), Joseph Tomelty (Jim Heeler), Julien Mitchell (Sam
         Minns), Gibb McLaughlin (Tudsbury), Philip Stainton (Denton),
         Dorothy Gordon (Ada Figgins), Madge Brindley (Mrs. Figgins),
         John Laurie (Dr. McFarlane), Raymond Huntley (Mr. Beenstock),
         Jack Howarth (Tubby Wadlow), Herbert C. Walton (Printer).

Running time   107 minutes

Distributed by British Lion (G.B.); United Artists (U.S.)

Released February 24, 1954 (G.B.); June, 1954 (U.S.)

Filmed at Shepperton Studios and on location in Salford beginning in
July, 1953

SUMMER MADNESS [SUMMERTIME (U.S.)] (1955, David Lean's
Production for Lopert Films)

Producer	Ilya Lopert
Associate Producer	Norman Spencer
Screenplay	David Lean, H.E. Bates, based on
	the play, *Time of the Cuckoo*, by
	Arthur Laurents, created on Broadway
	by Robert Whithead and Walter Fried
Director of Photography	Jack Hildyard, B.S.C. (Technicolor)
Art Director	Vincent Korda
Music	Alessandro Cicognini; Rossini's
	"La Gazza Ladra" (recorded in Rome)
Editor	Peter Taylor
Sound	Peter Handford
Rerecording Mixer	John Cox
Sound Editors	Winston Ryder, Jacqueline Thiblot
Camera Operator	Peter Newbrook
Chief Electrician	Archie Dansie
Assistant Art Directors	Bill Hutchinson, Ferdinand Bellan
Production Managers	Raymond Anzarut, Franco Magli

Production Assistant	Robert J. Kingsley
Assistant Directors	Adrian Pryce-Jones, Alberto Cardone
Make-up	Cesare Gamberelli
Hairdressing	Gracia de Rossi
Continuity	Margaret Shipway

Cast   Katharine Hepburn (Jane Hudson), Rossano Brazzi (Renato Di Rossi), Isa Miranda (Signora Fiorina), Darren McGavin (Eddie Jaeger), Mari Aldon (Phyl Jaeger), Jane Rose (Edith McIlhenny), MacDonald Parke (Lloyd McIlhenny), Gaetano Autiero (Mauro), Andre Morell (Englishman on train), Jeremy Spencer (Vito), Virginia Simeon (Giovanna).

Running time	99 minutes

Distributed by Lopert Films/United Artists

Released May 29, 1955 (G.B.); June, 1955 (U.S.)

Filmed on location in Venice in Summer, 1954.

THE BRIDGE ON THE RIVER KWAI (1957, Horizon Pictures, A Sam Spiegel Production)

Producer	Sam Spiegel
Screenplay	Pierre Boulle; also [uncredited] Carl Foreman, Calder Willingham, Michael Wilson, and David Lean, based on Boulle's novel[2]
Director of Photography	Jack Hildyard (Technicolor; Cinemascope)
Art Director	Donald M. Ashton
Music	Malcolm Arnold; "Colonel Bogey March" by Kenneth J. Alford (Royal Philharmonic Orchestra)
Editor	Peter Taylor
Sound	John Cox, John Mitchell
Sound Editor	Winston Ryder
Camera Operator	Peter Newbrook
Assistant Art Director	Geoffrey Drake

Production Manager	Cecil F. Ford
Production Executive	William N. Graf
Assistant Directors	Gus Agosti, Ted Sturgis
Construction Manager	Peter Dukelow; Bridge constructed by Equipment and Construction Company, Ceylon
Technical Advisors	Major-General L.E.M. Perowne
Engineering Consultants	Husband and Company, Sheffield
Wardrobe	John Apperson
Continuity	Angela Martelli

Cast   Alec Guinness (Colonel Nicholson), William Holden (Shears), Jack Hawkins (Major Warden), Sessue Hayakawa (Colonel Saito), James Donald (Dr. Clipton), Geoffrey Horne (Lieutenant Joyce), Andre Morell (Colonel Green), Peter Williams (Captain Reeves), John Boxer (Major Hughes), Percy Herbert (Grogan), Harold Goodwin (Baker), Ann Sears (Nurse), Henry Okawa (Captain Kanematsu), K. Katsumoto (Lieutenant Miura), M.R.B. Chakrabandhu (Yai), Viliaiwan Seeboonreaung, Ngamta Suphaphongs, Javanart Punynchoti, Kannikar Dowklee (Siamese girls).

Running time	161 minutes

Distributed by Columbia Pictures

Released November, 1957

Filmed on location in Sri Lanka (Ceylon) from October, 1956 to May, 1957 on a budget of $3.2 million.

LAWRENCE OF ARABIA (1962, Horizon Pictures, A Sam Spiegel-David Lean Production)

Producer	Sam Spiegel
Screenplay	Robert Bolt, based on various writings by and about T.E. Lawrence [A draft by Michael Wilson was discarded[3]]
Director of Photography	Fred A. Young (Technicolor; Super Panavision 70)

Production Designer	John Box
Music	Maurice Jarre; "The Voice of the Guns" by Kenneth J. Alford
Orchestrations	Gerard Schurmann
Conductor	Sir Adrian Boult (London Philharmonic Orchestra
Editor	Anne V. Coates
Casting Director	Maude Spector
Sound	Paddy Cunningham
Sound Editor	Winston Ryder
Camera Operator	Ernest Day
Chief Electrician	Archie Dansie
Second Unit Directors	Andre Smagghe, Noel Howard
Second Unit Cameramen	Skeets Kelly, Nicolas Roeg, Peter Newbrook
Art Director	John Stoll
Assistant Art Directors	Roy Rossotti, George Richardson, Terry Marsh, Anthony Rimmington
Set Decoration	Dario Simoni
Musical Coordinator	Morris Stoloff
Production Manager	John Palmer
Assistant Director	Roy Stevens
Construction Managers	Peter Dukelow; Fred Bennett (assistant)
Location Manager	Douglas Twiddy
Property Master	Eddie Fowlie
Costumes	Phyllis Dalton
Wardrobe	John Wilson-Apperson
Make-up	Charles Parker
Hairdressing	A.G. Scott
Continuity	Barbara Cole

Cast   Peter O'Toole (Thomas Edward Lawrence), Alec Guinness (Prince Feisal), Anthony Quinn (Auda), Jack Hawkins (General Allenby), Omar Sharif (Sherif Ali), Anthony Quayle (Colonel Brighton), Claude Rains (Mr. Dryden), Arthur Kennedy (Jackson Bentley), Jose Ferrer (Turkish Bey), Donald Wolfit (General Murray), I.S. Johar (Gasim), Gamil Ratib (Majid),

Michael Ray (Farraj), Zia Mohyeddin (Tafas), John Dimech (Daud), Howard Marion Crawford (Medical Officer), Jack Gwillim (Club Secretary), Hugh Miller (R.A.M.C. Colonel).

Running time	221 minutes (roadshow engagements); 200 minutes (general release); 184 minutes (1971 U.S. reissue cut by Spiegel)

Distributed by Columbia Pictures

Released December 9, l962 (G.B.); December 16, 1962 (U.S.)

Filmed on location in Jordan, Spain, Morocco, and England. Two years in production, shooting intermittently from May, 1961 through September, 1962 on a budget of $12 million and an actual negative cost of $13.5 million. [Lean himself has set the cost variously from $12 to $30.5 million, the latter figure being the total inclusive of prints and advertising used by Columbia to calculate profits.[4]]

DOCTOR ZHIVAGO (1965, A Carlo Ponti Production of David Lean's Film for M.G.M.)

Producer	Carlo Ponti
Executive Producer	Arvid L. Griffen
Screenplay	Robert Bolt, based on the novel by Boris Leonidovic Pasternak (Feltrinelli Editions, Milan)
Director of Photography	Freddie Young (Metrocolor; Super Panavision 70)
Production Designer	John Box
Music	Maurice Jarre (conducted by the composer)
Editor	Norman Savage
Sound	Paddy Cunningham
Rerecording Mixer	Franklin Milton, William Steinkamp
Sound Editor	Winston Ryder
Camera Operator	Ernest Day
Second Unit Director	Roy Rossotti
Second Unit Photogtaphy	Manuel Berenguer
Chief Electrician	Miguel Sancho
Art Directors	Terence Marsh; Gil Parrondo (associate)
Assistant Art Directors	Ernest Archer, Bill Hutchinson, Roy Walker

Set Decoration	Dario Simoni
Construction Managers	Gus Walker, Fred Bennett
Production Supervisor	John Palmer
Production Managers	Augustin Pastor, Douglas Twiddy
Assistant Directors	Roy Stevens, Pedro Vidal
Dialogue Coach	Hugh Miller
Costumes	Phyllis Dalton
Make-up	Mario van Riel
Hairdressing	Gracia de Rossi, Anna Christofani
Special Effects	Eddie Fowlie
M.G.M. Representative	Stanley H. Goldsmith
Continuity	Barbara Cole

Cast   Omar Sharif (Yuri Zhivago), Julie Christie (Lara), Geraldine Chaplin (Tonya Gromeko Zhivago), Tom Courtenay (Pasha/ Strelnikov), Alec Guinness (General Yegraf Zhivago), Siobhan McKenna (Anna Gromeko), Ralph Richardson (Alexander Gromeko), Rod Steiger (Komarovsky), Rita Tushingham (the girl, Tonya), Adrienne Corri (Lara's mother), Geoffrey Keen (Professor Kurt), Jeffrey Rockland (Sasha Zhivago), Lucy Westmore (Katya), Noel William (Razin), Gerard Tichy (Liberius), Klaus Kinski (Kostoyed), Jack MacGowran (Petya), Maria Martin (Gentlewoman), Tarek Sharif (Yuri at age eight), Mercedes Ruiz (Tonya at age seven), Roger Maxwell (Colonel in charge of replacements), Inigo Jackson (Major), Virgilio Texeira (Captain), Bernard Kay (Bolshevik deserter), Erik Chitty (Old soldier), Jose Nieto (Priest), Mark Eden (Young engineer), Emilio Carrer (Mr. Sventytski), Gerhard Jersch (David), Wolf Frees (Comrade Yelkin), Gwen Nelson (Comrade Kaprugina), Jose Caffarel (Militiaman), Brigitte Trace (Streetwalker), Luana Alcaniz (Mrs. Sventytski), Lili Murati, Catherine Ellison, Maria Vico (Women), D. Assad Bahador (Dragoon colonel), Peter Madden (Political officer).

Running time	200 minutes at New York premiere including Overture and Entr'acte, 192 without; 180 minutes in general release (cut by Lean)

Distributed by Metro-Goldwyn-Mayer

Released December 22, 1965 (U.S.); April, 1966 (G.B.)

Filmed on location in Spain, Finland, and Canada and at C.E.A.
Studios, Madid, from December, 1964 to October, 1965 on a budget of
$11.9 million.

RYAN'S DAUGHTER (1970, Faraway Productions/AG Film for M.G.M.)

Producer	Anthony Havelock-Allan
Associate Producer	Roy Stevens
Screenplay	Robert Bolt
Director of Photography	Fred A. Young (Metrocolor; Super Panavision 70)
Production Designer	Stephen Grimes
Music	Maurice Jarre (conducted by the composer)
Editor	Norman Savage
Sound	John Bramall
Rerecording Mixers	Gordon K. McCallum; Eric Tomlinson (music)
Sound Editors	Ernie Grimsdale, Winston Ryder
Camera Operator	Ernest Day
Second Unit Directors	Charles Frend, Roy Stevens (storm sequence)
Second Unit Photography	Denys Coop, Robert Huke
Art Director	Roy Walker
Assistant Art Director	Derek Irvine
Set Decoration	Josie McAvin
Construction Manager	Peter Dukelow
Special Effects	Robert Macdonald
Production Manager	Douglas Twiddy
Assistant Directors	Pedro Vidal, Michael Stevenson
Production Liaison	William O'Kelly
Location and Property Manager	Eddie Fowlie
Costumes	Jocelyn Rickards
Make-up	Charles Parker
Hairdressing	A.G. Scott
Continuity	Phyllis Crocker

Cast   Sarah Miles (Rosy Ryan), Robert Mitchum (Charles
          Shaughnessy), Trevor Howard (Father Hugh Collins), Christo-
          pher Jones (Major Andrew Doryan), John Mills (Michael), Leo
          McKern (Tom Ryan), Barry Foster (Tim O'Leary), Marie Kean
          (Mrs. McCardle), Arthur O'Sullivan (Mr. McCardle), Evin
          Crowley (Moureen), Douglas Sheldon (Driver), Gerald Sim
          (Captain), Barry Jackson (Corporal), Des Keogh (Private),
          Niall Toibin (O'Keefe), Philip O'Flynn (Paddy), Donal Neligan
          (Moureen's boyfriend), Brian O'Higgins (Constable O'Connor),
          Niall O'Brien (Bernard), Owen Sullivan (Joseph).

Running time   196 minutes (roadshow);
                              165 minutes (U.S. general release)

Working titles   MICHAEL'S DAY; THE IRISH REBELLION

Distributed by Metro-Goldwyn-Mayer

Released November 9, 1970 (U.S.); December 9, 1970 (U.K.)

Filmed on location on the West Coast of Ireland and in North Africa
from February, 1969 to March, 1970 on a budget of $13.3 million.

A PASSAGE TO INDIA (1984, A John Brabourne and Richard
Goodwin Production of A David Lean Film for Home Box Office,
Thorn EMI, and Columbia)

Producers	John Brabourne, Richard Goodwin
In association with	John Heyman and Edward Sands
Screenplay	David Lean, based on the novel by E.M. Forster and the play by Santha Rama Rau
Director of Photography	Ernest Day, B.S.C. (Technicolor, 1.85:1)
Production Designer	John Box
Music	Maurice Jarre (Royal Philharmic Orchestra conducted by the composer); "Freely Maisie" tune composed by John Dalby
Casting	Priscilla John
Editor	David Lean
Associate Editor	Eunice Mountjoy

Sound	John Mitchell
Rerecording Mixers	Graham V. Hartstone, Nicholas Le Mesurier, Michael A. Carter, Richard Lewzey, Lionel Strutt
Sound Editor	Winston Ryder
Music Editor	Robin Clarke
Dialogue/Effects Editors	Archie Ludski, Jack T. Knight
Second Unit Photography	Robin Browne
Camera Operator	Roy Ford
Camera Assistants	Frank Elliott, John Fletcher, Martin Kenzie (clapper)
Chief Electricians	Alan Martin, Bill Pochetty
Key Grip	Chunky Huse
Art Directors	Leslie Tomkins, Clifford Robinson, Ram Yedekar, Herbert Westbrook
Set Decoration	Hugh Scaife
Production Supervisor	Barrie Melrose
Production Managers	Jim Brennan, Shama Habibullah
Assistant Directors	Patrick Caddell, Christopher Figg, Nick Laws, Arundhati Rao, Ajit Kumar
Costume Designer	Judy Moorcroft
Couturier	Germinal Rangel
Set Costumers	Rosemary Burrows, Keith Morton
Locations and Props	Eddie Fowlie
Make-up	Jill Carpenter, Eric Allwright
Hairdressing	Elaine Bowerbank, Vera Mitchell
Production Assistant	Pat Pennelegion
Assistant to Maurice Jarre	Christopher Palmer
Production Accountants	Charles Cannon, Rex Saluz (location)
Publicity	Diana Hawkins
Stills	Frank Connor
Property	Bert Hearn (Master, U.K.), Mickey Pugh, Steve Short
Contacts & Liaison	Pamela Allen (London), Mohini Banerji (Delhi), P.N. Parthasarathy (government), Marcus Wilford

	(customs)
Unit Manager	Rashid Abassi
Secretaries	Eleanor Chaudhuri (production), Brioni Pereira (location)
Transportation	Pamela Wells
Assistant Editors	Anne Sopel, Kess't Hooft, Peter Dansie (sound), Jeremy Baylis (dialogue)
Sound Engineer	Ron Butcher
Boom operator	Keith Pamplin
Color timer	Ron Lambert
Continuity	Maggie Unsworth

Cast   Judy Davis (Adela Quested), Victor Banerjee (Dr. Aziz), Peggy Ashcroft (Mrs. Moore), James Fox (Fielding), Alec Guinness (Godbole), Nigel Havers (Ronny Heaslop), Richard Wilson (Turton), Michael Culver (McBryde), Art Malik (Mahmoud Ali), Saeed Jaffrey (Hamidullah), Clive Swift (Major Callendar), Ann Firbank (Mrs. Callendar), Roshen Seth (Amritrao), Sandra Hotz (Stella), Rashid Karapiet (Das), H.S. Krishnamurthy (Hassan), Ishaq Bux (Selim), Moti Makam (Guide), Mohammed Ashiq (Haq), Phyllis Bose (Mrs. Leslie), Sally Kinghorne (Ingenue), Paul Anin (Court Clerk), Z.H. Khan (Dr. Panna Lai), Ashok Mandanna (Anthony), Dina Pathek (Begum Hamidullah), Adam Blackwood (Mr. Hadley), Mellan Mitchell (Businessman), Peter Hughes (P&O Manager)

Running time   163 minutes

Distributed by Columbia Pictures

Released December 13, 1984 (U.S.), February, 1985 (U.K.)

Filmed on location in Bangalore, India and at Shepperton Studios from November, 1983 to June, 1984 at a cost of approximately $14.7 million

DOCUMENTARY FILM AS DIRECTOR

LOST AND FOUND, THE STORY OF COOK'S ANCHOR (1979, South Pacific TV/Faraway Productions)

Producers	George Andrews, Wayne Tourell
Teleplay	Robert Bolt
Photographers	Ken Dorman, Lynton Diggle, Eddie Fowlie
Editor	David Reed
Sound	Hugh Cleverly
Assistant Director	Wayne Tourell
Narrator	Kelly Tarlton
Running time	40 minutes

First broadcast by TV-2 of Auckland in May, 1979

PROJECTS AND OTHER WORK

1942-1950   Partner in Cineguild, which also produced **TAKE MY LIFE** (1947, directed by Ronald Neame and produced by Anthony Havelock-Allan) and **BLANCHE FURY** (1947, directed by Marc Allegret, produced by Havelock-Allan)

1950-1976   While working for Korda's London Films, Lopert, and Sam Spiegel's Horizon Pictures, several unrealized projects including adaptations of various novels: *The Cruise of the Breadwinner* by H.E. Bates (1950), who would co-script **SUMMER MADNESS**, *The Wind Cannot Read* by Richard Mason (1956), and *The Snow Goose* by Paul Gallico. Also biographies of Mary Queen of Scots (1951), Gandhi (1956-72), Galileo (1968), "The Taj Mahal Project" (for Korda, 1953), THE SLAVE (with Julie Christie for United Artists, 1967) and THE BATTLE OF BERLIN (for Carlo Ponti, 1967). Noel Coward reported that in 1951, Korda and Lean asked him to star in an untitled picture about allied convoys to the Soviet Union during World War II. Also in 1951, Korda reputedly approached Laurence Olivier to star in an adaptation of T.E. Lawrence's *Revolt in the Desert* by Terence Rattigan to be directed by Lean. When the project fell through, Rattigan used the work he had done on the script as the basis for his play, *Ross*.[5]

In 1963, Lean directed a number of scenes with Jose Ferrer and Claude Rains for **THE GREATEST STORY EVER TOLD** as a favor to George Stevens.

1977-1980   Work on the "Bounty" project, including script drafts with Robert Bolt and Melvyn Bragg, construction of a replica of the vessel, extensive location scouting, and casting sessions (favoring Oliver Reed as Bligh and Christopher Reeve as Christian)

1981-1991   Lean contemplated an adaptation of *Out of Africa* in 1982, which was dropped when the opportunity for **A PASSAGE TO INDIA** arose. After that film Lean considered two projects based on novels with Steven Spielberg: J.G. Ballard's *Empire of the Sun* (subsequently directed by Spielberg) and Joseph Conrad's *Nostromo*.

Work on the NOSTROMO project began in 1986 and included script drafts with Christopher Hampton and Robert Bolt, location scouting and set contruction supervised by John Box, and casting. Productions start dates were announced several times by Warner Bros. and Tri-Star and among the actors reported to be set were Kevin Klein (1986), Paul Scofield (1988), George Carafas, Irena Brook, Liam Neeson, Peter O'Toole, Marlon Brando (all 1989), and Mel Gibson (1990). Before Guy Hamilton was finally set as "back-up" director, similar arrangements were contemplated with Arthur Penn (for a reported $1 million fee), John Boorman, and Axel Corti.

AWARDS AND HONORS

1942   **IN WHICH WE SERVE**: Special Certificate from the Academy of Motion Picture Arts and Sciences to Noel Coward for production achievement.

1943   **IN WHICH WE SERVE**: Top-grossing British picture of the year.

1944   **THIS HAPPY BREED**: Top-grossing British picture of the year.

BLITHE SPIRIT: Academy Award for Best Special Effects

1945   **BRIEF ENCOUNTER**: Academy Award Nominations for Best Screenplay, Best Actress (Celia Johnson), and Best Director. Lean was the first British director ever nominated.

1946   **BRIEF ENCOUNTER**: Prix Internationale du Critique at Cannes.

        GREAT EXPECTATIONS: Academy Awards for black and white Cinematography and Art Direction; nominations for Best Picture, Director, and Screenplay.

1947   Elected as the first Chairman of the newly-formed British Film Academy.

1952   **THE SOUND BARRIER**: British Film Academy awards for Best Film and Best Actor (Ralph Richardson). Academy Award for Sound; nomination for Best Screenplay. New York Film Critics Award for Best Performance (Ralph Richardson).

1954   **HOBSON'S CHOICE**: British Film Academy award for Best Film.

1955   **SUMMER MADNESS**: Academy Award nominations (as **SUMMERTIME**) for Best Director and Actress (Katharine Hepburn). New York Film Critics Award for Best Direction.

1957   **THE BRIDGE ON THE RIVER KWAI**: British Film Academy awards for Best Film, Script, and Actor (Alec Guinness). Academy Awards for Best Picture, Director, Screenplay, Actor (Alec Guinness), Cinematography, Music, and Editing; nomination for Best Supporting Actor (Sessue Hayakawa). Top-grossing British picture of the year. Directors Guild of America Award for Theatrical Direction.

1962   **LAWRENCE OF ARABIA**: British Film Academy awards for Best Film, Script, and Actor. Academy Awards for Best Picture, Director, Cinematography, Art Direction, Music, Sound, and Editing; nominations for Best Screenplay, Actor (Peter O'Toole), and Supporting Actor (Omar Sharif). Directors Guild of America Award for Theatrical Direction.

1965   **DOCTOR ZHIVAGO**: Academy Awards for Best Screenplay, Cinematography, Art Direction, Music, and Costume Design; nominations for Best Picture, Director, Sound, Editing, and Supporting Actor (Tom Courtenay).

1970   **RYAN'S DAUGHTER**: Academy Awards for Best Cinema-
        tography and Supporting Actor (John Mills); nominations
        for Best Actress (Sarah Miles) and Sound.

1973   Directors Guild of America "D.W. Griffith Award" for
        Outstanding Achievement and Lifetime Contributions to
        Film.

1983   British Film Institute Fellowship for Lifetime Achievement.

1984   **A PASSAGE TO INDIA**: Academy Awards for Best Music
        and Supporting Actress (Peggy Ashcroft); nominations for
        Best Picture, Director, Screenplay, Cinematography, Art
        Direction, Sound, Editing, Costume Design, and Actress
        (Judy Davis).

        Knighted by Queen Elizabeth II.

1988   Special Tribute at Cannes.

1990   American Film Institute Lifetime Achievement Award

FOOTNOTES

INTRODUCTION

1. (i) David Lean, "The Film Director," (Essay) in Orwell Balkeston, ed., *Working for the Films* (London: Focal Press, 1947), page 34; (ii) Lean quoted in Douglas McVay, "Lean—Lover of Life," *Films and Filming*, August, 1959, page 9; (iii) Jay Cocks, "Adventures in the Dream Department," *Time*, December 31, 1984, page 62.

2. **BLITHE SPIRIT** and **BRIEF ENCOUNTER** were both released in 1945 but shot eleven months apart, the former in early 1944, the latter in 1945 for late fall release.

3. Lean speaking in "The Southbank Show: Lean and Bolt" and the documentary "David Lean: A Life in Film."

4. Andre Bazin, *What is Cinema?* (Berkeley: University of California Press, 1967), translated and edited by Hugh Gray, pages 91-92.

5. Neame speaking in "A Life in Film"

6. Bolt speaking in "The Southbank Show"

7. Andrew Sarris, *The American Cinema* (New York: E.P. Dutton, 1968), page 160.

8. Ian Cameron in Letter to Alain Silver, May 20, 1971.

9. I.A. Richards, *Principles of Literary Criticism* (New York: Harcourt, Brace & World, 1928), page 25.

10. Cf. Alain Silver, "Fragments of a Mirror: The Use of Landscape in Hitchcock," *Wide Angle*, vol. 1, no 3.

CHAPTER 1

1. Several reference sources, such as Denis Gifford's *British Film Catalogue* and Leslie Halliwell's *Halliwell's Filmgoer's Companion*, actually list all three, Pascal, French, and Lean, as directors. Both French and Lean have two credits on the film [see Biography section], but Lean's own recollections of what he did varied.

2. Rex Harrison, *Rex: An Autobiography* (New York: William Morrow, 1975), page 71: "David Lean was known to us as the 'whispering cutter.' It was part of his job to give Pascal guidance even on the set."

3. Lean in "A Life in Film"

4. Bazin, page 83.

5. Francois Truffaut, *Le Cinema Selon Hitchcock* (Paris: Robert Laffont, 1966), p 159.

6. Neame quoted in C.A. Lejeune, "The Up and Coming Team of Lean and Neame." *New York Times*, June 15, 1947, page 5.

CHAPTER 2

1. "A Life in Film"

2. Idem

3. Cf. the concept as described by Mary Shelley: "Then mighty are thou, O wind, to be throned above all other vicegerents of nature's power; whether thou comes destroying from the east, or pregnant with elementary life from the west; thee the clouds obey; the sun is subservient to thee; the shoreless ocean is thy slave." [*The Last Man*] Wind, sun, and water remain key emblems for Lean through **A PASSAGE TO INDIA**.

CHAPTER 3

1. Raymond Durgnat, *A Mirror For England*, (New York-Washington: Praeger, 1971), page 22 and James Agee, *Agee on Film*, (London: Peter Owen, 1963), page 267.

2. "A Life in Film"

3. Bazin, page 67.

4. Sergei Eisenstein, "Dickens, Griffith, and the Film Today" in *Film Form* (New York: Harcourt, Brace, and World, 1949), pages 213-14.

CHAPTER 4

1. George Orwell, *The Decline of English Murder and Other Essays* (London: Penguin, 1965), page 9.

CHAPTER 7

1. Although this apparently was at one time a concern for the filmmak-

ers as "rumors had preceded the arrival of the company for **SUMMER MADNESS**: that it was the story of unmarried love and the Patriarch of Venice would therefore forbid it, that there would be scenes of indecency, offensive to the sensibility of Venetians." [from Michael Korda, *Charmed Lives* (New York: Random House, 1979), pages 387-88.]

CHAPTER 8

1. David Lean, "Out of the Wilderness," *Films and Filming*, January, 1963, page 16.

2. Cocks, page 61 and Denise Worrell, *Icons* (New York: Atlantic Monthly Press, 1988), page 169. [Worrell, Elaine Dutka, and John Wright are credited as reporters in the *Time* article.]

3. Lejeune, page 5.

4. Korda, page 230.

5. Andrew Sinclair, *Spiegel: The Man Behind the Movies* (Boston: Little, Brown and Co., 1987), pages 3, 141.

6. Lean quoted in the Columbia Pictures press release for **LAWRENCE OF ARABIA**.

7. "The Southbank Show"

8. "A Life in Film

CHAPTER 9

1. The unproduced scripts: "Gandhi," "The Lawbreakers," "The Long Arm," and "Nostromo."

2. Robert Bolt, *A Man for All Seasons* (New York: Random House, 1962), page xvi.

3. Ibid., page xix.

4. "The Southbank Show"

5. T.E. Lawrence, *Seven Pillars of Wisdom, A Triumph* (New York: Doubleday, 1935), pages 253-254.

6. "The Southbank Show"

CHAPTER 10

1. Hollis Alpert, "The David Lean Recipe: A Whack in the Guts," *New*

York Times Magazine, May 23, 1965, page 98.

2. Silverman, page 153.

3. Betty Jeffries Demby, "An Interview with Robert Bolt," *Filmmaker's Newsletter*, October, 1973, page 30.

4. Stanley Price, "On the Spanish Steppes with **DOCTOR ZHIVAGO**," *Show*, May, 1965, page 41.

5. Giuseppe Lo Duca, *L'erotisme au Cinema* (Supplement), (Montreuil: Pauvert, 1968), page 44.

6. "The Southbank Show"

7. Lean in Balkeston, page 34.

CHAPTER 11

1. "A Life in Film"

CHAPTER 12

1. Lean comments to Maurice Jarre about the underscore in this sequence in "A Life in Film": "Don't be frightened about making it a little romantic. When she's going through that grass, it isn't a girl going on a nice country bicycle ride. There's something in the air that she doesn't know."

2. Chapter 26.

3. Lean in Blakeston, page 30.

4. Stephen M. Silverman, *David Lean* (New York: Abrams, 1989), page 188.

5. "A Life in FIlm"

6. Some of these observations are merely incorrect. For example: "Final important evidence from Lean's 'self portrait' about the nature of his genius is the explanation that after making **LAWRENCE OF ARABIA**, and **DOCTOR ZHIVAGO** with scriptwriter Robert Bolt, they decided to 'try an original' (**RYAN'S DAUGHTER**)." [Warren French, Editor's Foreword, in Michael Anderegg, *David Lean* (Boston:Twayne, 1984), page xi.] To say that **RYAN'S DAUGHTER** fails because it was not grounded in a preexisting literary work ignores that Bolt's first script was an adaptation of Flaubert's Madame Bovary.

7. Lean in Blakeston, page 36.

8. "A Life in Film"

9. Part of "la politique's" methodology was and is the shock value of such statements as "Nicholas Ray is the Cinema" (Jean-Luc Godard, 1957) or "a 'failure' by Aldrich greatly outvalues a 'success' by Lumet, by Pakula, or by Pollack" (Michel Maheo, 1987).

10. Richards, page 29.

11. Lean quoted in Cocks, page 60.

AFTERWORD

1. Lean quoted in Silverman, page 164.

2. Alec Guinness, *Blessings in Disguise* (New York: Knopf, 1986), page 216.

3. Elaine Dutka, "Judy Davis: A Not-So-Ordinary Actress," *Los Angeles Times*, April 24, 1991, page F5.

BIOGRAPHY

1. Lean interviewed by Jim Brown, "Today Show" (NBC).

2. Lean speaking at DGA/AFI Weekend, December 7, 1984.

3. Anthony Havelock-Allan, "A Man with Intent," *Bafta News*, June, 1991, page 2.

4. Michael Powell, *A Life in Movies* (New York: Knopf, 1987), page 379.

5. Lean quoted in Roy Moseley, *Rex Harrison: A Biography* (New York: St. Martin's, 1987), page 56.

6. The particulars of who recommended Lean (many including "rival" director Carol Reed claimed to have done so), how he made the demand for credit, and how Coward responded vary widely over nearly a score of books and articles that recount the story. The most recent, succinct, and probably most accurate recollection is Havelock-Allan's: "The question then arose as to who should act as technical advisor, since Coward admitted that he hadn't the faintest idea of what would technically be required. Coward had seen and admired Ronnie Neame's lighting camera work, so it remained to find someone who would tell Coward where to put his cameras, and what lenses to use. I suggested David. Del Giudice had been a director of the company which made 'French without Tears,' which David had edited, so he was in full

agreement. Coward liked David on meeting him and after the three of us, David, Ronnie and I, took over the writing of an abridged script—Coward's original draft outline had been a film about eight hours in length—there remained only the question of screen credit. When that came to be discussed David said with great courage and great conviction that he would not do the job of assisting the director without full co-director credit. Coward, who was not only a highly perceptive but also a fair-minded man, paused for only a second or two and said: 'Agreed'." [Havelock-Allan, page 3.]

7. "A Life in Film"

8. Powell, page 417.

9. Neame interviewed in Michael Singer, ed., *Film Directors: A Complete Guide* (Los Angeles: Lone Eagle, 1984), page 22.

10. Alan Wood, *Mr. Rank* (London: Hodder and Stoughton, 1952), page 247. In all the published interviews with and biographies about Lean, Neame, Ann Todd et al. including Silverman's vague statement: "Production was well under way when, displeased with the results, J. Arthur Rank called Lean into his office and asked that he take command of the picture" [page 83], Wood is the only source which specifically states that Lean replaced his Cineguild partner, Ronald Neame, as director. Neame himself recalls: "David and Stanley [Haynes] did not like the script and asked to rewrite it, so we put the picture back two weeks, and I started shooting with a 30 page script. By then, my confidence had been pretty heavily shaken; and about four days into shooting David asked me if he could take over as director. Not wanting to insist on continuing the picture with everything that had happened, I agreed." [Ronald Neame in a conversation with Alain Silver, June 17, 1991.] Neame also confirms Wood's statement that it was he who "suggested that David Lean should take over the picture" but adds that he went to Rank at Lean's urging and had not "left Cineguild" but finished the picture as producer.

11. David Lean, *Penguin Film Review* #4, October, 1947, pages 27-35.

12. Payn, Graham and Morley, Sheridan, eds., *The Noel Coward Diaries* (Boston: Little, Brown, 1982) page 78.

13. Neame, conversation with Silver.

14. Paul Tabori, *Alexander Korda* (New York: Living Books, 1966), page 255.

15. Sinclair, page 80 and Payn and Morley, page 370.

16. Powell, page 563 and Sinclair, page 96.

17. Lean quoted in Jerry Roberts, "Lean: Master of the Thinking Man's Epic," *Santa Monica Outlook*, April 17, 1991, page D7.

18. Richard Attenborough, *In Search of Gandhi* (Piscataway: New Century, 1982), page 137.

19. Silverman, page 127.

20. Not all the disagreements were financial. Lean and Bolt argued extensively over their drafts; and, after Bolt was incapacitated, according to Sinclair: "[Melvyn] Bragg agreed with Spiegel that Mr. Christian was a villain, but Lean saw him as a nautical Lawrence, a virtuous young man. There were terrible quarrels over the script with both Spiegel and Lean clutching their hearts and accusing the other of murder." [page 133]

FILMOGRAPHY

1. Some sources credit Eric Ambler as Producer possibly because he acted as unofficial co-producer when Ronald Neame was the film's director and/or possibly on the assumption that after Lean replaced Neame, the latter's producer credit was merely honorary. Neame affirms that he served as producer through the conclusion of production and secured the locations in Switzerland for Lean. [Neame, conversation with Silver]

2. Silverman, pages 118-19 and Sinclair, pages 77-79.

3. Sinclair, page 97.

4. Lean quoted in "Out of the Wilderness," *Films and Filming*, January, 1963, page 14 and in Roberts, page D7 respectively.

5. Rattigan quoted in *The New York Times,* December 24, 1961 and Adrian Turner in letter to Alain Silver, November 21, 1991

SELECTED BIBLIOGRAPHY

BOOKS

Aldgate, Anthony and Richards, Jeffrey. *Britain Can Take It.* London: Basil Blackwell, 1986. [Contains a lengthy chapter on **IN WHICH WE SERVE** in the context of wartime themes and productions.]

Agee, James. *Agee on Film.* London: Peter Owen, 1963. [Reprint of **GREAT EXPECTATIONS** review]

Anderegg, Michael A. *David Lean.* Boston: Twayne, 1984. [A detailed critical study of Lean's work in chronology through **RYAN'S DAUGHTER** with particular attention to the Dickens' adaptations, **LAWRENCE OF ARABIA**, and **DOCTOR ZHIVAGO**. Selected Bibliography and Filmography]

Armes, Roy. *A Critical History of the British Cinema.* New York: Oxford University Press, 1978.

Blakeston, Orwell, ed. *Working for the Films.* London: Focal Press, 1947. [Contains an essay, "The Film Director," by David Lean, pages 27-37. Lean discusses the job of directing, stressing the need for techinical knowledge about cameras and editing, working with actors, and the sensibility of the director in a slightly-dated, second person, and sometimes interrogatory style: "Have you got imagination? Have you extreme tenacity of purpose? Do you like hard work? Are you the sort of person who will use most known methods to see *your* ideas carried through to the end?" (page 27) Lean is candid about the necessity of being a "pretty big egotist. How can you be anything else if you are to make everyone else see the film your way?" (page 36) and also discusses the need to disguise technique and work from instinct: "You either have an instinctive sense of the dramatic or you haven't. You have a sense of timing or you haven't; and if you haven't don't try to be a director." (page 28)]

Castelli, Louis P. with Cleeland, Caryn Lynn. *David Lean.* Boston, Mass.: G.K. Hall, 1980. [A biographical sketch of Lean followed by critical notes providing structural analysis of Lean's characters, themes, and some visual usage. Chronological bibliography through 1979 with separate listing of reviews, filmography including synopses, guide to resources including library holdings, and a list of 16mm film distributors]

Durgnat, Raymond. *A Mirror for England: British Movies From Austeity to Affluence.* New York-Washington: Praeger, 1971.

Eisenstein, Sergei. *Film Form.* New York: Harcourt, Brace, and World, 1949. [Contains essay "Dickens, Griffith, and the Film Today"]

Fulton, A.R. *Motion Pictures.* Oklahoma: University of Oklahoma Press, 1960. [Discussions of **BRIEF ENCOUNTER** and **GREAT EXPECTATIONS**]

Gifford, Denis. *The British Film Catalogue.* New York: McGraw-Hill, 1973.

Houston, Penelope. *The Contemporary Cinema.* Middlesex: Penguin, 1964.

Huntley, John. *British Technicolor Films.* London: Skelton-Robinson, 1950. [Neame's photography on **THIS HAPPY BREED** and Calthorp's art direction on **BLITHE SPIRIT** are discussed]

Jarvie, Ian C. *Movies and Society.* New York: Basic Books, 1970.

Low, Rachael. *Filmmaking in 1930s Britain.* London: George Allen and Unwin, 1985.

Lyon, Christopher, ed. *International Directory of Films & Filmmakers, Volume II.* New York: Putnam, 1984. [Career article, filmography, bibliography by Charles Affron]

Manvell, Roger. *The Film and the Public.* Middlesex: Penguin, 1955.

_____. *What is Film?* London: MacDonald, 1965.

Oakley, C. A. *Where We Came In—Seventy Years of the British Film Industry.* London: George, Allen, and Unwin, 1964.

Phillips, Gene D. *The Movie Makers.* Chicago: Nelson-Hall, 1973. [Chapter on Lean's work, pages 150-163]

Perry, George. *The Great British Picture Show*. New York: Hill & Wang, 1974.

Pratley, Gerald. *The Cinema of David Lean*. New York: A.S. Barnes, 1974. [A career profile including filmographic information, synopses, quotes from Lean on all of his work presented chronologically, and a detailed interview on **DOCTOR ZHIVAGO**]

Reisz, Karel. *The Technique of Film Editing*. London: Focal Press, 1973. [Discussion of **GREAT EXPECTATIONS** and **PASSIONATE FRIENDS**]

Robinson, David. *World Cinema: A Short History*. London: Eyre Metheun, 1973.

Sarris, Andrew. *Interviews With Film Directors*. New York: Avon Books, 1967. [Contains an interview with Lean by Gerald Pratley]

Silverman, Stephen M. *David Lean*. New York: Harry N. Abrams, 1989. [A biography based on interviews with Lean and sundry collaborators, extensively illustrated and including many color plates. Selected bibliography and filmography.]

Sinclair, Andrew. *Spiegel: The Man Behind the Pictures*. Boston: Little, Brown and Co., 1987. [Biography of Sam Spiegel with chapters on **KWAI** and **LAWRENCE**]

Slide, Anthony. *Fifty Classic British Films*. New York: Dover, 1985. [Synopses, credits, and commentary on **IN WHICH WE SERVE**, **BRIEF ENCOUNTER**, and **GREAT EXPECTATIONS**]

Vermilye, Jerry. *The Great British Films*. Secaucus, New Jersey: A.S. Barnes, 1978. [Synopses, credits, and commentary on Lean's films from **IN WHICH WE SERVE** through **OLIVER TWIST**, **HOBSON'S CHOICE**, and **RYAN'S DAUGHTER**]

Wood, Alan. *Mr. Rank*. London: Hodder and Stoughton, 1952.

Worrell, Denise. *Icons*. New York: Atlantic Monthly Press, 1988. [Interview with Lean conducted for *Time* magazine in December, 1984, pages 144-171]

Zambrano, A(na) L(aura). *Dickens and Film.* New York: Gordon Press, 1977. [Contains sub-chapter on **GREAT EXPECTATIONS** and **OLIVER TWIST**]

PERIODICALS

Alpert, Hollis. "The David Lean Recipe: A Whack in the Guts." *New York Times Magazine,* May 23, 1965, pages 32f.

Andrews, George. "A Cinematographic Adventure with David Lean." *American Cinematographer,* v. 60, #3, March 1979, pages 242-44.

Anon. "As Long as David Lean . . . " *Daily Variety,* November 27, 1970.

_____. "Biofilmography Lean." *Film Dope No. 34,* March, 1986, pages 1-2.

_____. "Bridge on the River Kwai." *New York Times Magazine,* November 24, 1957, pages 44-5.

_____. "British Cinema—Where Is the Life That Once It Led." *Los Angeles Times,* January 27, 1963.

_____. "David Lean, the Bitterest Loser of Them All," *Movies International,* v. I, #3, 1966.

_____. "David Lean's Big Gamble." *Saturday Review,* November 14, 1970, page 53.

_____. "David Lean: the Grand Lion Still Roars." *American Film,* March, 1990, pages 20-27, 53. [Interview]

_____. "Fagin in Berlin Provokes a Riot." *Life,* March 7, 1949, pages 38-39.

_____. "Flying Director." Los Angeles *Herald Examiner.* February 7, 1971.

_____. "Mutiny Still in Dry Dock." *Variety,* October 10, 1979, page 39.

_____. "NOSTROMO Lensing Suspended," *Daily Variety,* January 29, 1991, page 2.

_____. "Oscar Bound." *Time*, December 24, 1965, pages 44-5.

_____. "Talk with a Star." *Newsweek*, December 24, 1962.

_____. "Unresolved 'Ifs' on de Laurentiis Pair." *Variety*, December 14, 1977.

_____. "What Directors Are Saying." *Action*, 6, 1, January/February, 1971, page 30.

Armbrister, Trevor. "O'Toole—Oscar Winner?" *Saturday Evening Post*, March 9, 1963, pages 22-26.

Bart, Peter. "NOSTROMO Illustrates Trend towards Standby Directors." *Daily Variety*, February 16, 1990, pages 10, 42.

Blum, Mary. "A Brief Encounter with David Lean." *After Dark*, December, 1970, pages 18-19.

_____. "Lean Directs His Films by Fussing for Perfection." *Los Angeles Times*, October 25, 1970.

Champlin, Charles. "The Phenomenal Persistence of David Lean." *Los Angeles Times* Calendar, December 31, 1989, pages 30, 33.

Cockburn, A. "Beat the Devil: Forster and All That." *Nation* 238, April 28, 1984.

Cocks, Jay. "Adventures in the Dream Department." *Time*, December 31, 1984, pages 58-62. [Portion of Cover Story, "An Old Master's New Triumph—David Lean Directs **A PASSAGE TO INDIA**"]

Combs, R. "David Lean: Riddles of the Sphinx." *Monthly Film Bulletin*, LII/615, April, 1985, pages 102-106.

Crabbe, Kathryn. "Lean's **OLIVER TWIST**: Novel to Film." *Film Criticism* 2, Fall, 1977, pages 46-51.

Dawes, Amy. "AFI Pays Tribute to Lean's 'Landscape of the Spirit'." *Daily Variety*, March 12, 1990, page 3.

Dawson, L. "An Englishman Abroad." *Photoplay* 36, April, 1985, pages 14-18.

Day, Ernest. "A Passage to India." *American Cinematographer,* February, 1985, pages 56-62.

Demby, Betty Jeffries. "An Interview with Robert Bolt." *Filmmakers Newsletter,* 6, #12, October, 1973, pages 28-33.

Eller, Claudia. "Outspoken Lean Feted at Cannes." *Hollywood Reporter,* May 23, 1988, page 25.

Farber, Stephen. "Look What They've Done to Lawrence of Arabia." *New York Times,* May 2, 1971, page 11.

Foreman, Carl. "Confessions of a Frustrated Screenwriter." *Film Comment,* VI, 4, Winter, 1970-71, pages 22-24.

Fuller, G. and Kent, N. "Return Passage." *Stills* 17, March, 1985, pages 29-36.

Furniss, Cathy. "Lean at SF." *Films in Review,* April, 1971, pages 237-38.

Halberstadt, Michele. "La Voie Royale." *Premiere* (France), April, 1985, pages 114-121. [Interview]

Harmetz, Aljean. "David Lean Films a Famed Novel." *New York Times,* December 9, 1984.

Havelock-Allan, Sir Anthony. "A Man with Intent." *Bafta News,* II, 5, June, 1991, pages 2-3.

Hill, Stephen. "Evaluating the Directors." *Films in Review,* 12, January, 1961, pages 7-13.

Holden, James. "A Study of David Lean." *Film Journal,* 1, April, 1956, pages 1-5.

Honan, William H. "For His Next Act David Lean Plans To Film a Conrad Story." *New York Times,* October 17, 1989, pages C17, 24.

Houston, Penelope. "In the Picture: Lean Time." *Sight and Sound* 54, #2, 1985.

Huntley, John. "The Music of **HAMLET** and **OLIVER TWIST**." *Penguin Film Review* No. 8 (1949), pages 110-22.

Joyaux, Georges. **"THE BRIDGE ON THE RIVER KWAI**: From the Novel to the Movie." *Literature/Film Quarterly*, Spring, 1974, pages 174-82.

Kael, Pauline. "Bolt and Lean." *New Yorker*, November 21, 1970, pages 116-118.

Kalish, Robert. "David Lean Romantics" [Two part article]. *1,000 Eyes Magazine* Nos. 3 & 4, October and November, 1975, page 22.

Kennedy, Harlan. "I'm a Picture Chap." *Film Comment* 21, January/February, 1985, pages 28-32.

_____. "Nostromo." *American Film*, March, 1990, pages 28-31, 53-55.

Lacayo, Richard. "Meeting of Two Masters." *Time*, August 27, 1984, page 54.

Laurenson, Helen. "Letter Home." *Esquire*, 64, December, 1965, pages 132f.

Lean, David. "Brief Encounter." *Penguin Film Review #4*, October, 1947, pages 27-35. [Lean writes about how the British cinema used the opportunity provided by World War II and being cut off from America to develop an indigenous following different from Hollywood where "only 4%" of the measureable feedback from filmgoers was from those over 21. After noting the lack of realism in Hollywood pictures, where heroines rise from bed each morning perfectly-coiffed and already made up, Lean describes a proto-typical movie-going couple, "Bill and Mary," and how post-War cinema brought them to accept "unglamorous" heroines such as Laura Jesson in **BRIEF ENCOUNTER**. Lean jumps back to discuss **IN WHICH WE SERVE** then extols Rank and Independent Producers in a brief history of their contribution to the new British cinema.]

_____. "The Film Director," see Blakeston, Orwell above under **BOOKS**.

_____. "Out of the Wilderness." *Films and Filming*, 9, #4, January, 1963, pages 12-15. [An "interview-article" as much an anonymous piece as authored by Lean, which mostly concentrates on the then-just-released **LAWRENCE OF ARABIA**. Lean does have a few comments on film-making in general and his past associations and working methods, for example: "Partnerships can be a very good thing, a part of growing up.

You want to have close pals with you."]

Lejeune, C(aroline) A(lice). "The Up and Coming Team of Lean and Neame." *New York Times*, June 15, 1947, page 5.

Levine, J.P. "Passage to the Odeon: Too Lean." *Literature/Film Quarterly* XIV/3, July, 1986, pages 138-150.

Lightman, Herb. "On Location with Ryan's Daughter." *American Cinematographer*, August, 1968, pages 748f.

Lukas, Anthony J. "Doctor Zhivago: Approved by India." *New York Times*, January 25, 1967, page 35.

Mann, Roderick. "After Fifteen Years Lean Returns to Action." *Los Angeles Times*, December 9, 1984, page 37.

Martin, Harold H. "The Two Loves of Doctor Zhivago." *Saturday Evening Post*, 239, January 15, 1966, pages 26-31.

McBride, Joseph. "Virtuoso Director David Lean Dies." *Daily Variety*, April 17, 1991, pages 1, 22.

McCarthy, Todd. "Directors Guild Devotes a Weekend to David Lean." *Daily Variety*, December 11, 1984, page 6.

_____. "Silberman Backs Lean's NOSTROMO." *Daily Variety*, May 23, 1988, pages 1, 27.

McInerny, J.M. "Lean's 'Zhivago': A Reappraisal." *Literature/Film Quarterly* XV/1, 1987, pages 43-48.

McVay, Douglas. "David Lean—Lover of Life." *Films and Filming* (August, 1959), pages 9-10, 34.

Moss, Morton. "How To Make a Movie." Los Angeles *Herald Examiner*, March 9, 1971.

Murphy, A.D. "As Long as David Lean Films Draw, 'Will Be Able to Get Backing'." *Daily Variety*, November 25, 1970, page 6.

Norman, Barry. "Somebody Had to Say It . . . and David Lean Did." *Variety*, December 10, 1964. [Comments on **DOCTOR ZHIVAGO**]

Parisi, Paula. "Filmmakers in Focus." *Hollywood Reporter*, February 17, 1989, page 12.

Pickard, Ron. "David Lean: Supreme Craftsman." *Films in Review*, May, 1974, pages 265-284.

Price, Stanley. "On the Spanish Steppes with **DOCTOR ZHIVAGO**." *Show*, May, 1965.

Ptacek, Greg. "David Lean Dies at 83." *Hollywood Reporter*, April 17, 1991, pages 1, 7, 19.

Quincannon. "Double Takes." *Sight and Sound*, 51, # 2 (1982), pages 121-3.

Rainer, Peter. "David Lean, Master Director." Los Angeles *Herald Examiner*, February 10, 1989, pages 7, 11-12.

Reynolds, Charles. "David Lean on What You Can Learn from Movies." *Popular Photography*, 42, March, 1958, pages 108f. [Interview with Lean]

Roberts, Jerry. "Lean: Master of the Thinking Man's Epic." Santa Monica *Outlook*, April 17, 1991, page D7.

Ronan, Margaret. "David Lean and the Fat Box Office: Movie Audiences Don't Change." *Senior Scholastic*, 98, February 15, 1971, page 18. [Interview with Lean]

Ross, Steven. "In Defense of David Lean." *Take One*, 3, #12, July/August 1972, pages 10-18. [Interview with Lean]

Rushdie, S. "Point of View: Outside the Whale." *American Film* 10, January/February 1985, page 16.

Sacluna, N. and Van der Wyst, F. "A Passage to India." *Skoop* XXI/3 (May, 1985), pages 18-21.

Schickel, Richard. "Epic Beauty and Terror." *Life*, January 21, 1966, pages 48-60.

_____. "A Superb **PASSAGE TO INDIA**." *Time*, December 31, 1984, pages 54-57. [Portion of Cover Story, "An Old Master's New Triumph—

David Lean Directs **A PASSAGE TO INDIA**"]

Silver, Alain. "The Untranquil Light: David Lean's **GREAT EXPECTA-TIONS**." *Literature/Film Quarterly* 2, Spring, 1974, pages 140-52.

Sragow, M. and Kennedy, H. "David Lean's Right of Passage." *Film Comment* XXI/1, January/February 1985, pages 20-32.

Stewart, R.S. "**DOCTOR ZHIVAGO**: The Making of a Movie." *Atlantic Monthly*, 216, August, 1965, pages 58-64.

Thomas, Bob. "David Lean." *Action*, November/December, 1973, pages 17-22.

Thompson, Howard. "Career Inventory from the Lean Viewpoint." *New York Times*, November 9, 1952, page 5.

Turner, Adrian. "In Quest of Screen Silver." *London Times*, November 18, 1990, pages 7.2, 7.3.

Tusher, Will. "Tri-Star Gazing at $360 Mil Slate." *Daily Variety*, December 10, 1990, pages 1, 22.

Viviani, C. "David Lean: l'Ami Passionne." *Positif* 291, May, 1985, pages 2-5.

Watt, Ian. "Bridges Over the Kwai." *Partisan Review*, 26, Winter, 1959, pages 83-94.

Watts, Stephen. "David Lean." *Films in Review*, 10, April, 1959, pages 245-47.

Westerbeck, Colin L., Jr. "Lean Years." *Commonweal*, December 18, 1970, pages 302-3.

Wolf, William. "Lean Rejects Drawing Room Comedies." *Los Angeles Times* Calendar, October 26, 1969, pages 1, 24, 25.

Zambrano, A(na) L(aura). "**GREAT EXPECTATIONS**: Dickens and David Lean." *Literature/Film Quarterly* 2, Spring, 1974, pages 154-61.

DOCUMENTARIES

DAVID LEAN, A SELF-PORTRAIT (Pyramid Films, 1971). Produced and Directed by Thomas Craven.

DAVID LEAN: A LIFE IN FILM (London Weekend Television, 1984). Produced by Nick Evans. Directed by Nigel Wattis. Edited and Narrated by Melvyn Bragg.

CHAMPLIN ON FILM: LAWRENCE OF ARABIA RESTORED (Z Channel, 1989). Produced by Susan Aldisert. Directed by Bob Worden. Hosted by Charles Champlin.

THE SOUTHBANK SHOW: LEAN AND BOLT (London Weekend Television, 1990). Produced and Directed by David Thomas. Executive Producer, Nigel Wattis. Edited and Presented by Melvyn Bragg.

INDEX

[Page numbers of illustrations are in italics. Abbreviations: (a) actor, (au) author, (c) composer, (d) director, (e) editor, (pd) production designer, (ph) photographer, (pr) producer, (sc) screenwriter. Page numbers after the semi-colon refer to the Filmography. Footnotes are deginated by an "f."]

Addinsell, Richard (c); 245, 249
Agee, James (au), 44
Aldrich, Robert (pr/d); 271f
Allegret, Marc (d); 263
Alwyn, William (c); 250
Ambler, Eric (sc); 249, 273f
American Film Institute, 226, 229, 239
Archers, The (production company), 18
Arnold, Malcolm (c), 111, 120, 149; 251-252, 255
Ashcroft, Peggy (a), *219*, 223; 262, 266
Ashton, Donald M. (pd); 255
Asquith, Anthony (d); 242
AS YOU LIKE IT; 242
Attenborough, Richard (a/d), 225; 243
Autiero, Gaetano (a), *132*; 254

BALACLAVA; 241
Ballard, J.G. (au); 264
BALL AT SAVOY; 242
Banerjee, Victor (a), *221*; 262
Banks, Leslie (a), *93*; 251
Barnard, Ivor (a), *48*, *75*; 247, 249
Bates, H.E. (sc); 253, 263
BATTLE OF BERLIN, THE (film project), 237, 264
BATTLESHIP POTEMKIN, THE, 182

Bax, Arnold (c), 248
Bazin, Andre (au), 3, 20, 24, 71
Beethoven, Ludwig von (c), 204
BIG PARADE, THE, 172
BLANCHE FURY; 263
Blithe Spirit (play), 20
BLITHE SPIRIT (film), 18, 22-27, 132, 220, 234; 244-245, 265
Bogart, Humphrey (a), 143
Bolt, Robert (au/sc), 8, 153-155, 157-159, 161, 166, 169-170, 174, 179-180, 189, *201*, 209, 227, 237-239; 256-257, 259, 263-264, 273f
Boorman, John (d); 264
Booth, Shirley (a), 138
Boulle, Pierre (au/sc), 145-146, 150, 236; 254
BOUNTY, THE (film project), 231, 238; 264
Box, John (pd), 237, 239; 256-257, 261, 264
Brabourne, John (pr); 260
Bragg, Melvyn (au/sc/pr), 231; 264, 273f
Brando, Marlon (a), 224, 237; 264
Brazzi, Rossano (a), 126, 134-*138*, 138-139; 254
BREAKING [THROUGH] THE SOUND BARRIER see **SOUND BARRIER, THE**

BRIDGE ON THE RIVER KWAI,
   THE, 2, 102, 141-151, 169,
   180, 184-185, 236; 254-255, 265
Bridge over the River kwai
   (novel), 236
BRIEF ENCOUNTER, 2, 6, 7, 16,
   18, 29-42, 43, 52, 82, 91, 110,
   121, 123-125, 130-131, 168,
   176, 184, 188, 192, 203-204,
   206, 224-226, 234, 238; 245-
   246, 265
British Dominion Studios, 232
British Lion, 234
British Movietone News, 232
Brontë, Emily, 11, 199
Brook, Irina (a); 264
Brooks, Richard (sc/d), 170
Brothers Karamazov, The
   (novel), 169
BROTHERS KARAMAZOV, THE
   (film), 170
Browne, Winyard (sc); 252
Brownlow, Kevin (au), 231
Bryan, John (pd); 247-250
Bulwer-Lytton, Edward (au), 55
Buñuel, Luis (d), 173
Byron, George Gordon, Lord
   (au), 97

Cahiers du Cinema, 226
Calthrop, G(ladys) E. (pd); 243-246
Cameron, Ian (au), 9
Carafas, George (a); 264
Carroll, Lewis (au), 11
Cavalcade (play), 19
Chabrol, Claude (au/sc/d), 2, 227
Chaplin, Geraldine (a); 258
Christie, Julie (a), *173-174, 177,
   179*; 258, 264
Cicognini, Alessandro (c); 253
Cineguild (production company),
   18, 21, 27, 43, 234-235; 263,
   272f

Clare, Mary (a), *75*; 249
Coates, Anne V. (e); 256
Coleridge, Samuel Taylor (au),
   32, 96, 100, 169, 175
Collins, Sewell (d); 241
Conrad, Joseph (au), 153, 239; 264
Cooke, Sandra, 233
Corti, Axel (d); 264
Courtenay, Tom (a), *179*; 258, 266
Coward, Noel (au/sc/pr/d), 11-
   24, *13, 17,* 27, 29-30, 43, 82,
   227, 233-236; 242-246, 264,
   271-272f
Cruikshank, George, 73
Cruise of the Breadwinner
   (novel); 263
Cummings, Constance (a), *23*; 245
Currie, Finlay (a), *46*; 247
Czinner, Paul (pr/d), 232; 242

D(enham) & P(inewood) Studios,
   234
DANGEROUS GROUND; 241
Davies, John Howard (a), *67-68,
   74;* 249
Davis, Judy (a), *221,* 224, 229;
   262, 266
Day, Ernest (ph); 261
De Banzie, Brenda (a), *117;* 253
de Laurentiis, Dino (pr), 238-239
Del Giudice, Filippo (pr), 18,
   233-234; 271-272f
De Sica, Vittorio (a/d), 134
Desny, Ivan (a), *84, 87, 89;* 251
Devi, Leila, 233
Dickens, Charles (au), 43-49,
   55-56, 61-63, 65-68, 70-71,
   73-74, 76, 82, 111, 235; 247-
   248
Dickinson, Thorold (e/d); 241
Dineson, Isak (au), 238
Directors Guild of America, 226,
   229

Doctor Zhivago (novel), 169, 185
DOCTOR ZHIVAGO (film), 2, 7,
    125, 141, 169-185, 200, 209,
    229, 237-238; 257-259, 266
Donald, James (a); 243, 255
Donaldson, Roger (d), 239
Downey, Kenneth (a), *75*; 249
DREAMING LIPS; 242
Durgnat, Raymond (au), 44

Eisenstein, Sergei (au/d), 76, 182
Elliott, Denholm (a); 252
Ellstree Studios, 232
Elvey, Maurice (d); 241
Empire of the Sun (novel), 239;
    264
"Eolian Harp, The" (poem), 32,
    169, 175
ESCAPE ME NEVER; 242

Far From the Madding Crowd
    (novel), 199
Fellini, Federico (d), 9
Ferrer. Jose (a); 257, 264
Finney, Albert (a), 237
Flaubert, Gustave, 209; 270f
Foot, Geoffrey (e); 250-251
Ford, John (d), 142, 225, 239
Foreman, Carl (sc/pr/d), 236; 254
Forster, E. M. (au), 211, 213-214,
    216, 218, 220, 222, 239; 261
49th PARALLEL, 12, 233; 242
Fox, Edward (a), *224*; 262
French, Harold (d), 12, 233; 242
FRENCH WITHOUT TEARS;
    242, 272f
Frend, Charles (e); 242
Freud, Sigmund (au), 44

Gallico, Paul (au); 263
Gandhi, Mahatma, 237
GANDHI (film project); 263
Gaumont British News; 241

Gaumont Studios, 232; 241
General from the Jungle, The
    (novel), 141
GHOST CAMERA, THE; 241
Gibson, Mel (a), 239; 264
Godard, Jean-Luc (au/sc/d), 227;
    271f
Goehr, Walter (c); 247
Goodwin, Richard (pr); 260
G.P.O. Films, 98
Grant, Cary (a), 143
Great Expectations (novel), 43,
    57-60, 71, 81
GREAT EXPECTATIONS (film),
    7, 16, 43-67, 73, 91, 109, 168,
    180, 182, 203-204, 212, 230,
    235; 247-248, 265
**GREATEST STORY EVER
    TOLD, THE**; 264
Green, Guy (ph); 247-250
Gregg, Everley (a), *39*; 246
Griffen, Arvid L. (pr); 257
Griffith, D(avid) W(ark) (d), 225,
    232
Grimes, Stephen (pd); 259
Guinness, Alec (a), *6, 54, 56, 68,
    73, 147, 150, 156, 160*, 224-
    225, *224*, 229, 236; 247, 249,
    255, 257-258, 262, 265

Hamilton, Guy (d), 240; 264
Hammond, Kay (a), *23*, 27; 245
Hampton, Christopher (sc), 239;
    264
Hanbury, Victor (d); 242
Hardy, Thomas, 187, 199
Harris, Jack (e); 244-249
Harrison, Rex (a), 12, *23*, 27,
    232; 245
Havelock-Allan, Anthony (pr/sc),
    18, 30, 232, 234; 242-247,
    259, 263, 271-272f
Havers. Nigel (a); 262

Hawkins, Jack (a), *160*; 255, 257
Hawks, Howard (d), 142
Hayakawa, Sessue (a), *147, 149-150*; 255, 265
Hayes, George (a), *52*; 247
Haynes, Stanley (sc/pr), 235; 248-250, 272f
Heart of Darkness, The (novel), 153
Hepburn, Katharine (a), 126, *131-132, 134-138*, 138, 236; 254, 265
Heyman, John (pr); 260
HIGH TREASON; 241
Hildyard, Jack (ph), 144; 251-254
Hiller, Wendy (a), 12
Hitchcock, Alfred (pr/d), 8, 9, 25, 138, 225, 239
Hobson, Valerie (a), *61, 64*; 247
HOBSON'S CHOICE, 22, 109-120, 179, 185, 199, 203, 236; 252-253, 265
Holden, William (a), 143; 255
Holloway, Stanley (a); 244, 246
Hope, John, 79
Hopkins, Anthony (a), 239
Horne, Geoffrey (a), *149*; 255
Hotz, Sandra, 233
Howard, Leslie (a/d), 232; 242-243
Howard, Trevor (a), *32, 123*, 138, *190*, 224-225; 246, 249, 260
Hunt, Martita (a), 54; 247
Hunt, Peter (au), 80

Independent Producers, 234
INDISCRETION OF AN AMERI-CAN WIFE, 134
Inglis, John, 82
Ingram, Rex (pr/d), 9, 232
INSULT; 241
INVADERS, THE see **49TH PARALLEL**

IN WHICH WE SERVE, 7, 11-19, 33, 97, 123-124, 233-234; 242-243, 264

Jacoby, George (D); 241
James, Henry (au), 125
Jarre, Maurice (c), 184, 213, 237; 256-257, 259, 261, 270f
JAVA HEAD; 241
Jennings, Humphrey (d), 98
Jesse, F. Tennyson (au), 80
Johnson, Celia (a), *8, 19*, 21, *32, 35-37, 39*; 243-244, 246, 265
Jones, Christopher (a), *193-194, 201. 205*, 224-225; 260
Joyce, James (au), 209
Justin, John (a); 252

Keats, John (au), 29
Kellino, Roy (d); 242
Kellino, W. P. (d); 241
Kennedy, Arthur (a); 257
Kinski, Klaus (a); 258
Klein, Kevin (a); 264
Krasker, Robert (ph); 246
Korda, Alexander (pr), 142, 235-236; 263-264
Korda, Vincent (pd); 251, 253

Lachman, Harry (d); 241
LAST ADVENTURERS, THE, 233; 242
Last Man, The (novel); 268f
Laughton, Charles (a), 111, *117, 119-120*, 236; 253
Laurents, Arthur (au), 126, 138; 253
LAWBREAKERS, THE (film project), 238
Lawrence, Thomas Edward (au), 153-154, 161, 237; 256, 263
LAWRENCE OF ARABIA, 2, 7, 78, 124, 141-142, 153-168,

185, 206, 226, 230, 238-239; 256-257, 265-266

Lean, David (photographs of) *160, 179, 183, 201*

Lean, Francis William LeBlount, 231

Lean, Isabelle, 233

Levine, Joseph E. (pr), 238

"Lines Written in Early Spring" (poem), 30, 42

London Films (production company), 235; 263

LONG ARM, THE (film project), 238

Lopert, Ilya (pr); 253, 263

LOST AND FOUND; 263

Lubitsch, Ernst (pr/d), 232

Lumet, Sidney (d); 271f

MacDonald, David (d); 242

Madame Bovary (novel), 238; 270f

MADELEINE, 2, 79-96, 109-110, 122, 124, 172, 196, 199-200, 230, 235; 250-251

Madeleine Smith Affair, The (book), 80

MAJOR BARBARA, 12, 14, 235; 242

Man for All Seasons, A (play), 154

Mann, Anthony (d), 9

Marcus, Steven (au), 80

Marx, Karl (au), 44

MARY QUEEN OF SCOTS (film project); 263

Mason, Richard (au); 263

"Match with the Moon, A" (poem), 179

McKenna, Siobhan (a); 258

McKern, Leo (a), 224; 260

Merchant of Venice, The (play), 109

Miles, Bernard (a); 243, 247

Miles, Sarah (a), *190, 193, 201, 205,* 224; 260, 266

Mills, John (a), *48, 50, 53-54,* 54, *56, 61, 65, 114, 194,* 224; 243-244, 247, 253, 260, 266

Miranda, Isa (a); 254

Mitchum, Robert (a), *193-194,* 224-225; 260

MONEY FOR SPEED; 241

Morley, Robert (a), 12

Mountbatten, Lord, 11, 233

M.P.A.A., 73

Myers, Thelma (e); 243

National Society of Film Critics (U.S.), 229

Neame, Ronald (ph/sc/d), 8, 18, 27, 30, 142, 229, 234-235; 242-245, 247-249, 271-273f

Neeson, Liam (a); 264

Newley, Anthony (a); 249

Newman, Paul (a), 225

Newton, Robert (a), 12, *19, 67, 69,* 244, 249

NIGHT PORTER, THE (1930); 241

Norman, C.P. (pd); 243-245

Nostromo (novel), 239; 264

NOSTROMO (film project), 176, 229; 264

Notable British Trials, 80

"Ode to the West Wind" (poem), 32, 175

Oliver Twist (novel), 67

OLIVER TWIST (film), 3-7, 37, 53, 67-78, 109, 121, 172, 199, 233-235; 248-249

Olivier, Laurence (a), 232; 263

ONE OF OUR AIRCRAFT IS MISSING, 12, 14; 242

ONE WOMAN'S STORY (U.S. Titlte) see **PASSIONATE FRIENDS, THE**

Orwell, George (au), 80
Other Victorians, The (book), 80
O'Toole, Peter (a), 154, *156,*
    160, 162, 164, 225, 237;
    257, 264, 266
Out of Africa (novel), 238; 264

Pakula, Robert (d); 271f
Pascal, Gabriel (pr/d), 12, 233; 242
Passage to India, A (novel), 211,
    214, 218, 239
PASSAGE TO INDIA, A (film), 2,
    42, 82, 124, 138, 179, 211-
    227, 230; 260-262, 264, 266
Passionate Friends, The (novel),
    121
PASSIONATE FRIENDS, THE
    (film), 2, 7, 82, 121-126, 134,
    176, 217, 224, 235; 249-250
Pasternak, Boris (au), 169, 237;
    257
Patrick, Nigel (a), *106;* 252
Penguin Film Review, 235
Penn, Arthur (d); 264
Phipps, Nicholas (sc); 250
PHYSICIAN, THE; 241
Pollock, Sydney (d); 271f
Ponti, Carlo (pr), 169, 237; 257,
    264
Powell, Michael (pr/d), 12, 18,
    232-234; 242
Pressburger, Emeric (pr/d), 18,
    232, 234, 237
"Prometheus" (poem), 97
PYGMALION (film); 242

Quaid, Dennis (a), 239
Quayle, Anthony (a); 257
Quinn, Anthony (a); 257
QUINNEYS; 241

Rachmaninoff, Sergei (c), 35, 40,
    110, 184, 204; 246

Rains, Claude (a); 250, 257, 264
Rank, J. Arthur (pr), 142, 234-
    235, 237; 272f
Rank Organization (production
    company), 18
Rattigan, Terence (sc), 98; 251, 263
Rau, Santha Rama (au); 261
Rawsley, David (pd); 243
Ray, Michael (a), *160;* 257
Ray, Nicholas (d); 271f
Raymond, Cyril (a), *8;* 246
Reed, Carol (d); 271f
Reed, Oliver (a); 264
Reeve, Christopher (a); 264
Renoir, Jean (d), 9, 225
Return of the Native, The (novel),
    187, 199
Richards, I.A. (au), 9, 227
Richardson, Ralph (a), *98, 104,*
    106-107; 252, 258, 265
Rohmer, Eric (au/sc/d), 227
ROMEO AND JULIET, 184
Rosmer, Milton; 241
Rossellini, Isabella (a), 239
Rossetti, Dante Gabriel (au), 179
Rossini, Gioacchino (c), 135
Ruben, J. Walter (d); 241
Rutherford, Margaret (a), 27; 245
RYAN'S DAUGHTER, 2, 103,
    139, 170, 172, 184, 187-209,
    213, 223, 226, 229-230, 237-
    238; 259-260, 266

SAILORS DON'T CARE; 241
Sands, Edward (pr); 260
Sarris, Andrew (au), 8
Savage, Norman (e); 258-259
Scofield, Paul (a); 264
SECRET OF THE LOCH, THE; 241
Seven Pillars of Wisdom, The
    (book), 153, 158, 161
Sharif, Omar (a), *173-174, 177,*
    225, 237; 257-258, 266

Shaw, George Bernard (au), 12, 232
Shelley, Mary Wollstonecraft (au); 268f
Shelley, Percy Bysshe (au), 32, 175
Shingleton, Wilfred (pd); 247, 252
Silberman, Serge (pr), 239
Silverman, Steven (au), 231; 272f
Simmons, Jean (a), *53*; 247
SLAVE, THE (film project); 263
Smith, A. Duncan (au), 80
Smith, Madeleine, 79-82
Snow Goose, The (novel); 263
SOUND BARRIER, THE, 18, 97-107, 149, 151, 168, 202-203, 235; 251-252, 265
Spencer, Norman (sc/p); 252
Spiegel, Sam (pr), 142, 150, *160*, 169, 227, 236-238; 254, 256-257, 263, 273f
Spielberg, Steven (pr/d), 239; 264
SPIES OF THE AIR; 242
STALAG 17, 143
STAZIONE TERMINI, 134
Steiger, Rod (a), *179*; 258
Stevens, George (pr/d); 264
Still Life (play), 30, 234
Stuart, Josephine (a), *77*; 249
Sullivan, Francis L. (a), 48-*49*, 54, 73, *74-75*; 247, 249
SUMMER MADNESS, 2, 82, 121, 124, 126-139, 176, 192, 203, 214, 217, 236; 253-254, 263, 265
SUMMETIME (U.S. Title) see SUMMER MADNESS

"Taj Mahal" (film project); 263
TAKE MY LIFE, 235; 263
Tale of Two Cities, A (novel), 76
Tangye, Helena Annie, 231

Taylor, Peter (e); 252, 254-255
Tess of the D'Urbervilles (novel), 199
This Happy Breed (play), 19
THIS HAPPY BREED, 18-22, 27, 132, 233-234; 243-244, 264
Thomson, Ian (e); 241
TIGER BAY (1933); 241
Time of the Cuckoo, The (play), 139
"To a Child Dancing in the Wind" (poem), 32, 187, 228
TO CATCH A THIEF, 138
Todd, Ann (a), 82, *84*, *88*, *92-93*, 94, *95*, *104*, 121-122, *123*, 233; 250-252, 272f
Traven, B. (au), 141
Tri-Star Pictures (production company), 239
Truffaut, Francois (au/sc/d), 227
Turner, Adrian (au), 231
Tushingham, Rita (a); 258
Two Cities (production company), 18, 233

Vajda, Ladislas (d); 242
Valentino, Rudolph (a), 19
Vidor, King (d), 170, 172
Vorhaus, Bernard (d); 241

Wager, Anthony (a), *46*, *53*, *65*; 247
Walker, Norman (d); 241
"Walrus and the Carpenter, The" (poem), 11
Walsh, Kay (a), 121, 233; 243-244, 247, 249
Walton, William (c), 12
War and Peace (novel), 169
WAR AND PEACE (film), 170
Warner Bros. (production company), 238
WAY WE WERE, THE, 184
Welles, Orson (pr/d), 239
Wells, H(erbert) G(eorge) (au),

121-122, 124-125, 137; 249
Westmore, Lucy (a), *174*; 258
"When I Have Fears" (poem), 29
White, Merrill (e), 232; 241-242
WIFE OF GENERAL LING, THE;
    242
Wilder, Billy (sc/d), 143
Williams, Emlyn (a), 12
Willingham, Calder (sc); 254
Wills, J. Edler (d); 241
Wilson, Michael (sc), 236; 254,
    256
Wind Cannot Read, The (novel);
    263
Wordsworth, William (au), 30, 42
Wyler, William (pr/d), 239

Yeats, William Butler (au), 32,
    187, 203, 209, 228
Young, Fred(die) A. (ph), 167,
    226, 229, 237; 256-257, 259

Zeffirelli, Franco (d), 184
Zinnemann, Fred (d), 142